Praise for Jenifer Ringer's *Dancing Through It*

"Ms. Ringer is that rare double threat: a ballerina who can write."
                                                    —*The New York Times*

"Provides a glimpse into the fragile psyche of a dancer. These are accounts to cherish."   —*The Washington Post*

"A charming and unflinchingly honest account of Ringer's career, particularly her battle with eating disorders."   —*Pointe*

"Jenifer Ringer's book is an honest and exhilarating look into the life of a young dancer, with both the excitement of achievement and the desperate anxiety given proper treatment. This is a must-read for anyone entering the dance community, but even more broadly, for any young person passionately following their dream. Jenifer was fortunate to have help in conquering her eating disorder and other demons, and this book may be a help to those wrestling with their own issues. Besides, for those of us who wish we could dance, knowing about it from the inside is a rare privilege."
                —Kathy Keller, coauthor of *The Meaning of Marriage*

"Ringer now offers a frank and open account of her demanding dance life, revealing seldom-seen technical aspects of this rigorous art form. A sure hit for balletomanes and everyone concerned about body-image issues."   —*Booklist*

"As a dancer, Jenifer Ringer offers quintessential musicality, brilliant technique, infectious humor, and a good old dash of gorgeous. As a writer, she offers all of this and more, providing us with a rare opportunity to look behind the curtain and understand the pressures, challenges, and rewards faced by this remarkable individual. *Dancing Through It* is one of the most candid and insightful books about classical ballet I have ever read. An honest portrait of the rarefied world of the New York City Ballet, Jenny's writing will make you tear up, roar with laughter, and reflect on the myriad pressures and rewards of being a dancer and an artist. Long before you've put this book down, you will want to shout 'Brava' once again for this treasured ballerina and gifted author."
                —Peter Boal, artistic director, Pacific Northwest Ballet

"Told with modesty and humility, Ringer's memoir exposes the unrelenting rigor of a dancer's life and the passion and exhilaration of dance itself."
—*Kirkus Reviews*

"One of New York's most beautiful dancers, Jenifer Ringer brings idealism, humor, and a raw, searing honesty to this poignant memoir. I had a hard time putting the book down, and I teared up several times."
—Wendy Perron, author of *Through the Eyes of a Dancer,* and editor at large, *Dance Magazine*

"With disarming candor, she relates devastating low points she experienced as a young dancer, invited to join City Ballet at age sixteen, as well as years of ascension through the hypercritical ballet world. . . . Ringer infuses her narrative with a deep appreciation for the magic of the theater and a moving sense of gratitude toward her success in such an arduous profession. . . . Her memoir is an eloquent reminder that moving forward often involves a few falls, missteps, and leaps of faith." —*Publishers Weekly*

"In her new book *Dancing Through It* [Ringer] opened up . . . about enduring nearly twenty-five years in the pressure-cooker world of elite professional ballet." —ELLE.com

PENGUIN BOOKS

DANCING THROUGH IT

Jenifer Ringer retired as a principal dancer with the New York City Ballet in 2014 and is now the director of the Colburn Dance Academy in Los Angeles, California. She is married to James Fayette, also a former principal dancer with the New York City Ballet. They live in Los Angeles.

DANCING THROUGH IT

My Journey in the Ballet

Jenifer Ringer

PENGUIN BOOKS

PENGUIN BOOKS

Published by the Penguin Group
Penguin Group (USA) LLC
375 Hudson Street
New York, New York 10014

USA | Canada | UK | Ireland | Australia | New Zealand | India | South Africa | China
penguin.com
A Penguin Random House Company

First published in the United States of America by Viking Penguin,
a member of Penguin Group (USA) LLC, 2014
Published in Penguin Books 2015

Photograph credit appears on page 275

THE LIBRARY OF CONGRESS HAS CATALOGED THE
HARDCOVER EDITION AS FOLLOWS:
Ringer, Jenifer
Dancing through it: my journey in the ballet/Jenifer Ringer.
pages cm
Includes index.
ISBN 978-0-670-02649-4 (hc.)
ISBN 978-0-14-312702-4 (pbk.)
1. Ringer, Jenifer. 2. Ballerinas—United States—Biography. 3. New York City Ballet.
I. Title.
GV1785.R484A3 2014
792.802'8092—dc23
[B]
2013036975

Printed in the United States of America
10 9 8 7 6 5 4 3 2

Set in Granjon with Diotima display
Designed by Carla Bolte

To Mom and Dad, my encouragers and prayer warriors

To Becky, my sister and best friend

To Grace and Luke, my precious lights

To James, my husband and hero

CONTENTS

DANCING THROUGH IT

Prologue

There is a ballet that is like an ocean: it seems to stretch beyond the horizons of the stage. No matter how many times I see or dance this ballet, George Balanchine's *Serenade*, I always find something new to discover, something so beautiful that I wonder if the audience should laugh or cry.

When the curtain opens, it reveals seventeen women grouped in two diamonds that touch at one central tip. They wear long, light blue tulle skirts that blow softly in the breeze stirred by the curtain as it rises up from the stage. There is a dim blue light that makes the dancers seem like indistinct angels. They each have one hand raised toward the front corner of the stage, where the light is the brightest, as if they are shielding their eyes from a divine glow. As the orchestra begins to play Tchaikovsky's quiet strings, the dancers slowly begin to move, each placing the wrist of her upraised hand against her temple as she turns her face away from the light. The movement and music build from there.

Soon, dancers are rushing on and off the stage, and key figures emerge: one woman, tall and statuesque; another, smaller, dancing quickly with light leaps; there will eventually be a third, the Waltz Girl, who comes in many measures later, finds love with a strong young man, but then loses him when the wind sweeps him and the rest of the women offstage. At the end of the third movement, this last woman falls to the ground, alone.

Then, though nothing visible changes on the stage, it seems that now the dancers are in some land in between heaven and earth. The tall woman, the Dark Angel, enters, hair down, leading a new man to the fallen Waltz Girl. The Dark Angel shields the man's eyes, as if they have traveled through lands that he is not allowed to see. He picks up the Waltz Girl, encouraging her to stand again.

The man dances in this hinterland with the three main women, all of them reaching and yearning for something they cannot quite grasp. Eventually, the Waltz Girl falls to the ground and cannot get up again. The Dark Angel covers the man's eyes, and takes him away.

Six angels come, awakening the Waltz Girl once more. A motherly figure, flanked by three men, appears, and the Waltz Girl runs to her, embracing her and then once more sinking to her knees. The three men lift the Waltz Girl first to her feet and then even higher to stand on their shoulders. Finally, accompanied by the flock of angels, the men carry their fragile burden toward a new, brighter light that beckons to them from offstage. The Waltz Girl reaches for the light and then opens her arms, leading with her heart as she flies up to the heavens.

If I were to distill into one event what made me want to dance, I would say that dancing in *Serenade* was what ultimately led me to a career in ballet. Though I tiptoed through my childhood, often prancing instead of walking and locking myself in my room to dance wildly to disco music, I always thought of ballet as my hobby, my after-school activity. Even as I had successes at my ballet schools and got caught up in making myself the perfect ballerina, I always figured that after high school I would go to college, get a job, and get married, like regular people.

But when I was fourteen and a student at the Washington School of Ballet, the Washington Ballet was performing *Serenade* at the Kennedy Center and needed some of the advanced students to fill in the corps de ballet. I was one of the four students chosen. The moment I heard the music and began to learn steps that fit the music so well that they seemed inevitable, I knew my life had been changed. This was *dancing*. This felt completely *right*. If I were not allowed to dance these steps to this music, something would always be missing from my life. And there was a moment during my first performance of *Serenade* that was like a light taking up residence in my chest.

I did become a professional ballerina, but six years after all of my dreams came true, I found myself trapped inside them. I had been a bright and talented sixteen-year-old when the New York City Ballet offered me the chance to join its elite corps de ballet, one of the four girls chosen that year out of a country of talented teenagers. At twenty-one, I was promoted to soloist, an even greater achievement. To the outside world, I appeared to be one of those successful young people who would have an amazing career in a specialized world experienced by only the lucky few.

But the public saw only my upward trajectory as I went from one featured role to the next, slowly gaining the confidence and experience that might one day earn me the ultimate prize: principal dancer rank. Few noticed my absences from the stage during the times that I battled injuries, normal enough occurrences in the life of every elite athlete, and no one knew about my eating disorders. No one knew that I alternated between anorexia and compulsive overeating, completely unable to control my relationship with food. When I was in the phase of my cycle in which I under-ate, my weight for ballet was "good," and I was onstage dancing almost every night. I took a weird pleasure in the bones showing through my skin. When I was in the overeating phase, I would slowly start gaining weight, which caused me to panic and grow paranoid as I imagined critical looks aimed in my direction.

The dangerous thing was that always, no matter what was happening during my days, I could lose myself in performances, and *Serenade*, in particular, could inevitably raise my spirits to a higher place—dangerous because it meant I never focused on addressing the identity and self-image battles I was facing. But over time, the overeating won out over the anorexia, and my weight gain became pronounced. Thinness is prized on the ballet stage; overweight dancers are considered failures who have no self-control, or just do not "want it" badly enough. People at work avoided eye contact with me and left me isolated in my own little bubble of shame.

Inside that bubble I curled continually into myself, growing ever more still, until there was nothing of the dancer left in me. Outside the theater, if I heard music anywhere, my muscles would become leaden and I felt as if there were a great dark weight pressing on me, freezing me motionless where I stood. There came a time when even performing *Serenade* couldn't make me feel beautiful, or even feel as if I were a part of something beautiful. There was just shame and self-hatred. I would gaze at my fellow dancers during a performance of *Serenade* as they swept like blue angels flying across the stage and yearn to be like them again. I felt separate, ugly, unworthy, worthless. I felt a desperate need to change, to fix myself, to escape this paralyzing, shadowy place in which I was bound. I watched the Waltz Girl as she was lifted up to heaven, and wished hopelessly that I were she. And I wondered how it was that I could be the same person as that little girl who had freely danced in her bedroom, compelled by something inside her to respond to the joy of music by *moving* with complete abandon.

Due to my weight struggles, I was eventually forced out of the ballet world, but after a year away, I was able to return to dancing professionally with the New York City Ballet as an entirely new person. And several years later, when a writer for the *New York Times* publicly criticized my body, I had the ability to perceive the criticism as untrue. I had a great deal of help with my personal struggles from so many people, and the story I tell in this book includes many but not all of them. I have dear, close friends who I know will be there for me throughout my life, as well as three people who are so necessary to my well-being that they seem to be woven into my makeup—my parents and my sister—but during my hardest times, I shut them out. So much of the time I describe in these pages is my journey alone and separate from my friends and family as I struggled to learn how to be a freestanding adult who could meet life's problems and deal with them in a healthy way. I love my family with all of my heart and know that I have always had their unconditional love and support. This period of my life, however, involved learning and growing that I needed to do on my own.

I also cannot tell my story without including, in an overt way, my Christian faith, and writing this book has made this clearer than ever to me. I have never been particularly public about my faith and have kept it fairly personal, which some would say does not reflect well on me as a Christian. In writing this book, I realized how compartmentalized I have kept my faith, and have been trying to more successfully integrate it into my life so that I am the same person everywhere I am, no matter who I am with or what I am doing. Indeed, saying that I am a Christian does not make me perfectly good by a long shot; it just means that as I fail and struggle, I know that I have a Savior who came to rescue me. Here, I describe one aspect of my Christian journey that has an element of closure to it because my eating disorders and depression have, by God's grace, ceased to exist, but there are so many other areas of my walk in which I fall down or make poor choices and continue to need God's grace and mercy and guidance.

Another reason it has been challenging for me to talk about my faith in this book is that it is so important to me, and I desperately want to get it *right*. That, I suppose, is a bit of the perfectionist ballerina still inside me. But I did not go to seminary and cannot argue about faith with logic and learned examples. All I can do is relate my own experience with God and hope that my honesty will come through with the sincerity and humility I intend. And I must trust that God and those who read this book will extend me grace if I fail to get something right.

I feel so blessed to have been allowed to dance for a living. To have lost dancing so completely and then regain it has made me appreciate every chance I have to dance, not only on the stage in the professional sense but also in life, for the pure joy of it. Dancing was returned to me, and now when I hear music anywhere I can move freely, unchained, and be glad.

Chapter One

❧

Tiptoe

Tiptoe, tiptoe, tiptoe . . . my seven-year-old feet stabbed into the carpet as I wandered through the house looking for my mother. I had a plan for the next bit of time, and she needed to be informed. I finally found her coming out of her bathroom with a towel wrapped around her head.

"Mommy," I said gravely, "I'm going to be in my room dancing, so if you call me, I won't hear you."

She looked at me for a second, her expression not changing. This was very important to me because I wanted to dance to very loud music, and it was an established rule in our house that when the parents called for the children, the children must respond immediately.

"I won't hear you because of the music, Mom. So you will have to come to my room to get me if you need me."

She smiled slightly. "Okay, sweetheart."

Relieved that I had solved my one little worry, I pranced back to my bedroom and closed the door. Under my window, waiting openmouthed, was my record player with the front panel disco lights. I turned out my lights and closed my curtains to dim the outside sunshine as much as I could. Then I turned to my record collection. I had only a couple of records, but one was always on top, and that was the one I now chose. The magical-looking singers from ABBA grinned at me from the cover.

I lovingly put the record on the turntable and set the pin onto my favorite track. With the first downward swoop of the piano, the lights on the front panel of the record player began to pulse. I turned up the volume. The lights grew brighter. Soon my room was changing colors with every beat of "Dancing Queen" and I was dancing wildly; there was no technique or thought involved. I spun and leaped and rolled on my yellow carpet in pure instinctual reaction to the music. I ricocheted off my bed and then bounced on top of it to flop and flip like a fish on land. I climbed off the end of the bed and onto my trunk and then jumped to the floor like a cat. When the song ended, I was sweaty and out of breath. I immediately started the song all over again.

This dancing was serious business to me. I loved it and danced every chance I got, but it was wrapped up in my imaginary world where I was a beautiful princess, a real dancing queen, who had adventures and needed rescuing and wore beautiful dresses all the time. I was always pretending to be a part of some story or another and was very happy to be alone in worlds of my own creation. I was not picturing myself as an actual dancer or ballerina; in my "pretends" I was not identifying myself as someone who danced for a living. I just danced for the joy of it.

Weeksville, North Carolina, was a perfect place for a girl with a vivid imagination. It was small and quiet and had few organized activities; children had to entertain themselves. We lived down a long gravel road that took us far away from any town. My dad used to let my sister and me sit on his lap and steer our pickup truck as we left a dust trail rising in our wake. Beside our house was a neighbor's orchard. Behind was a soybean field. To the left of us was an empty lot overgrown with waist-high grass and threaded with paths for the neighborhood children to run along. Across the street, behind another row of houses, was a wide, gentle river. In our yard was a giant wooden and rope swing set, complete with monkey bars and a balance beam. My father had built it by hand. In the summers, I would leave the house and wander the neighborhood, running wild or coercing the neighboring children to play parts in my pretend games, not coming home until the sun was setting and my mom issued her high-pitched clarion call to return to the house for dinner.

If I was stuck inside, I would dress up in my "princess outfits," which consisted of a collection of my mom's old nightgowns and my prized floor-length red-velvet Christmas dress. Or I would spend hours in my walk-in closet, acting out some kind of scenario with my favorite dolls. My family jokes that they never saw me or knew what I was doing; I was always in my room by myself.

With such a temperament, it would seem that dance classes were a perfect fit for me. So when I was five, my mother took me to a local dance studio for classes. Though I tried some and enjoyed the tap and jazz and baton twirling, ultimately I found them boring; we spent all our time learning our routines for the recitals. The performances themselves were a blast, but they were too few. And the one time I tried ballet, I thought I had never known a more boring hour in my life. Why was I just hanging on to a pole on the wall, repeatedly bending my knees? This was no way for the Dancing Queen to spend her time.

I had a lot of energy and imagination, but I wasn't actually that healthy as a very young child, and spent much of my first-grade year of school home sick with a string of viruses. My parents were very worried, but I didn't mind much; I found school boring. I have a memory of donning my Christmas dress and sitting down to put my new tiara on my head, only to be disappointed because of the chicken pox bumps all over my face. Then I remember my mom coming to me one day and saying gently that she thought there was a chance that some part of me actually wanted to be sick so I would have to miss school. She was not being harsh and did not disbelieve that I was really sick; she just wanted to pray with me about it.

My parents were Christians and were doing their best to raise their daughters in a stable family centered on a strong faith. When I was young, I think my parents were just becoming more serious about their own faith and were trying to incorporate Christianity more strongly into our family. There were bumps and inconsistencies, but my mother, particularly, was determined, and we started to go to church regularly. It became a habit—it was just something we did every Sunday. And when we had struggles or uncertainties, we began to pray about them.

I have a vivid memory of my mother sitting beside me as I lay in bed and telling me that if I opened up the doors of my heart and asked Jesus to come in, He would come into my heart. I really wanted it, and I did ask, and felt that something was different afterward. Though I was a child, I knew that something important had happened.

So even at a young age, when my mom suggested I pray about the possibility of wanting to be sick and therefore resisting getting well, I did. I told God that I was ready to stop being sick and wanted to be well again. And it happened—I became a very healthy child who rarely got sick. I went back to school consistently. I do not believe my parents said anything to the school about my being bored or uninterested, but the next thing I knew, I was sitting in a room with a very nice lady, answering questions and solving problems for her. I enjoyed it because I was missing my regular classroom time. Soon thereafter I was told I would skip second grade and go directly into third grade when school started again.

My first day in third grade was rocky; the teacher announced to the class, "This is Jennifer Ringer. She is new in our grade this year because she skipped over second grade."

Every head swiveled toward me, and I was fixed with the blank-faced stares of big third-grader eyes. I got along as best I could without drawing too much attention to myself—until it came time for our writing exercise. The teacher came by my desk, stopped, and proclaimed loudly, "Oh, here in the third grade, we write small, in only one line, not two." I was mortified as every student in the class once again stared at me. Perhaps that is why my handwriting is so bad even today.

But despite my embarrassing start, I flourished in third grade and had made a good start in fourth grade when we suddenly moved in the middle of the year to Summerville, South Carolina. My father, a marine biologist, had taken a new job with the Naval Criminal Investigative Service (NCIS) and been transferred once again. We had always moved around a lot for his work, so this move was not that big a deal to me. And Summerville, just outside Charleston, was a great place for our family.

I brought with me to Summerville my love for dance, though I had stopped taking dance lessons because they were just too tedious. I moved on to other things: cheerleading, softball, tennis, piano. My sister, Becky, who is four years older than I, was very athletic and talented in many areas. She made everything look easy: she was a gifted pianist who would later go on to get her doctorate in musicology, she was captain of her tennis team, she played first base and shortstop on her softball team, and she won many of her heats on the swim team. I would go to all of her events and watch her and think, That looks fun. I'm going to do that too.

Well, it turns out that sports were not necessarily for me. I was good enough at them when I applied myself, but they just didn't capture my fancy, and all the ability in the world gets you nowhere if you're not motivated or focused. My softball coaches would yell at me because while I was out in right field, instead of paying attention to the game and thinking about my position, they'd find me turning cartwheels or seeing how high I could throw my glove and still catch it. In tennis, my wrist would give out every time I tried to whack the ball, leaving me feeling unsatisfied. During piano recitals, I would unconsciously swing my legs so wildly that they would kick the piano, resulting in a loud discordant *gonk* of a sound. Cheerleading was more fun for me; I enjoyed kicking my legs and learning cheers that I got to yell at the top of my lungs. But then they decided to make me the top of all the pyramids, and I really didn't trust my fellow nine-year-olds to hold me up. Sports star, then, did not seem my destiny.

I was more interested in the actual academics in school, and was in the "good" crowd that got straight A's. I got along well with my classmates and threw myself into extracurricular activities of the non-athletic sort. I was voted onto the student council and eventually became president, which meant I read the morning announcements to the whole school over the loudspeaker and got my picture in the local paper when the school started a program for planting trees. I continued to be an overachieving student—one of my good friends and I shared an exclusive prize called the Fred L. Day Award for academic excellence. And I even won a prize at the regional science fair because of some icky experiment I did, with my dad's help, where we tested for the bacteria that came off cooked and uncooked meats. To this day, I am afraid of raw meat and wash my hands and my entire kitchen repeatedly if a package of meat is even cracked open. The things that grew in those petri dishes . . .

My best friend at the time was Tanya Nikitas. She was the one who had gotten me into cheerleading. We were mostly inseparable, except for the times that, like all young girls, we suddenly got mad at each other for who knows what reason and had to air out our problems. The rest of the time, we were tape-recording ourselves singing popular songs or working on our dance routine for the school's talent show. Tanya loved to dance, too, and was taking ballet lessons at a studio in Summerville. One day she asked me to come and spend the night at her house, and our moms arranged for me to be dropped off at Tanya's ballet school to wait for her to finish her class. This little bit of scheduling between two moms would turn out to change my life.

I remember walking up a long stairway. The building wasn't in the best condition, and the stairway was dusty and dark. Then I walked down the hallway to a door through which I could hear classical music playing. The door opened directly into the ballet studio. I paused uncertainly at the threshold, looking at Tanya and the other girls in their leotards holding on to long wooden bars—or as I eventually learned to spell them, barres—that ran the length of the long rectangular room. The floor was wooden as well, and there were pictures and posters of dancers on the walls. The teacher was a petite blond woman wearing a thick sweater unitard and smoking a cigarette. She spoke with a confident British accent.

Someone directed me to the dressing room area, where I could sit and wait for Tanya to finish class. Through the door of the dressing room, I could see the class proceeding. I sat on a bench and cracked open my giant schoolbooks so that I could get a head start on my weekend homework. Wouldn't it be great if I finished it all now and then had the whole weekend free? But before long, I was distracted by what was going on in the studio.

The girls were really dancing. They were doing complicated steps that moved them all over the room with turns and leaps. The teacher would stop them to correct all sorts of little things that I couldn't really see and certainly didn't understand, and then make them try the step over and over again until she was satisfied. She would sometimes yell, but it didn't seem mean. It seemed challenging. This class looked nothing like the boring ballet classes I had taken before. It looked thrilling. I wanted to do it.

In December 1983, when I was ten years old, I started taking ballet with this very teacher, Terry Shields. I instantly loved it. Terry taught ballet as if it were very important and precious. She was the first person to instill in me an extremely important virtue for any dancer: discipline, combined with high standards. I learned that the steps needed to be done exactly right, not just "good enough."

Ballet was difficult, and I did not do everything well right away, even though I was beginning to sense that I was good at it. My body moved in the right ways by both natural instinct and learned new habits. The challenge and the idea of striving for excellence appealed to me; the hard work was attractive because it got results. Furthermore, I was being given the tools to really dance. I had never known there were so many steps or so many different and intricate ways to move. There were jumps and turns and poses that went so far beyond my imaginary homemade choreography. Now when I danced in my room, I wasn't just flopping on my bed or spinning to the floor. I knew what I was doing. I had a repertory of movements to choose from depending on my mood or the beat of the music, and I could string them together to make something more than just a little-girl dance. I was becoming a dancer, and I was hooked.

Around this time I took another big step toward becoming a new, more complete person, building my spiritual character along with my dancing one. My family was attending a large charismatic church in Charleston. It had wonderful praise music and seemed filled with people really living out the Christian life. It was far away from our home, however, and I often resisted going. Sometimes I begrudged the fact that church took up much of our Sunday. But I did have an unusual experience there. They often called for people to voluntarily come up to the front to recommit themselves to God, and during one such call, I really felt the desire within me to go. I was around ten or so, and I shocked my family and myself by leaving my seat and going forward when people were asked to come and be baptized in the Holy Spirit. I felt scared to do it, but it also felt right. I didn't talk much to my family or to anyone about what it was like; it felt too private. But it seemed afterward that I had a much deeper, more sensitive relationship with God. The experience was life changing because I was beginning to take ownership of my faith. It was not just something that my parents were making me do. I could make my own decisions about where I wanted to place my faith and could have my own personal relationship with God. The seeds had been planted, but time would tell whether or not these seeds had fallen on fertile soil.

Both my new relationship with God and my time with Ms. Shields came together to open a whole new phase of my life. I was praying every day, in every situation, and felt comfortable having God a constant part of my day. I was suddenly part of a small ballet school community, which meant my family got to know the other girls and their mothers and fathers very well. Even though I had only recently started formal training, I had moved fairly quickly into the advanced class, which ranged in age from ten to sixteen, and we got to do special performances and lecture/demos at local schools. In Summerville, the performance opportunities were limited, but Ms. Shields took what she could get.

One such performance took place during a hot spring day on the tennis courts in the middle of town. We were part of the entertainment for the annual Flower Festival, dancing ballets choreographed by Ms. Shields. Another time we were the intermission performance for a local beauty pageant, which was a real eye-opener for me. I still remember being backstage and watching the strange things the women would do to their bodies to make themselves look a certain way in their bathing suits.

However odd the setting, though, I loved the performances and the opportunity to dress up and dance without being stopped for corrections.

When I was eleven, Ms. Shields determined that my class was ready to go *en pointe*. We would be wearing real pointe shoes and dancing on our toes! We were beside ourselves with excitement.

When exactly any given student goes *en pointe* is up to the judgment of the teacher, and many factors are considered. Is the dancer strong enough? Can she rise up on to the ball of her foot with her leg in proper alignment? Will her technical ability support this added level of difficulty? Dancing *en pointe* is entirely different from dancing in the soft pink ballet slippers, and many ballet steps have to be relearned. Ms. Shields had been watching all of us carefully, and she felt that it was time for us to start beginner pointe classes.

She took us to the nearest ballet shop and fitted each one of us individually for pointe shoes. I thought I had never seen anything more beautiful. Ms. Shields sent us home with a stern warning not to wear our shoes in the house; we needed to be trained properly in how to go *en pointe*, otherwise we could twist an ankle. We were instructed to wait to put on our shoes until the next week, when we had our first pointe class.

I compromised. I did not actually walk in the pointe shoes or go up *en pointe* in them, but I put them on my feet, lay back on my bed, and kicked them in the air, marveling at how wonderful these mysterious shoes were. I couldn't wait until our first class!

My first experience *en pointe* was not exactly what I imagined. It felt weird, as if my toes were inside bricks, and standing on my toes, though thrilling at first, was decidedly uncomfortable by the end of class. Ms. Shields had taught us how to put lamb's wool around our toes to cushion them, but during the class the lamb's wool had shifted around and holes had formed that left my tender skin unprotected. I got blisters.

Later, I learned that dancers actually taped their toes with masking tape to prevent blisters. But for now, I was a ballerina with blisters on her feet! From her pointe shoes! How wonderfully thrilling.

A number of us were ahead of the other students, and when Ms. Shields decided we had progressed far enough, she started an actual little performance company that she called the South Carolina Children's Ballet Theatre. This was exciting for all of us, because it meant we were going to put on real productions in a real theater. Ms. Shields rented a small auditorium, and rehearsals began for our first show; we would be dancing a mixed bill of choreography Ms. Shields made for us. As exciting as it was, however, suddenly there was a new element of pressure and competition in the ballet studio. It became apparent that now all the girls would not be treated equally on the stage. In class, we all danced together, but for the performances, some girls were being given special featured parts, and some were not. The stakes were being raised for everyone: Ms. Shields was very demanding. She had high expectations for the performance, and would sometimes become short-tempered. Since she was choreographing, producing, and designing the entire production by herself, she was under a lot of stress as well.

I knew that I was one of the better girls in the class, and I desperately wanted a special part, so I was anxious about the rehearsals. Ms. Shields became even more demanding in classes and occasionally lost her patience with me.

"What are you doing over there, Jenny?" she would ask me, her eyes on fire. "You are too lazy. You think ballet is always going to come easily to you. It's not! It takes constant hard work. You can't let up for a minute!"

After lectures like that, given before the entire class, I would cry all the way home. But it never stopped me from coming, and besides, she was right: I was certainly lazy at times. I liked to daydream, and not just in right field—I'd find myself drifting away during the less interesting parts of ballet class, like the barre work. I was used to not having to try very hard for things, and while I was learning discipline, I also relied to a large degree on my natural abilities. There was a complacent part of me that thought ballet would just be something else I was good at and that I wouldn't really have to try that hard. But her words sank in, and the fact that it took an extra level of work and determination challenged me and ultimately paid off enormously—having to apply myself over and over actually inspired me to stick with ballet. The fact that Ms. Shields did not just automatically give me all the best parts was good for me; I would have assumed that my mild and minimal efforts were enough and ended up just a passable dancer. Instead, starting at ten or eleven, I was driven to prove myself, to gain Ms. Shields's approval and admiration. My competitive side came out, and I wanted to be the best in the class and get the best parts in our productions. I worked harder.

I did end up getting featured parts in Ms. Shields's performances, but she was a generous director and tried hard to give each of us something special to do, thus spreading out the spotlight. And I never took my place for granted. I remember one bad day when I had to miss a weekend rehearsal so that my family could go to my sister's piano competition, which was out of town. Ms. Shields at first penalized me for that, saying nothing but going forward and starting the new choreography without me, and I thought I was not going to be in her new ballet at all. Great tears were shed. But then she added me to the ballet, creating a late entrance for me, and I was saved.

From the very beginning, I have loved the excitement of performing, and even with our little shows, I was always sad when a weekend of performances was over. Performing was stressful and anxiety provoking, sure, but it brought so many fun and new elements together. Ironically, to me it was the ultimate pretend game, a total break from reality.

I still remember sitting on the floor of the ballet studio with the other girls, staring into the mirror for our first stage-makeup lesson. We learned that to look our best onstage, we had to exaggerate the features of our face to make them seem bigger and more beautiful. The bright stage lights and distance from the audience would cause our features to wash out otherwise. With a white waxy substance we covered up our eyebrows, a difficult feat for me with my thick black brows, and then redrew them perfectly, a little higher than they were naturally. This was the way Ms. Shields had done her makeup in her youth; I was to discover later that dancers no longer whited out their eyebrows for stage unless it was for a particular character part. After the eyebrows came the base: with thick cake makeup we made our preteen complexions smooth and even. We gave ourselves pink, blooming cheeks and red glossy lips and drew lines around our eyes to make them appear huge and doll-like. Best of all, we got to wear false eyelashes. We were transformed into more glamorous versions of ourselves. And then we put on our costumes and pointe shoes, further changing ourselves into different creatures entirely. We were ballerinas: perfect, exotic, separate.

During the fall of 1985, when I was twelve, my father was transferred to Washington, DC. My mother and sister and I had to stay behind in Summerville while we tried to sell our house, but we knew we would eventually be moving as well. Then my father received an award for some outstanding work he had done on a case with NCIS. The award was to be given in Washington, and my mom and I went to watch the award ceremony while my sister stayed with friends. It was my first time on an airplane, and I was thrilled. My family never flew because it was just too expensive. I loved every minute of it, but my mother discovered she did not like flying.

"Isn't this wonderful?" I remember exclaiming to my mother when I managed to tear myself away from the airplane window.

"Uh-huh," she replied with a strange grimace on her face while she gripped the armrests hard enough to break them. We took the train home.

The real reason I went to DC that weekend and my sister didn't was that I was going to audition for the summer intensive program at the Washington School of Ballet. Mom and I wanted to see if we liked the school, and we needed to find out how I stacked up against the ballet students in a big city. Terry Shields had told my mother that she thought I "had it all" and could be a professional dancer if I wanted to, but we just didn't know for sure. I was only twelve years old, and I had no particular aspirations to be a professional dancer. I loved to dance, but ballet was just an after-school activity for me; I presumed that, like everyone I knew, I would go on to college after high school and then get a regular job. Was dancing even a real job, or did dancers have to wait tables to make money? Besides, after reading James Herriot's *All Creatures Great and Small*, I wanted to be a veterinarian.

Anyway, the audition was set up at the school. My mom had done research and found out that the Washington School of Ballet was the best in the area. She had kept her quest a secret from Ms. Shields, afraid that Terry would give me lesser parts in our upcoming performances if she knew I was leaving. For the audition, I was just to take a regular class with girls my age so the director of the school, Mary Day, could come and watch me. When we arrived at the white-and-gray building that housed the Washington School of Ballet, I was overcome by terror. All my confidence drained away, leaving me feeling like the biggest small-town ballet dancer in the world. What if those big-city teachers were mean and scorned me for even trying to take classes at their school? What if the other girls did bad big-city things to me, and I was humiliated? What if I got lost inside that huge building and never found the studio? I sat in our truck and cried, telling my parents that I had changed my mind and I didn't want to go there after all.

Somehow my parents convinced me that I needed to try. We had a long prayer in the truck, and I poured out all of my fears to God. I gathered up my courage, and we all went inside together. The predominant color was gray—gray walls, gray floors, gray sky outside the windows. Everyone inside seemed very serious. Mothers sat on benches, whispering to each other and assessing every passerby, no matter what age. Students dressed in the uniform leotard of steel gray scurried about purposefully, knowing where they were going. Directed to the dressing room by a distracted secretary, I somehow made it to the studio for the class. I wore a black leotard and stuck out like a sore thumb.

The other girls, hair slicked back into tight buns, stared at me while they stretched their long legs around their heads. One or two asked me why I was there and seemed nice enough, but the others remained aloof. A man came in. Was he the teacher? No—he proceeded up a very small flight of stairs that led to an elevated platform in the corner of the room.

Upon that platform, miraculously, crouched a piano. Live piano music. My intimidation increased. I had never danced to anything but a record.

Another man came in. He was dressed all in black and had gray hair to match the ambience, a straight back, and an unsmiling face. This was the teacher, Michael Steel. Class began, and I had the definite feeling that serious work was about to happen.

The style of the class and the combinations of steps were totally new to me, and I felt that I was floundering and constantly having to catch up. I had only ever taken ballet class from Ms. Shields, and I was used to her combinations of steps and her style. Here at Washington Ballet, they had a different syllabus and a different training style, even to the way they canted their heads while they did the combinations at barre. The other girls were extremely good, much better than the girls I had been taking class with in South Carolina. For the first time in a long while, I was not the best in the class. Mr. Steel never said a word to me, for which I was thankful; everything seemed difficult enough. When he corrected the other girls, he was very stern and demanding, not mean, but I did not think I could handle a correction or criticism of any kind during this class.

At one point a plump, owlish woman came in and watched the class, peering sharply through her large brown glasses. She was unsmiling the entire time and seemed to watch all the girls, not just me. I quickly figured out she was Mary Day. As the class progressed, I started to get my bearings, and my confidence grew as I was able to execute some of the combinations respectably. The hardest part was not knowing how to navigate with the other girls; I did not know whether to stand in the front or in the back of the groups when we began to do our center work after the barre. When doing moving combinations across the room, I did not know whether to go first or last. What impression was I making, and what was the etiquette? The other girls, I was sure, would prefer that I stay back and out of their way and only dance when they were finished. But would Mary Day expect me to be more assertive, to show that I had gumption? When the class was finally over, I was terribly relieved. Though the hour and a half had felt horribly stressful, I had a sense of accomplishment: I had faced a huge fear, walked through it, and come out the other end.

A few weeks later we learned through the mail that I had been accepted to the summer course, but I still could not decide how I felt about the whole experience. There were many ballet school options for me in the DC area; we would be living in West Springfield, Virginia, near multiple dance schools, some casual, some more serious, including the Virginia Ballet School. In Maryland there was also the well-respected Maryland Youth Ballet School, but that was too far of a commute. I was torn about how serious I wanted to be in my ballet studies. My mom and I prayed often that we would make the right decision about where I should go.

Meanwhile, we finally sold our house in Summerville and moved to Virginia. We went through the motions of settling into a new home, which were pretty familiar to us now, since we rarely lived in one town longer than four years. My sister and I set up our rooms. My mother got us registered for school. We began the great "church search," looking for a Bible-based community with good preaching.

And we had to make a decision about where I would study ballet. I leaned toward Virginia Ballet, which seemed friendlier and less intimidating. Washington Ballet, with its grayness and unsmiling students, seemed too scary, and my mother was terrified of the drive into the city in the infamous DC traffic. But we wanted to say we had given it a chance, so we decided I would take a summer course at both schools, a couple of weeks at Virginia Ballet and then a couple more at Washington Ballet.

I loved the teachers and classes at Virginia Ballet. I studied with a teacher called Oleg Tupin, who had danced with the Ballet Russe de Monte Carlo. He was wonderful and gave me a lot of attention in the classes. Oleg taught in the Russian classical style, my first experience with this technique, which stresses dramatic, more extended positioning of the body and high leg extensions. This school seemed perfect for me because it combined serious training with a friendly atmosphere, and I even got to take pas de deux, or partnering, classes for the first time. There were no boys taking ballet in Summerville, hence no pas de deux.

Dancing with a male partner was one of the things real ballerinas did, and it was a thrill to try it myself. The men taking the class were older than the girls and had probably consented to come just to give the students some partnering experience. I felt shy around them at first, and it seemed odd to be doing such things as holding a strange man's hands or feeling his hands intimately on my waist. But the men were very professional, and it soon became apparent that this was work. Pas de deux is difficult, subtle, and technical and there is a lot to learn, even for experienced partners. In fact, partnering is a skill that professional dancers are constantly working on to maintain and improve.

My favorite thing was being lifted; the first time my partner seized me and held me in the air, I felt a "Gee, golly" smile spread over my face. The sense of flying through the air in beautiful positions as classical music soared around me was exhilarating. The instructor of the class knew that many of us were new to partnering, but he went ahead and plunged into some of the trickier, more spectacular moves. One of these moves was a *grand jeté* lift where my partner tipped me backward over his head so that I was in a backbend, staring at the wall behind us, my front leg pointed straight up to the ceiling. I loved it, but it took lots of tries to get the balance just right. Not only does the man have to hold the woman in the correct position, but the woman also has to have the strength to hold her position for a sustained time. I was never dropped, but we had some ungainly dismounts. My partner figured out exactly where on my hips he needed to hold me to find the balance point of my body, and I was told how to hold my position so that I did not cause him to injure himself. We tried it over and over.

I was having so much fun that I ignored the pain I began to feel on the skin of my back every time I was lifted. When I got home and looked at my back in the mirror, I saw that the material of my leotard, pressed repeatedly against my skin by my partner's thumbs, had chafed two sores on my lower back.

I did not think too much of my wounds until the next partnering class, when we tried the overhead *grand jeté* lift again. Every time my partner picked me up, it felt as if someone were holding two lit matches against my back. I couldn't believe how much it hurt, but I didn't want to miss the opportunity to try this glorious lift, which I might never have again. I continued, not telling anyone, and eventually we moved on to another lift in other classes. It was my first experience dancing silently with pain, something that professional dancers do on a daily basis. Even today, when I am doing a lot of partnering, I will actually build up slight calluses on the skin of my back that prevent me from hurting during certain lifts. Of course, I wish now that I had had the courage to tell the instructor that the lift was hurting me, but that communication skill was something I would not learn for a long time.

I also suddenly had a pain behind my ankle during the classes at Virginia Ballet. Perhaps it was the newly intensive schedule. I was doing multiple classes a day, five or six days a week. We went to a foot doctor and discovered that I had a heel spur, an extra growth of bone that was impeding the motion of my foot when I pointed it. Heel spurs were very painful and often meant surgery.

This news was devastating to me, but before we did anything, my family and I prayed about it. My mother found out that there were people in our new church who felt called to pray for other people's healing, and she asked if they would consider praying for me. One night we went over to the group's regular Bible study, and some of them prayed for my foot. I felt a little uneasy about it because I had never been prayed for by a group of strangers. It was extraordinary to meet people who cared enough about what they felt God had called them to do that they would pray for someone they did not know, and for something that was horrible to me but not necessarily that important in the scheme of the world. But these generous Christians assured me that God cared about even these things in my life, and they prayed for my healing.

Well, to my surprise, the pain went away. We never went back to the foot doctor, as it seemed pointless—the problem was gone. I was never bothered by that issue again and gave it little thought after the fact. I was thirteen and felt invincible.

After the two-week intensive course at Virginia Ballet, I felt pretty sure that I would end up there for the year. But we went ahead and tried the summer intensive at Washington Ballet as well—six days a week, three to five hours a day, for two weeks. I was very nervous in the beginning. The studios were huge, the classes large, with roughly twenty-five students, and the teachers difficult and strict. At one point the choreographer for the Washington Ballet, Choo San Goh, even came and taught our class. He was very quiet and gentle, but I couldn't believe that I was taking a ballet class from a real, famous choreographer. I felt breathless every time he walked by my barre because I was trying so hard to please him and be noticed.

At one point in the class he asked me my name.

I thought I said, "Jenny."

"Genie?" Choo San asked.

I remembered that with my very southern accent, people in the North often didn't understand that my name was Jenny, short for Jennifer, but instead thought I was saying, "Ginny," short for Virginia.

I overcorrected. "Jahny," I said.

"Johnny?" he asked.

"*Juney*," I replied, with emphasis. Had that sound really just come out of my mouth?

"Pardon me?" he said.

"Jeeny!" I blurted.

Choo San looked at me with a bemused expression. The students laughed. What was wrong with this girl, that she couldn't say her own name? I felt my face turn bright red. Finally inspiration struck.

"Jennifer!" I gasped.

"Ah," said Choo San, and the class continued. I felt like a wet noodle.

Despite that one incident, I soon discovered that I loved being at the Washington School of Ballet. Yes, it was harder and stricter and more serious than anywhere else I had been. Yes, the girls there were better dancers than I'd ever seen in my age group. But I loved the difficulty, and I loved the challenge. Everything was at a higher level, and I found I wanted to conquer the heights. I saw something in myself that was inspired by the conflict and wanted to triumph over it; I felt that I actually could succeed in this school and that the school would make me better. I wanted to stay.

We had some backtracking to do because I had pretty much committed to the Virginia Ballet School. We asked the Washington School of Ballet if I could attend their year program after all, and I was accepted on a half scholarship. I wrote Oleg a letter, telling him how much I had loved studying with him but that I'd decided to go to Washington Ballet for the year. He wrote back, telling me all of the plans he had had for me that year, which of course confused me and made me feel guilty.

The program for advanced students at the Washington School of Ballet was early release, which meant that I would have to get out of my high school one period early. My school allowed ballet to be my physical education credit, so we could make it through traffic and be at the Washington Ballet in time for the first of my two daily ballet classes. My mother started doing dry runs into DC with my dad so that she could get used to the forty-five-minute route before it really counted. We found another student who was willing to carpool with us so that we could all save on gas money. It felt like we were preparing for a lot, but I was so excited about this new beginning.

I was thirteen when I began studying at Washington Ballet in the fall of 1986. For my mother and me, life in the afternoons revolved solely around ballet. My mornings were those of a normal high school student. My sister and I were both going to the same high school, she as a senior and I as a freshman, since I had skipped second grade all those years ago. My sister was extremely busy with extracurricular activities as well; her piano studies were intense, and she was also captain of the tennis team. But now that she could drive, she was becoming more self-sufficient. She drove us both to school most mornings.

My mother had a part-time job as a school nurse and would pick me up early at school. During our forty-five-minute commute into DC, I would have a snack, do some homework, twist my hair into a bun, and even change into my leotard and tights if the traffic was bad and I thought we might be late. We also started praying together on the days when we didn't have a carpooler with us.

Initially the prayers were just for our safety during the commute; my mom was petrified of driving in the notoriously bad traffic of the Beltway, and she needed the reassurance of God's protection all the way there and all the way home. But soon our prayers blossomed to other areas, and we ended up praying for everything in our family's lives, no matter how small. It was a wonderful time of growth for both of us because we had never had such a long uninterrupted, undistracted time to pray. I learned how to pray, and how to watch for the results of those prayers. I felt more peaceful about things because I knew that even when I was scared or feeling out of control, God was there and His wisdom was working, whatever the outcome might be.

My first months at the Washington School of Ballet were invigorating and eye-opening. We had a variety of teachers, not just one, as I was accustomed to in South Carolina. The student body was large, and there were three good-size studios. We were grouped roughly by age and also by talent, and there were a couple of boys in our classes as well. The teachers were demanding but pleasant.

The charismatic Julio de Bittencourt taught us ballet and character dancing. In character, we wore heeled shoes and did stylized czardas and mazurkas like those I had seen in folk festivals or European national dance exhibitions on television. Mr. de Bittencourt tried to draw the fire out of our young souls and instill some passion into our dancing. We studied the subtly precise art of Chinese dancing with a company member from the Washington Ballet, learning ritualistic processions and poses. We had regular technique classes in soft ballet shoes with the challenging and funny Suzanne Erlon. She would lead us through barre to the center work, which included turns and then jumps. After a short break during which we put on our pointe shoes, we had pointe classes with the feminine and ladylike Patricia Berrand, who taught us the finer elements of dancing *en pointe*. Mary Day herself came in to teach us when she could, and that was always cause for extra nerves and more attention to how our hair was fixed.

It was fascinating for me to be exposed to all of these different styles of teaching and dancing. I felt myself growing as a dancer every day as new ideas or techniques were offered to me. My competitive side also came out, and I found that I wanted to be the best in the class at every step. I never completely succeeded, but there were certain movements in which I felt, proudly, that I had perhaps been the closest to perfect. Looking back now, I'm not so sure I was always correct in my assessment!

I began to form friendships with the other girls in the class and soon became closer to them than to the students at my high school. But when we were actually in the studio, there was always a subtle competition for the teachers' approval and attention. The Level B class that I was in was very talented, and we all wanted to stand out. I surprised myself by becoming more assertive than I ever had been; in those larger classes, it was important to try to stand in the front line of girls, or at least at the center, so as not to be overlooked. I don't remember our ever being overtly mean to each other, but I do remember silently jockeying for the best position in line or trying to get my leg the highest just so that I could "win," not necessarily for the pure reason of improving myself. The talent in the other girls definitely drove me to improve. I wanted to be able to tell myself that I was the best, at least at a certain combination.

My mother was receiving an education as well. On every available surface sat what we came to call the Ballet Mothers. These women, who loved ballet, were very involved in their daughters' progress, and waited at the school for the duration of their daughters' classes, striving to catch glimpses of the studios when the door was accidentally left cracked open. My mom started to joke that she was becoming one of them, and that I would one day write a book called *Ballet Mommy Dearest*.

During my second year at Washington Ballet, something happened that would alter the course of my life. I came in contact with a ballet called *Serenade*, choreographed by a man named George Balanchine of the New York City Ballet. I had never heard of George Balanchine, and I assumed that the New York City Ballet must be some small regional company in Manhattan. In fact, Balanchine was the most influential and innovative choreographer ever to arrive on the ballet scene, and his company, the New York City Ballet, is one of the best in the world. *Serenade* was the first ballet the Russian-born choreographer made in America when he arrived in 1934. It is as heart stopping now as it was then.

The Washington Ballet was going to perform *Serenade* at the Kennedy Center, and they needed four students to fill in the corps de ballet because they didn't have enough women in the company. With much excitement, I learned that I was to be one of the four. The rehearsals were incredible. I'd never danced steps likes these to music that stirred me as much as did Tchaikovsky's Serenade for Strings in C. These steps *were* the music, and my body *was* the instrument playing the notes. It almost seemed that with every new step I learned, my heart had to grow bigger.

Finally, during my initial performance of *Serenade* at the Kennedy Center, I felt a new light dawning inside of me. It was at the end of the first section of the ballet, when all of the women return to the pose they were in when the curtain arose—double diamond formation, palms and faces lifted to the light. Then, on a deep chord, they turn as one and take a stately step, followed by successive steps in time with the slow rhythm of the music. As I did this, surrounded by my fellow dancers, I lifted my eyes and looked toward the bluish stage lights illuminating our path. Like the other women, I trailed my right hand behind me as if I were running my hand over the tops of tall grasses or letting my fingers pass across the surface of a body of water.

And the thought rose up in me, distinct: This. I want to do *this* for a living.

Chapter Two

New York

&In 1987, when I was fourteen, my mom and I began to realize
that the thing for advanced students to do was to go away to summer
ballet intensives. A lot of Washington Ballet students went to the
Chatauqua program in upstate New York. Some students chose to go to
the School of American Ballet in New York City, a choice that wasn't
very popular with Mary Day because of the very different training to be
found there.

After asking the Ballet Mothers and reading some ballet books, my
mother found out that the School of American Ballet, the ballet school
attached to the New York City Ballet, was reputed to be the finest ballet
school in America, and we felt that even if Ms. Day didn't approve, it
would be a good indication of my level of talent to go to SAB's Summer
Course audition and see what happened.

I had never auditioned for anything before, and I was very nervous.
The audition was held at a studio in the Kennedy Center, and after I'd
safety-pinned my number to my leotard, I went and stretched with the
rest of the silent, unsmiling girls. The teacher walked in; I found out
later it was Susan Hendl, one of the ballet mistresses for the New York
City Ballet. She gave us a full ballet class. It was very difficult—some of
the steps were faster than I was used to, and many of the accents were
placed at different points in the music. During the *grand battement* combination at the barre, where the students perform high, fast kicks, the
teacher zeroed in on me.

"Get your leg back into fifth quickly!" she said, standing right next to
me. Fifth position is where ballet dancers close their legs together, feet

pressed against each other, the toe of each foot touching the heel of the other. "Into fifth and hold it there on the count of one."

She began to clap her hands on the downbeat when she wanted me to freeze in fifth position after kicking my leg all the way up to my ear.

"And fifth!" Clap.

"And fifth!" Clap.

"And fifth!" Clap.

She looked at me consideringly. "A little better."

She walked away, and I stood in place, panting. I'd never been asked to do *grand battement* that way. It was much, much harder. But I could see that it was also better.

After the audition came weeks of waiting to see whether I'd been accepted to the summer program. When the letter came, we learned that I had been accepted, on scholarship.

We were thrilled, but after looking at what it would cost to stay in New York City for five weeks, we didn't think we could afford it. My grandmother came to the rescue.

Marie Brown, my mother's mother, loved the arts; she herself was a chorus teacher and often brought her students to New York City so that they could be exposed to the best opera and Broadway shows. She told my mother, "You should go. I'll pay for your hotel." And it was settled.

That first summer course was terrifying and exhilarating. Terrifying because we were in big, bad, scary New York City. Would we get mugged daily? And I would be going to the biggest, baddest ballet school in the country. Would the students scorn me? Would they lock me in the lockers? Would I even be able to keep up?

But it was exhilarating for exactly the same reasons. The city was amazing—busy, fascinating, and ever on the move. We toured every inch of it and went to as many Broadway shows as we could afford to. And SAB was a revelation. The other students were nice, the teachers were demanding but kind, and the instruction was eye-opening.

Everything at SAB was on a higher level. The other students were better dancers than any I had yet encountered. We took our technique class, which I'd always danced in soft leather ballet slippers, in pointe shoes; I had to learn to dance every step, even the beginning steps at the barre, in pointe shoes. The standards were extremely high, and my learning curve was steep. I was challenged every moment of class. The Balanchine technique they taught was quick, precise, and intensely musical. When George Balanchine came to America to start his new company, he had first opened a ballet school, the School of American Ballet, because he knew that he was going to have to train dancers from a young age to dance in the revolutionary way he wanted them to dance. He wanted to open up classical ballet, make it more extreme and at the same time more efficient, and he needed to teach a whole generation of dancers to move in a completely different way. Once he had laid down this new technical foundation for his school, he felt that he could start his company.

For me, I felt as if I were starting over, because even the most basic ballet steps were taught differently at SAB. Something as easy as a plié, where the dancer bends and straightens her knees, was executed with a different impetus and musicality than I was used to doing it. The barre exercises were often set to a faster pace than I was accustomed to, but as a result, my muscles were more ready to move quickly once I was in the center. Even when we were dancing the slower adagio movements, the instructors wanted a sense of power and purpose in our movements. Something in me thrilled to every class.

The school asked me to stay for the year, an honor given to very few summer course students. We declined, as I would have had to leave my family and live on my own in New York, and my parents thought I was too young for that. I returned to Washington Ballet that fall a much different dancer, stronger and more confident. I missed the challenge I'd felt at SAB and couldn't wait to go back to New York the next summer.

During that year, a surprising turn of events brought change to my family. My father, continuing to work for the U.S. government, was given the opportunity to transfer to New York City. There were many considerations, but ultimately my parents decided that he would take the transfer. It would be a great job for my father, my sister could study piano with some of the best teachers in the world, and I could attend the School of American Ballet while still living with my parents. It seemed as if God had paved the way for my sister and me to pursue our arts in the city known for some of the best artistic instruction in America. And my mom had fallen in love with New York City, so she would be pleased just to wake up every morning as a New Yorker. She would be able to get a job there as well.

In the summer of 1988, when I was fifteen, my family moved to New York City. We sold our cars and felt a sense of freedom that we could just walk out of our building and go anywhere without worrying about traffic or parking. And we felt very safe; we were in the busy Lincoln Center neighborhood and lived in a doorman building.

Our New York existence was in fact a bit unrealistic, as I discovered a couple of years later when I moved out on my own. It is common knowledge that New Yorkers live in cramped, expensive apartments, but since my father's job considered New York City an undesirable "hardship" post, they provided incentives to those employees willing to work there. One of those incentives was help with housing costs. Because of that aid, we were able to get a large and lovely apartment on the thirty-third floor of a doorman building that had a pool and a gym in the basement. On a clear day, I could see the Statue of Liberty blinking far away in New York Harbor from my bathroom window. My family thought that living in New York was a piece of cake; why were people always complaining?

My sister was home from college and was looking for a summer job. I had a bit of time to settle into my new room; I remember unpacking while listening to the one country music station in New York City. We searched for a church and started going to a church called All Angels' Church, which was about twenty blocks away from our apartment. Very soon, however, the summer course at the School of American Ballet had started up, and I was busy dancing again.

It felt very different going back to SAB this time around, having done it once before and knowing that I would be staying for the year. I was fifteen now and felt a curious mixture of confidence and insecurity. On one hand, I was now experienced, and I knew that I was liked at SAB. But on the other hand, what if I got there and learned that I was just one of many they liked and ended up getting lost in the crowd? What if I was good, but not really *that* good?

And there was a whole new set of other students to be concerned about. I was used to the competition with the other girls at Washington Ballet. They were a known factor, and we had worked out whatever little things we needed to work out. But now at the SAB summer course, I was in a new class. There were some familiar faces, but also many new and talented girls whom I hadn't seen last year. And what about the girls who regularly attended the year-round course? Most of them were off at other summer courses, so I would have to wait and see what they were going to be like.

Since I was now in the highest level at the summer course, I was eligible for the SAB summer workshop performance, in which students performed new choreography in the small theater at the Juilliard School. It would be the last year for these summer performances, though the year students would still have their annual spring workshop performances, and the school would be taking the dancers to perform upstate in Saratoga Springs, where the New York City Ballet toured in the summer. This summer workshop meant rehearsals after our regular classes, but it was a chance to work with new choreographers and to perform in New York City, and I was really hoping to be picked.

Three different up-and-coming choreographers from different ballet companies came to watch our classes, and all of the students struggled to dance well and be noticed. I wasn't sure whether I would be singled out or not; I wasn't one of the flashier dancers in the class. There were others who could jump higher or turn around more times as they pirouetted on one pointe-shoe-clad foot. I was coordinated, had good movement quality, and could generally dance well; I also had a pleasing line and could make good-looking shapes with my body, excelling at adagios, where dancers moved slowly in a sustained manner. But I didn't have any technical "tricks" that might set me apart.

One student in particular daunted me. Her name was Monique Meunier, and she was my age and new to SAB that summer. She was the sensation of our class, everything I was not: strong, confident, she could do multiple turns with ease. It seemed there was nothing she couldn't do. Beside her I often felt small, weak, and mousy.

Somehow, however, I was chosen to do workshop and ended up being one of three leading women in one of the ballets. Monique and a student named Anne from South Africa were the two other leads. Best of all, I was going to do a pas de deux, a "dance of two" between just one man and one woman; my movement was an adagio, and I was paired with a very tall boy who could lift me in soaring lifts around the studio. To my terror and excitement, the choreographer even wanted us to do a "bird" lift, where I was held over my partner's head by my hip bones, with my feet and head arching up to the ceiling. It is the same lift made famous by the end of the movie *Dirty Dancing*. The balance was really tricky to get, and there were definitely times I feared I would be dropped on my head. Luckily I was with a good, conscientious partner.

The summer course sped by particularly quickly because I was so busy with the extra rehearsals. Suddenly the performances were over—I honestly don't remember them, which has often been the case in my career. Only if something unusual happens during a performance do I recall it with any clarity. This may be because performances are adrenaline-filled moments where I become something else and express myself using the more emotional, unreasoning part of my brain. I experience them deeply, but after a couple of days or weeks, I forget what it felt like to dance them.

Once the summer workshop performances were over, I was just waiting for the fall to begin so that I could become an official student of the School of American Ballet. One of my teachers from the Washington

Ballet, Suzanne Erlon, told me that I should audition for the American Ballet Theatre, the more classical and traditional of the two major New York ballet companies. But I was fifteen, and it felt too soon. Many students start to think about auditioning for companies around the age of sixteen, but even that is on the youngest margin of professional dancer hopefuls. I knew that I wanted to dance for a living—I loved it utterly— and it was starting to look like I might have a chance, but I still felt very much like a student, not ready for the audition circuit.

Finally the fall season started up, and I once again entered an entirely different world from the one I'd existed in before. My days were split up between school and ballet, and my adventures all took place within a six-block radius. I would leave my home on Sixty-first Street and walk to Sixtieth to go to my morning academic classes at the Professional Children's School (PCS). I was now a junior in high school, and because of the advanced classes I had taken in Virginia, I didn't have that many more credits to go before I could graduate. Also, the school was specially created to work around the schedules of artistically minded children. The class schedule was very flexible, and the school even offered private correspondence classes where students met regularly with their teachers one on one and were then responsible for a large part of their work on their own. The school catered to kids who were in television shows and movies, performed on Broadway every night, were musical prodigies at Juilliard, or were ballet students at SAB.

Looking back now, I can see that already my parents and I were subconsciously willing to sacrifice normal but important things so that I could pursue ballet as a career. I didn't think about it. Ballet just seemed more important, more rare and valuable, than seemingly ordinary activities like school and church, and everyone from the ballet world told us that it would take all of my dedication to "make it." It didn't matter to us very much that at the age of fifteen I was hardly doing any academic work; in fact, we were thrilled that I had advanced so much in Virginia that I rarely had to think about my homework. I would get the credits to graduate early, leaving more time for me to focus on ballet.

I was nervous about my first day as a New York City high school student. My mom took me to the Gap and bought me a new outfit, as she always did for my sister and me on our first day of school. I felt pretty cute in my outfit and it did give me confidence, until I got home and realized that all the price tags and size stickers were still on the outside of the clothes and had hung there all day for everyone to see.

After two early-morning high school classes, my fellow SAB students and I would troop over to the old entrance to the Juilliard building on Sixty-sixth Street, where SAB was located at the time. The first ballet class of the day was from ten thirty to twelve. We would arrive with our heavy book bags balancing out our equally heavy dance bags and head to the dressing rooms to change into our leotards and tights. There was usually about a half hour before classes began, so there was plenty of time to primp, fix our hair, get on our pointe shoes, and stretch before class.

I prepared very carefully for my ballet classes. I was now a full-time student of the School of American Ballet, which meant I was now officially a student of Balanchine technique. His style was called neoclassical: turning away from the heavy costuming and dramatic story lines of classical ballet, he instead choreographed ballets that were sleek and modern, with simple costumes and no story. His choreography focused on the dance itself and used classical ballet steps but often added a twist—a flexed foot here, a more extreme, off-balance pose there. Though he had died in 1983 and his choreographic works in America began in 1934 with *Serenade*, the ballet that stole my heart, his work looks more modern and innovative today than some ballets that were choreographed just yesterday.

At SAB, I was being trained to be a modern neoclassical ballet dancer: a Balanchine dancer. We learned not only to dance rapidly with precision but also to dance any step from any position at any time with hardly any preparatory movements. Even a moment of stillness couldn't be just a pretty, static pose; we needed to look and feel ready to move at all times, and there were supposed to be invisible lines of energy radiating from our extremities. Balanchine's technique is very difficult to master and was extremely challenging for me. But I felt energized and stimulated by the classes at SAB, and though every day I failed at many of the steps I was being taught, it seemed as if I were learning to really dance for the first time.

My main teachers that first year were Suki Schorer, Antonia Tumkovsky—"Tumey," as we all called her—and Susan Pilarre. Susan was an expert on Balanchine technique and style who focused on musical precision and dynamics blended with confidence and strength. Tumey's classes were exercises in endurance and stamina; her loving spirit would somehow shine through her tough Russian standards, and even when she made us jump until I thought I would pass out, I still adored her. Suki, whose class seemed to me to be the perfect interpretation of what Balanchine would have taught himself, tried to hone and refine us, searching for elegance and femininity on top of a strong base of musicality and technique.

After surviving our morning class, we would go to the Juilliard cafeteria to get some lunch. I would have yogurt and fruit and a half bagel, chat with some of the girls, and sometimes do some last-minute homework. But we didn't have much time. Soon it was time for us to grab our bags and troop back over to PCS for an afternoon school class and perhaps a quick "correspondence lesson" with one of our teachers.

Once that was done, school was over for the day. It was time for us to go back over to SAB for our second ballet class of the day. These classes, usually from two or two thirty and lasting an hour to an hour and a half, were pointe or pas de deux classes, variations classes where we worked on real solos from various classical or Balanchine ballets, or sometimes even ballroom classes, where we added another layer of elegance to our partnering skills.

We had so much to learn, and SAB wanted us to be thoroughly schooled in everything they thought a Balanchine dancer would need. In our technique classes we learned the basics, the ABCs of ballet, sometimes simplifying steps to the extreme and repeating them over days and weeks. In our pointe classes, we fine-tuned our work *en pointe*, emphasizing steps that would enhance our strength and precision. Variations class taught us how to sustain a ballet "paragraph"; most combinations in a technique class are short, only seconds long, like sentences for the body. In a variation, or solo, a dancer must have the strength and stamina to dance excellently for a minute or more, transitioning from one "sentence" to the next, and this takes practice. Both the pas de deux and ballroom classes focused on our ability to work with and trust a male partner and were in many ways the highlight of my week.

Once again, Suki and Susan were our main teachers for pointe and variations, Andre Kramerevsky taught us pas de deux, and once a week we had variations with Madame Danilova, a famous old Russian prima ballerina who was one of the stars of her generation. Though she had left Russia with Balanchine and been involved in his early European companies, Danilova rounded out SAB's curriculum by teaching the students very classically. Her classes were something special during the week.

Danilova was a treasure. She seemed to step out of an old daguerreotype when she emerged from her dressing room. Perfume wafted around her, and her hair was always perfectly set. She wore a leotard and a sheer chiffon skirt with a colorful scarf around her waist. Dainty ballet slippers with heels graced her feet, and her matching earrings and necklace twinkled in the studio lights.

Her classes were of an older style of ballet, slower and more poetic than the classes of the other teachers. She encouraged us to find subtle nuances in our dancing and to use contained and understated port de bras—the way we carried our arms—to make beautiful pictures with our bodies. In her classes we learned to dance in a way that would invite an audience into our world to see the luminescent shapes and phrasing we were creating onstage. She didn't want us to bash the audience on the head with our audacious technical daring. The good technique should be there—just underneath a layer of artistry. The variations she taught us were from the classic full-length ballets; that first year we worked on the fairy variations from the prologue to *The Sleeping Beauty*. She was quiet, ladylike, and frail with age, and throughout my adult career I often wished that my fifteen-year-old self had taken more time to soak up her style while I could. Even just an hour and a half with her taught me how to dance and behave like a lady, with poise and dignity.

Most days, this second afternoon class was the last of the day, and I would return to my family's apartment to do homework. By this time I was walking on the sidewalks by myself; I would have been horrified to still be picked up by my parents. Most of the other students, even though they were just teenagers, came from out of town and lived in their own apartments with roommates. I was already an oddity to be living at home with my parents, and I was at the age where I was trying to get as much independence as possible. Looking back now, however, I'm glad that I wasn't as independent as the other students. Fifteen was too young for me to be entirely on my own, dealing with the various pressures facing teenagers, in New York City.

On Fridays a special third class was added to our day. A five thirty–to–seven pointe class with the wonderful Stanley Williams, it was one of my favorite classes. I would hang out in the Juilliard lounge or in one of the hallways at SAB wearing warm-up clothes and doing homework or having a snack with the other students. Then we would go up to the studio early and stretch or just mess around and be silly the way only ballet dancers can be, asking each other, "Can you do this crazy thing on pointe?"

Then Stanley would come into the studio wearing his trousers and button-down shirt, smoking his pipe, and chuckling at all of us. Utter silence would descend as we prepared our brains to decipher his mysterious monosyllable of the moment. Some weeks the only word he would say was "in." Other weeks it was "toe." He asked for very simple steps and preferred uncomplicated music, mostly just chords. The other students and I would attempt his combinations, trying to figure out what he meant by "in" when he was correcting the way one rose onto pointe.

Every now and then a student would earn a nod from him, which was highest praise. Whenever I got a nod, I would think wildly to try to figure out what it was exactly I had done right so that I could do it again. I never really knew. But somehow I danced differently in his class; the mixture of his particular combinations, with the minimal music, silent studio, and simple words, would cause me to glide and float silently on pointe. I had greater mental focus on where I was putting my weight as I moved through the combinations of steps, and much more control over my body's balance. I couldn't reproduce this feeling in anyone else's class.

After the Friday-night class, my parents and I, and sometimes my sister, had a new tradition where I would meet them in the lobby of the Juilliard building and we would go for a slice of pizza and then an ice-cream sundae at Diane's, a burger-and-ice-cream parlor on Seventy-second Street. I could eat whatever I wanted because I had a teenage metabolism and was dancing a rigorous three hours a day. I was not worried about my weight and really had no awareness of anyone my age being worried about her body. If any of my friends had weight concerns, we never spoke of it. After our meal, my family would walk home, passing shops that were fully lit and open for business despite the lateness of the hour and marveling that we were now living our regular life in New York City.

The fall and winter leading up to Christmas was a blur of adjustments for me. School wasn't overly difficult, but given my busy ballet schedule, it was always a push to get assignments in on time. Classes at SAB were intense and challenging; the class size was very small, perhaps only fifteen or twenty girls per class. And every student was talented. I felt that I had a lot of catching up to do; my training had made me a pretty dancer, but not necessarily a strong dancer.

Indeed, there was a new level of competition for me at SAB. I was certainly not the best dancer, though I had my good moments. For every type of ballet step, there was one girl to whom the skill and movement came naturally. I would try to learn from her, always aspiring to be as good as or better than her at some point in the future. For turns, I would watch Monique. For fast, precise footwork, I would watch Elizabeth Walker. For high, effortless jumps, I would watch Tatiana Garcia-Stefanovich. I'm not sure they watched me for anything—perhaps for the way I used my arms in port de bras, a carryover from Washington. Ballet class for us was a silent, beautiful struggle, as each of us strived to be the best and garner the praise of the teachers. Outside class, we were giggly teenagers, but in the studio it was hard, serious work.

During this time, my family was still attending All Angels' Church, located beside the famous food store Zabar's on Eightieth and Broadway, about fifteen blocks from SAB and Lincoln Center. It was a small church with a dedicated family of congregants who knew one another well, a strange thing for New York City. Many of the members were professional artists, actors, and singers, and the leaders of the music ministry were talented songwriters with experience on Broadway. Needless to say, the music during the services was excellent.

Going to church was just something my family did on Sundays now, an accepted fact of our life. With the amazing worship music and the genuine, friendly members of All Angels', it was a pleasure to go. I had a personal and real faith as a Christian, but it had never been tested. It was easy for me to believe, and I didn't put much intellectual thought into my faith. I wonder now if we really know and have a good grip on our faith in God until we go through a major trial in our lives; is our Savior really a personal one until we have had to go through a true crisis of faith? As ballet began to take over more and more of my life over the years, I unfortunately found it easy to let God slip away. But here, with my family's traditions, I was laying down what would be good "muscle memory" for faith, and it would serve me well many years down the road. And though I gave up on God for a while, He never stopped pursuing me.

One Sunday during the church service, All Angels' had a dance offertory instead of the usual music. It was understated and beautiful and moving. I learned that the two girls who had danced were sisters who were both in New York City Ballet: Margaret and Kathleen Tracey. An actress and choreographer, Cornelia Moore, had choreographed their dance. I met them, and they welcomed me into their circle. Meg and Katey took me under their wing and talked to me about their years in SAB and what it was like being professional dancers in the company. And they asked me to join them the next time they danced in church.

We were careful about how we danced in church, since people can be opinionated about how they want their church services done. Our pastor, Martyn Minns, was very much in support of dance as an expression of praise to God, but he helped guide us as to how best to proceed with a dance ministry. We started with very simple steps and movements; most of what we did was gestural at first. We made sure our clothing covered our bodies well and that nothing in our appearance or choreography could be construed as suggestive. And we tried to make clear by the way we danced that we were not actually performing for the congregation sitting in the church. Rather we were using our bodies to worship God and glorify Him with the gift he had given us; we were an augmentation of the congregation's own worship.

I loved dancing during the church services. It was a chance for me to really feel like I was dancing for God alone, and a way to participate as a server in a church service using the special skills that God had given me. I loved the sense of freedom from criticism that I felt when I danced in the sanctuary. These short moments were about expressing certain feelings or thoughts or ideas that might arise in our relationship with God; since there were no words, the people watching could be touched in a more personal, subjective way because they were engaging their emotions and not the rational sides of their brains that they had used during the sermon. It was wonderful to think that I was touching people in a spiritual way through my dancing.

My family had our first New York Christmas, and my mother ran us around the city, doing every special holiday activity she could find. We gazed at the windows on Fifth Avenue and battled the crowds under the Rockefeller Center tree. We primly held our pinkies aloft at a Christmas Eve high tea at the Plaza Hotel. We stood in the twilit darkness of the Metropolitan Museum of Art to watch the lighting of its Christmas tree. We waited in frigid temperatures at the finish line of the Central Park New Year's Eve Run, which started at the stroke of midnight along with glorious fireworks. The runners dressed up in costumes and paused at champagne stops along the course. My dad ran in the race, dressed up in a tuxedo T-shirt and a yellow bird mask.

Before we knew it, the holidays were over and SAB started up again. And suddenly we were into Workshop rehearsals. Workshop was the final performance at the end of the regular school year, different from the now-discontinued summer workshop, and it was a big deal. Students from the two top classes got to participate, and everyone got to dance. All the students placed a great deal of importance on these performances because they were the main gateway, besides open auditions, to a career in dance after SAB. Although most of the senior students would be involved in the performances, only a few would get principal parts. Casting of the ballets was a good indication as to who might be asked to be in City Ballet. Furthermore, directors from around the world came to watch the performances and scout out the talent. Often job offers were made directly following the performances. I was turning sixteen that spring, an age at which very few dancers are asked into a professional company. I didn't expect to be getting offers this year and assumed I would have another year at SAB. After that, I was hoping to be asked into City Ballet, which almost every student at the School of American Ballet wanted to join.

We learned that there would be three ballets in the Workshop program this year: Balanchine's *Serenade*, staged by Suki Schorer; an August Bournonville pas de trois, staged by Stanley Williams; and Balanchine's *Symphony in C*, staged by Susan Pilarre. Slowly, as rehearsals began to be posted, we started to learn our casting. Although several of us might be learning the featured parts, not all of us would get a chance to actually perform them.

I had mixed feelings about the parts I was slated to learn. In one instance, I was absolutely thrilled. Suki decided to have me learn the part of the Waltz Girl in *Serenade*. From my previous experience with *Serenade* at Washington Ballet, I was already in love with the ballet, and the Waltz Girl was my dream part in it. This was the role of the girl who danced with the young man, fell down, and was left alone onstage, and then was lifted to the sky in the end. I couldn't wait to start rehearsals. I'd hoped to be in Stanley Williams's ballet because it was seen as the most exclusive of the ballets—it only had three dancers in it, as opposed to the other two ballets, which each had large casts. I wasn't chosen for that piece, however; instead, I would be one of the demis in the fourth movement of *Symphony in C*, a ballet with four separate movements, each with its own set of principals and demi-soloists.

The hardest thing for me was to keep my eyes on my own path and not look at what the other girls were getting to dance. Some of my classmates had principal parts in all of the ballets. I had to remind myself that it was my first year; I should be thrilled to be doing anything special at all. I could have been chosen to be in the corps for all of the ballets. And I was so grateful about *Serenade*. Rehearsing that ballet was the highlight of every week.

Soon after rehearsals started, we learned that students from the school would also be performing an excerpt from *Serenade* on the New York State Theater stage as part of New York City Ballet's annual Dancers' Emergency Fund performance in February. There could be only one cast for this performance, and suddenly the whole school was focused on who that cast would be. We learned that the Russian Girl would be danced by Tatiana, even though she had already been made an apprentice with the company and was technically not still a student at SAB. Arch Higgins, one of my friends and a sought-after partner in pas de deux class, was considered by all to be one of the top boys at the school and would be dancing the Waltz Boy. Bryce Jaffe, one of the senior girls, would be dancing the Dark Angel. The big question became Waltz Girl, the role I was training for in the ballet that had made me want to become a professional dancer.

Suki took another girl in my class, Tanya Gingerich, and me aside and told us that they were still deciding which of us would be Waltz Girl for this special performance. Tanya was a gorgeous girl and a beautiful dancer who was older than me and had been at SAB for a while, as had the other dancers chosen to do the lead roles. I felt intimidated by her and thought that by seniority, she automatically should have been chosen. In reality we were in the same class and therefore at the same level, but as the new girl, I felt like the usurper. I was of course terribly excited and wanted to dance the performance more than anything, but I felt stressed and anxious because I knew that the other students weren't happy with the situation.

Over the next weeks, Tanya and I alternated during every rehearsal, each of us dancing with Arch, who ended up having to do each section twice. Every rehearsal felt like a deciding performance, with Suki watching Tanya and me critically and never letting on what she was thinking. Ballet masters from City Ballet were brought in to work with us. Sean Lavery and Karin von Aroldingen, both legends from the Balanchine years, came in to give us their wisdom on the ballet. Sean helped us with the partnering, telling the girls how to hold their bodies in the lifts and Arch where to place his hands so that he could more easily control our weight. He made everything richer and more exciting. Karin worked with us on the feeling of the role. "Run through the light," she said, demonstrating with her chest lifted and arms held back as if she were about to fly. Both of these dancers had worked with Balanchine, so it was a thrill to hear what they had to say.

Tanya and I could both do the steps well; it was a deceptively difficult part that was physically hard to get through without tiring out. I pushed myself to never let any weakness or tiredness show, no matter how out of breath I got. Tanya and I were both dancing under feelings of stress and tension as we awaited the big decision.

Ultimately, there was a rehearsal scheduled to which every major faculty member of the school came. We were to dance the ballet twice, first with Tanya as the Waltz Girl, and then with me. I felt a mixture of nerves and resolve. I knew I was the underdog but really wanted to prove that I was strong enough and good enough to dance the part. I gave the rehearsal my all, attempting to dance it as if I were performing it onstage. Afterward, I sat at the back of the studio, spent, sweaty, and flushed, while the powers that be discussed things at the front of the room.

Finally, Tanya and I were taken aside one by one. I saw Suki pull Tanya to the side of the room to speak with her. I rummaged around in my dance bag so that it would not look like I was listening, but I stayed in the studio: good or bad, I would be getting my news next. I heard footsteps and looked up as Suki approached.

"Jenny. So we have decided that you are going to be dancing at State Theater with Arch," she said, a tiny pleased smile on her face.

"Wow!" I said quietly, thrilled but trying hard not to celebrate too obviously. I was euphoric but contained my excitement out of respect for Tanya. I learned later that the school had actually decided on a compromise, where though I would be dancing this excerpt at State Theater, Tanya would be doing the more important evening performances of Workshop while I did the less attended matinees.

"But we have to keep working on your *jeté battu* into the *soutenu*," she said, suddenly demonstrating how she wanted me to do a particularly difficult passage in the ballet. It was hard for Suki to pass up the opportunity to give me a couple more corrections. I adored Suki and would do anything for her, so I stayed and worked with her on my aching legs until she finally released me to go home.

Ecstatic but also exhausted, I went home to let the stress roll off me for the first time in weeks. That night, I woke up with a 102-degree fever and ended up being sick and unable to dance for three days. I think my body crashed under the weight of the anxiety and physical exertion I'd forced upon myself; some subconscious part of me wanted to ensure that my body would rest in bed for a few days. There were still two weeks until the performance, so the days off didn't affect my rehearsal time too much.

The day of the performance at the New York State Theater came quickly. My parents and I had a long prayer that morning and committed the performance to God; I had done all the work I could, and now it was just time to dance and let God be in control. The day passed rapidly, and then suddenly my fellow students and I were backstage, waiting for our stage rehearsal. Shaky with nerves, I tried to laugh and joke with my friends, but mostly I was too tense to talk. Company members lingered onstage and looked at the students, their expressions mostly shuttered, though a few offered smiles of encouragement. Meg and Katey Tracey came to check on me and offered hugs and wishes of *merde*, the way company members bade each other good luck. I was surprised to learn that *merde* was French for, well, what you might step in if you walked through a cow pasture.

The company ballet masters were on hand for the stage rehearsal. These were the coaches who taught and rehearsed the individual ballets; they were responsible for making sure the steps were correctly danced and the technique looked polished. A little woman with short reddish brown hair and a giant cat T-shirt that reached to her knees placed us in our spots onstage. She was Rosemary Dunleavy, the main ballet mistress for the company. Kind but firm, she obviously knew what she was doing. Peter Martins, a former principal dancer with New York City Ballet who had become ballet master in chief after Balanchine's death, was also there. He had been a famous dancer in Denmark before he came over to join the New York City Ballet, and was one of the most notable of Balanchine's choice male dancers. Now he was in charge of everyone and everything in the company. For this rehearsal, he sat on a stool at the front of the stage and watched with interest, smiling and laughing at us a bit and jumping up to fine-tune certain moments from time to time.

The rehearsal was brief, really just a run-through of the ballet. The company had other ballets to put on the stage that night and couldn't spend a lot of time on us. When it was over, I sat backstage for a moment and sorted through my emotions. There was excitement because I'd just rehearsed with Peter Martins on the State Theater stage, and it had gone well. There was relief that the rehearsals were finally over, and all that was left to do was perform. There was also terror that the rehearsals were over, and I would never get to rehearse my problem spots again. What if everything went wrong? What if I fell out of the two consecutive double pirouettes? What if even just *one* thing went wrong? Would that mean I had blown it and my chance to join the company was over forever? Should I put my pointe shoes back on, find Arch, and practice again? No, there was nowhere to rehearse, and company members were all over the place, watching. I needed to stay cool. I had done my best. Obviously I would just have to deal with the nerves fluttering in my stomach for another few hours until the performance began.

My fellow students and I were sent down to the basement of the theater to get ready for the show. The New York State Theater is located in Lincoln Center, a complex of buildings on the Upper West Side of Manhattan. The three main buildings are grouped around a great fountain; the State Theater, renamed the David H. Koch Theater in 2008, is to the left of the fountain. In the center, behind the fountain, is the Metropolitan Opera House, and on the right is Avery Fisher Hall. The New York State Theater was built in 1964, and Balanchine was involved from the beginning in making the theater perfect for dance. From the sprung floor, to the acoustics meant to dampen the clicking sounds of ballerinas' toe shoes, to the great sight lines and lack of center aisle so that every seat in the house was good, Balanchine had thought of it all. A cement block of a building, with its face made almost entirely of long windows, it is actually not that beautiful inside; the primary colors are white and gray, and there are hardly any windows back in the working part of the theater. But the stage is the perfect place to dance ballet. The basement of the theater, quaintly called the Lower Concourse, is a labyrinth of dim hallways lined with large crates and filing cabinets. I'd never been in the backstage area before, and the only way I found my way to our dressing area was by following the sound of excited chatter.

Meg and Katey came down to visit me and offer encouragement. They checked out my stage makeup and told me it was fine. I slicked my frizzy hair back with an enormous amount of hair spray, until it was hard and shiny. If I was anxious about a performance, I usually took my nerves out on my poor hair. I felt a surge of confidence, knowing that at least I could depend on my hair not to pop out of my bun and let me down. I don't remember warming up or putting on my costume. All of a sudden I was backstage, waiting the final ten minutes before *Serenade* would begin.

Suki came up to me and assessed my appearance.

"You look good! Good luck," she said encouragingly. Then she cocked her head and started brushing the hair on my forehead downward, against the hair spray. "You could do your hair a little softer though, you know." She gave my hair a dissatisfied grimace and moved on to another girl.

I silently screamed inside my head.

I ran to a backstage mirror and was horrified to see that she had made my hair stick up like Alfalfa's in *The Little Rascals*. Breathless, I took water from the water fountain and attempted to reslick my hair. Luckily, the quantity of hair spray I'd applied made my hair like glue, and my problem was quickly solved.

Arch appeared beside me.

"Do my shoes look the right color?" he asked, looking panicked. "They told me to dye them blue to match the unitard, but there were a million shades of blue spray paint! I tried to mix colors, but I don't know . . . and I think I did it too late. My shoes are still wet! And look, my hands are BLUE!" I later learned that for the boys, *Serenade* blue is a notoriously difficult color to achieve on ballet slippers. And no one had told Arch to wear protective gloves.

He held his shaking hands up to my eyes. Obviously I wasn't the only one trying not to freak out.

"I'm sure you won't be able to see that from the stage," I told him, trying to reassure him. I needed a calm partner. It was too late to worry about blue hands.

"Places, please," we heard the stage manager call. Feeling unreal, I went to stand in my place at the front of one of the two diamond formations. The audience noise dwindled to silence. The stage lights went blue. For our excerpt, we were starting with the Waltz section. While the other girls turned and walked offstage, trailing their hands behind them as I had done as a student at Washington Ballet, I would stay onstage, repeating the famous arm movements that began the ballet, and wait for Arch to come and tap me on the shoulder so that we could begin our dance together.

Just feet away from me, on the other side of the lowered curtain, the strings burst forth with Tchaikovsky's opening chords, like cries of the heart. My stomach rose into my neck, making it impossible to breathe for a moment. I raised my right hand toward the lights, a gesture that half reached, half shielded. Then the curtain rose with a quiet, zipping hum. I felt the breeze from the rising curtain blow my skirts gently around my ankles.

A strange thing happened when I looked out from the New York State Theater stage for the first time. The audience looked warm and inviting. The large jewel-like lights placed along the different audience levels glowed gently. The floor felt soft under my pointe shoes. My nerves suddenly left me, and I felt comfortable, at home. I felt a gladness rise up in me, and I knew that I was going to be able to dance with ease and confidence.

The whole performance was a joy that ended all too quickly. Arch and I danced like soul mates, everything going perfectly. I made my double pirouettes and got through those *jetés battus* that Suki had been worried about. I felt as if I were flying, lifted up on soaring winds. I wanted to do it again, right away if possible.

I could hardly sleep that night, reliving the entire day over and over in my head. After the experience of dancing on that stage, I craved a repeat and started to dream of being asked into City Ballet right away. Yes, I was young. But I thought I was ready. I wanted to be a City Ballet dancer.

And then the next week started, and it was as if nothing had happened. I was back to the normal routine. However, Peter was apparently impressed enough with my performance that he wanted to change my casting in the Workshop performance. To my surprise, Susan informed me that I would now be learning the principal women in both the second and third movements of Balanchine's *Symphony in C*.

I was of course excited by this, but also a little daunted. It didn't mean I was going to perform the roles, but there was a good chance I would if Peter had asked that I learn them. I knew Susan was skeptical that I was strong enough, so I felt that I had a lot to prove. Also, the girls already doing these parts were currently the unspoken stars of my class; Elizabeth was dancing the third movement, and Monique was dancing the second movement. Both of them intimidated me; when I watched them dance I saw everywhere I was lacking.

I pushed myself, though, and felt that I could rise to the occasion. I was used to succeeding, and after the performance at the State Theater, I had more confidence.

Then disaster struck.

It was springtime, and a few weeks before Workshop. I had just turned sixteen and was taking Susan's class. She had stopped the class to give me a correction on my *ballonnées*, scissorlike pointe steps. I was trying to do them sharper and cleaner and stronger. Something happened, and I kicked my working leg so hard that it pulled my standing leg out from under me and I fell.

Embarrassed, I got up, but I couldn't put weight on my foot. I looked at Suzy, who cared intensely about her students. She looked horrified.

"Sit down," she told me. "We'll get some ice."

She looked very upset, and I sat against the wall under the barre, trying not to cry. I was brought a pack of ice and watched the class with blank eyes as it resumed, not really seeing anything. I took the ice off my foot to check on it. It was turning purple, and a ridge of swollen skin was rising as if it were on a fault line.

In disbelief, I called my mom to come pick me up. She was just as devastated as I was and in full protective mode. She refused the offer of crutches, probably because that would mean we were admitting defeat. We went to a doctor in a taxi.

He took X-rays and then presented us with the news.

"Looks like you've broken your fifth metatarsal," he told me kindly. "Now, it's just a hairline fracture, so if you really want to do those performances, I can tape you up real good so that you can do it."

I looked at the doctor for a moment, taken aback. Is that what real dancers did? Did they dance on broken bones? Should I do that? Perhaps he was just testing me. I couldn't tell. I knew that Workshop was the most important event of an SAB student's year. I knew that to be asked into the New York City Ballet, or any other company of repute, for that matter, I had to dance Workshop. I knew that if I didn't do Workshop, I would have to put my dreams on hold and come back next year to try again. It was a devastating thought.

But my foot *hurt*. I couldn't bear to stand on it at all. It looked like an eggplant. I knew there was no way I could dance on it, and I knew that even Workshop was not important enough to make me crazy enough to dance on a broken foot.

I was given crutches and sent home. That night my mom somehow sweet-talked another doctor, Dr. Louis Galli, into paying a house call to give us a second opinion. I believe it was Dr. Galli's first and only house call, and he became my favorite doctor for the rest of my career. He often reminds me of how he came to my pink bedroom and looked at my eggplant foot while I was in my flowered pajamas. Dr. Galli confirmed the diagnosis, and I resigned myself to six weeks without dance to allow my foot to heal.

I didn't go to watch Workshop. It was just too hard to be missing it.

In a lot of ways, that first catastrophic injury was good for me. I learned a lot of lessons during the recovery that I was able to apply during the course of future injuries. Even while my foot was broken, I learned there were other things I could do to stay strong. Since the year was almost over at SAB, I didn't have to go and watch classes while I recuperated. The teachers told me to heal and come and take the summer course classes when I was ready. I started going to Pilates and discovered that I could hop one-legged around the studio from machine to machine. The instructors would put a cuff around my ankle so that I wouldn't use my foot. They loved having ballerinas and would come up with all kinds of crazy exercises to confound me and make me sore. This was probably the first time I realized I had stomach muscles.

I also learned that it was important to come back slowly and methodically from injuries. Stanley Williams saw me on the sidewalk one day, and in his typical Zen master fashion he gave me a nugget of wisdom to take home with me.

"The slower you come back, the faster you come back," he said, gazing at me with his deep brown eyes. I smiled and nodded, but didn't understand his advice.

As soon as I could, I was back in ballet class and even in rehearsals, trying to be ready to go on a fantastic trip SAB was taking to Holland in order to perform with the Kirov Ballet School as part of an early fall festival. I was to dance *Serenade* and the lead in another Balanchine ballet, *Valse-Fantasie*. But in the middle of one of my rehearsals, my foot began to hurt again.

This time I had a stress reaction on one of my metatarsals, a precursor to a stress fracture. It came from coming back to ballet too quickly and not having the muscular support around my bones to protect them from the difficult physical activity. I was sidelined again, though I was allowed to go to Holland with the group anyway, since my ticket was paid for.

I was happy to be going to Holland with the school because I'd never been overseas and all of my good friends were going. But I was bitterly disappointed and felt worthless. I was surrounded by dancers preparing for performances and talking about their roles; all I could do was take part of their ballet classes, and even the steps I was allowed to dance with my injury I couldn't do very well because I was not in the top form that all of the other students were in.

It was from this trip that I have my first memory of compulsively eating. It was not what I ate or how much of it I ate, but how I *felt* about the food and how the food would make me feel after I ate it. We would eat in a cafeteria for every meal, and I remember eating a lot of the fried cheese sticks they had there. I didn't overdo it necessarily, but I had a strange need to eat them, and I knew they were not the healthiest choice I could have been making. I was unhappy to be on this fabulous trip as just an observer. There was something about those cheese sticks that I ate every day that made me feel better. I looked forward to them because they made me feel happy.

Around this time I also became aware of my body's appearance for the first time. Up until then, I really hadn't put a lot of thought into my shape. I was confident in myself and felt pretty. I knew that every young woman came in a different shape and size, but I just assumed that everyone felt comfortable in her own body. God made us all different, and our differences were part of what defined us and made us unique. I suppose I was a bit Pollyanna-ish in that respect. I didn't look critically at myself, just as I didn't look critically at others. It was just not in my thought process to assess and compare and critique.

But during my sixteenth summer I began seeing changes in my body. I had been injured and so was not as physically active as I had been. Also, I'd only recently started my period and was beginning to see myself cross the line from girlhood into womanhood. My leotards were not fitting me the same, and I began to worry about parts of my body peeking out if my dance clothes were too small. In regular clothes I felt fine, but in the more revealing ballet wear, I was seeing my body blossom and I didn't feel comfortable with it.

I remember being taken aback by some conversations with my mother.

"You may need to watch what you eat more now that you are older and your metabolism is changing," she remarked offhandedly one day. The comment made me feel a little resentful and controlled, even though she couldn't have said it in a milder way.

Another day she said, "I see a difference in your thighs since you have been injured. It might be something you need to watch in terms of ballet." She said it as casually as she could, but she was worried about the possibility of my being criticized by SAB and wanted to somehow protect me. My mother loves her family fiercely and has always been our staunchest advocate. She had an idea of the body issues facing young women in the ballet world and was hoping I could avoid them altogether.

But her comment gave me pause. My thighs? I hadn't thought about my thighs. I went to the mirror and looked at my legs. Yes, my thighs were different. My hips were now more womanly, and my thighs were now thicker at the top than they were at the bottom. Was that bad? Should I not feel good about that? It was confusing, and instead of talking to my mother about it, I kept my insecurities to myself.

Much has been written about what the perfect ballet body is, and what Balanchine's ideal of the perfect ballerina was: small head, long neck and limbs, slim hips, arched feet, tall and very thin. I knew all of this and had always felt that my body was a close approximation to this ideal. I wasn't tall and my torso was probably a little longer than it should be, but all in all I thought I was pretty good.

I'd been around enough now that I'd heard the girls in the school talking about their weight and how they would eat a lot one day and then not eat the next, but I never put much thought into it. I had my head in the clouds much of the time, and the girls who were my closest friends were all pretty normal with their eating. They were healthy. But most of us, because of our low body weights due to all the physical activity we did throughout the day, tended to start our periods later than the norm, and so we were only now, at fifteen and sixteen, beginning to see changes in our bodies. Would I still have a "ballet body" in a year? I wondered if the other girls were having similar feelings. But I didn't talk to anyone about it.

Over the rest of the summer and fall of 1989 I took the time to heal properly and was soon strong and ready to dance fully again. I was in my last semester at Professional Children's School because I had enough credits to graduate early. Hopeful that this would be My Year, I was eager to get started at SAB and see what exciting things were in store for me.

Things felt different, however. It seemed that the teachers were not that interested in me anymore, and I often felt ignored. I wondered if I had been written off because of my injuries or if I had somehow fallen behind. Had I somehow missed my chance?

Feeling very upset about the sudden turnaround at SAB, my mom and I, at her urging, prayed a lot and searched the Bible for guidance. I was now "all in" as far as ballet was concerned; I wanted to be a dancer for a living and was desperate to get into New York City Ballet. It wasn't even a question anymore; I *had* to be a dancer at City Ballet. I had no other plan. My life was geared perhaps too much to just this one goal. At SAB, the only company ever talked about was City Ballet, and it seemed that to go anywhere else would be a failure. This was of course a misconception on my part; there are a good number of gorgeous ballet companies in America producing great art and excellent dancers. But I was almost brainwashed into believing that City Ballet was the only place worth dancing.

And truly, when I saw the company dance for the first time, it caused a complete change in how I viewed the dance world. I'd only ever seen classical ballet companies dancing classical ballets. But City Ballet dancers moved like no other company I had seen. Their energy and power swept them across the stage like whirlwinds, yet they could stop and be delicate on a dime if they needed to. The choreography was riveting, and small dramas unfolded within the nuances and subtleties of each particular dancer. My mother and I had gone to see every ballet company that passed through New York—American Ballet Theatre, Joffrey, the Royal Ballet, the Kirov—but in no other company did the dancers sometimes appear to be roaring with their bodies. City Ballet dancers growled in their quest to eat up the space of the stage, yet they somehow contained this fierce beauty within strong technique and musicality. This was how I wanted to dance, and I didn't think I could bear not getting into City Ballet.

My mom and I searched the Scriptures, looking for answers or reassurances. We wondered if I should perhaps jump ship and audition for American Ballet Theatre. I would have to rethink everything—but perhaps being a professional dancer somewhere, anywhere, would be enough? Then we did come across a verse that seemed meant for us: "Will I prepare the baby for birthing and not let it be born?" (Isaiah 66:9).

We got the sense we should wait things out and see what happened. It was still early in the year, after all, and apprentices were not usually taken into the company until the spring. So I waited, and trusted that God had a plan for me that was better than any plan I could envision.

A few weeks later, at the end of October, I was roaming the halls of SAB in sweatpants and fuzzy lion slippers waiting for my Friday-evening pointe class with Stanley. I saw Peter Martins at the end of the hallway, watching a class through the doorway. My stomach did a flip, as it always did when I saw him.

As I passed, I caught his eye, and he came toward me with a smile on his face.

"You're just the person I was looking for," he said.

I grinned vacantly at him, having no idea what to say.

"I wanted to tell you that I'll be making you an apprentice," he continued. "You can start with company class on Tuesday."

I felt a rush of . . . something indescribable. My dream had just come true. The greatest desire of my sixteen years had just been granted to me during a conversation in a hallway while I was wearing fuzzy lion heads on my feet. I wanted to squeal, but Peter was still there looking at me, and there were other students passing back and forth on all sides. I contained my joy and tried to be dignified and adult about the news.

I gushed my thanks to Peter anyway and attempted to look suitably happy without completely losing my head. He might have given me a hug, but I don't remember. I went into the girls' locker room, not knowing what to do with myself. I didn't tell anyone, because I didn't know who else had been chosen as apprentices and I didn't want the other girls to feel bad. I opened my locker and stared inside. My toothbrush was there, offering me an activity to perform. So I went into the bathroom and brushed my teeth.

I soon learned that I was one of four girls to be made apprentices. At the time, an apprentice didn't have full rights or pay and could perform in only four ballets a season. Apprentices were paid by the hour or by the performance, not with a weekly salary. It was a probationary position, but it was how most of the girls from SAB were transitioned into the company. Except in very rare situations, New York City Ballet only took students from SAB into the company; they wanted dancers well trained in the Balanchine technique. Two boys, Arch and Ethan Stiefel, were taken in as full company members.

I look back on that weekend, my last as a student, and my heart goes out both to those of us who were taken in and to those of us who were not. For many of the students at SAB, the knowledge that they have been passed over when apprentices are chosen feels world-ending. They might stay on another year, hoping to get chosen for the next round, but many start looking to go to auditions for other companies in the spring. This isn't a bad thing at all, but they have to change their mind-set and adjust their dreams. And the anxiety of auditions adds a whole new stress to the life of a ballet student; there are very few professional jobs to be had, and the competition is great. Many of the dance jobs don't pay a living wage, and dancers have to get second jobs. And those who don't get jobs in dance companies must further shift the goals for their lives, looking to colleges or applying the skills of discipline and excellence that they learned in ballet school to other, nonperforming careers.

For those of us who were taken into the company, I see our euphoria and enthusiasm, our idealism and our naive certainty that this was just our first step on our way to being great stars in the ballet world. But we were wholly unprepared for the difficulties awaiting us in the professional world of City Ballet. We had no idea that this dream of ours was actually grueling work, with long days spent trying to live up to extremely high standards of excellence. We were teenagers, and we had just won the ballet lottery. It would take a while for us to realize that the world we were entering might well prove impossible to survive in.

Chapter Three

❧

The Company

℘My first day as an apprentice with New York City Ballet was Halloween in 1989. I'd planned a funny costume to wear at SAB, and I had debated with myself over whether to wear it after all. What if all the company members dressed up for Halloween, and I ended up looking ridiculous because I had no costume? But then what if I wore a costume, and no one else did?

I ended up not wearing the costume, but I did bring it just in case. It is indicative of my complete unpreparedness for company life that I thought the company members might dress up for Halloween. I was still firmly rooted in the student mentality. I hadn't crossed over into the dance-is-work thought process yet.

My first company class was a bit of a shock. Whatever I'd been expecting, it was not what I got. The theater was rather dingy and dirty, and Main Hall, the biggest studio where company class was held, was drab and gray. I arrived at the studio forty-five minutes early to warm up. The only other person in the room when I got there was my friend Inmaculada Velez, also a new apprentice. Fifteen minutes passed, and we were still the only ones. I wondered if we had gotten the time or place wrong.

Slowly dancers began to trickle in about twenty minutes before class was due to start. The company members looked cool and mature, ambling into the studio in their well-worn warm-ups and sloppy hair. They studied us curiously or ignored us completely. Some offered smiles tinged with amusement or something like sarcasm. The jokers in the company loudly remarked, "Hey, we have new apprentices!" making us blush.

Class finally started, and I was a mass of tension. Barre was much harder than it would have been had I been relaxed. Even the first combination at the barre, the simple leg bends called pliés that are supposed to start a dancer's muscles flexing and stretching, left me sweaty and slightly out of breath. Was everyone assessing my technique already? Was this class my one shot? During center, when the dancers left the barre and did moving combinations in the middle of the studio, I stayed in the back out of everyone's way, just trying to take the atmosphere in and figure out where my place would be. Even though I was about the same size as the rest of the company, I felt dinky and small and insignificant. The company members looked so confident and self-assured. They knew the routine and how to get through the day. I'd felt that way as one of the "big girls" at SAB; now, I was starting all over.

We were called into the administrator's office and told some basic rules about our new life: we were supposed to write down all of our rehearsals so that the company could give us our hourly fee, we were only allowed to perform a total of four ballets as apprentices, and there was a phone number we should call every night so that we could listen to the tape-recorded message detailing the next day's rehearsal schedule. Oh, and how did we want to spell our names in the program?

Now, in my defense, I was sixteen and wanted to be unique. There were twelve Jennifers at SAB and already five Jennifers in NYCB when I became an apprentice. I couldn't bear the thought of being one more Jennifer. I'd thought about using my middle name, Ellen, as my new stage name, but it just felt weird to suddenly have everyone calling me by a different first name. My big move toward originality was to drop one of the *n*'s from *Jennifer*. I'd seen a street in Washington, DC, called Jenifer Street and had always liked the way it looked. So from that day forward, I was Jenifer Ringer.

My fellow apprentices and I were called to understudy all the ballets being rehearsed throughout the day. This meant we were working on three or four ballets a day. Sometimes we were all called together, and sometimes we were called to different ballets based on our size; I learned that some ballets were for the shorter girls and some were for the taller girls. At the time, there were many very tall girls in the company, so at five foot six I was considered medium to small.

I was amazed at how fast the dancers learned the steps. The main ballet mistress for the Balanchine repertory, Rosemary Dunleavy, was extremely clear and methodical, and the dancers responded well to her teaching technique. Rehearsals were serious business once they began. Everyone was very focused and eager to get as much accomplished as possible in the time allotted.

The first ballet I performed as an apprentice with the New York City Ballet was the Scherzo section of George Balanchine's *Tschaikovsky Suite No. 3*. The ballet comprised four sections. The first three sections were danced behind a sheer scrim that from the audience's perspective made it look as if the dancers moved through a mist. The women wore long chiffon dresses and had their hair down. My section, the Scherzo, was the third. The last section, called Theme and Variations, had bright lights and no scrim, and the ladies wore tight buns and tutus.

I'd been understudying ballets for hours every day, weeks on end, and I was so excited to finally be actually dancing in the center of the room during the rehearsal. It didn't matter that it was a part usually reserved for the newest and youngest members of the company because the other dancers had risen to better things; I was just thrilled to be dancing. I was doing it—I was dancing with a professional company.

We didn't have much time—when my fellow apprentices and I began to learn our parts, we were only a week away from the performance. I was soon to learn that there was often very little rehearsal; with forty or so ballets to put on every season, there just wasn't the time, space, or people power to rehearse ballets for a long time. One of the amazing things about the dancers of New York City Ballet is that they can be given steps for a piece one day and be ready to perform it the next with at least the appearance of confidence and poise.

Rosemary was the ballet mistress in charge of *Suite No. 3*, and she taught us the steps in a rational, systematic way that somehow made them easier to learn. I still retain many of the steps and counts that Rosemary taught me, even now, twenty years later. She was strict and businesslike with us, though I'd seen her laughing with some of the older girls, and she made sure the choreography was correct in every detail. I was a little scared and very eager to show how well I could do—she definitely seemed to be sizing up us new girls those first rehearsals. We never ran the piece straight through because someone was always making a little mistake, but I learned all the steps in that first rehearsal, even though I'd never seen the ballet before.

A few days later, the night of the performance came. I was nervous about where I would sit in the dressing room. Since at this time we shared the theater with the New York City Opera, the dancers moved into the dressing rooms anew at the beginning of every performance season. I found out that most of the spaces already had designated, but unlabeled, owners. The rows of mirrors and lights were reserved already by the senior girls, and I was too intimidated to try to find a spot. Luckily, the two girls I'd met at my church—Meg and Katey Tracey—were senior dancers themselves, and they took me under their wing and gave me a spot between them in their dressing room. They helped me with my stage makeup as well, often laughing kindly at my inexpert attempts.

The Scherzo section, named for the piece in Tchaikovsky's musical score, was one of the hair-down sections behind the scrim, and the corps girls actually wore soft ballet slippers, not pointe shoes. For these reasons, I felt that it was a minor piece not to be worried about, but I wasn't certain, since we had never done the whole ballet without stopping. Meg seemed to confirm my thoughts. She remarked, "I danced that part when I first got into the company. It's a puff."

Puff? Well, surely that must mean it was a light and fluffy ballet, just fun and dancey. Since my ballet was the last of the evening, I warmed up backstage while the first ballets were going on, fascinated by the difference between the effortless, ethereal beings onstage and the panting, groaning beasts they became once they had exited into the wings. I will never be like that, I thought.

During the intermission before my piece, I put on my costume and waited for the ballet to start, dancing around a bit both to stay warm and to generally look like I knew what I was doing. The Scherzo was the third movement, so I waited backstage during the first two movements, the butterflies in my stomach increasing in their violence with every passing moment.

Finally I realized the second movement was winding down and it was time to take my place in the wings for my entrance. I saw my opposite and fellow apprentice, Inma, in her place across the stage in her wing. We stared wide-eyed at each other. We were waiting for our music—there were only four very fast counts of music before we were supposed to leap onto the stage, and we needed to be ready.

There was applause after the second movement and then an anticipatory silence. I was so nervous I thought I would either throw up or explode.

Then one-two-three-four, and I was suddenly leaping onto the stage. It was glorious. I felt as if I were dancing above the ground and flying across the air. This is what I was meant to do, I exulted to myself. Everyone must be able to see!

Quite soon, however, I started to have trouble breathing. This is kind of hard, I thought. I was only a quarter of the way through. I kept my feet moving, but they were definitely grounded now. Shuffling, really. Halfway through, my arms felt oddly heavy, as if they had lost the blood that was supposed to be in them. Did that mean my body was going into shock?

Three quarters through, and I looked hazily over at Inma, dancing across from me. Her lips were blue. I wondered if I looked the same.

Finally the Scherzo was over, and I was one of those panting beasts in the wings, doubled over and wondering where the oxygen had gone. I made my way shakily to the dressing room, thrilled that I'd survived but a little surprised by how hard the ballet had been. The tissues I used to remove the thick stage makeup on my face revealed stripes of bright red, sweaty skin.

I later said to Meg, "I thought you said the Scherzo was a puff."

"It is," she replied. I stared at her until she said, "Well, here at the theater, that means it's really hard. You get really out of breath, or puffed."

Ah. I had much to learn, apparently. But still, I was here. I was doing it. I was a professional dancer.

Soon after my first performances of the Scherzo, the company got ready for *The Nutcracker*. Christmastime in New York is about giant Christmas trees, shopping, and huge snowflakes made of lights hanging over the avenues. But for City Ballet dancers, it is all about *The Nutcracker*— eight shows a week for six weeks straight.

As the time for our first performance of the ballet drew near, I looked every day for a *Nutcracker* rehearsal on the daily schedule but none showed up. At SAB we had rehearsed for months for the Workshop performances; for the Scherzo, we had only a week. But certainly for a big ballet like *The Nutcracker* they would rehearse far in advance? The days went by, and I started to panic. *Nutcracker* was only a week away!

Finally, three days before opening night, we had our first rehearsal. The older dancers all knew the ballet well because they had danced it every December for years, but for us new dancers, there was a lot to learn in very little time. I was to be a Maid in the party scene at the beginning of the ballet, a Snowflake during the transitional snow scene, and one of the Hot Chocolates dancing the Spanish divertissement in the second-act Land of the Sweets. I also understudied the famous second-act Waltz of the Flowers.

That initial week of *Nutcracker* performances was a shock to me; to suddenly jump into eight consecutive performances, where I was expected to perform every single minute onstage at my highest level, was exhausting even as I was exhilarated to be working a real dancer's schedule. A couple of days into the run, there were multiple injuries among the corps ladies, and Rosemary discovered she didn't have enough dancers to cover all of the roles. The solution was to have Monique, an apprentice along with me, and I do something very unusual. In the second act, we were to dance in both the Hot Chocolate dance and the Waltz of the Flowers. Normally dancers do only one of these at a time.

My schedule, therefore, was very busy. The only part I alternated with another girl was that of the Maid in the party scene. Otherwise, I did every Snow, every Hot Chocolate, and every Flowers. After Hot Chocolate, while the other divertissements such as Marzipan and Candy Canes were being performed, Monique and I would run to the greenroom, where the ladies' costumes were kept, get out of our Hot Chocolate dresses, colored tights, and specially dyed pointe shoes, put on pink tights and the Flowers costume, and run out to the hallway without our shoes on. Before the mirror just outside the greenroom, we would take off the giant Hot Chocolate headpieces, smooth anything out of place on our hair, and then put in the Flowers headpiece. Then we would run to the pointe shoe station on stage right with our pink pointe shoes, resin up our tights so they would not slip inside our shoes, put paper towels around our toes, stuff our feet into our shoes, and then quickly tie our ribbons around our ankles. We would resin up the outside of our pointe shoes to prevent any slipping onstage and then run to the wing through which we would enter the Land of the Sweets as a Flower. It was hectic.

The worst was doing it all over again in reverse order so that we could come out in the finale of the ballet as Hot Chocolates once more. The company simply cut out some of the Flowers from the finale so that the numbers would work out evenly. Monique and I did this every show for the rest of the run that year. It was an eye-opener to see how hard it was possible to work as a ballet dancer, and even as I thrilled to be living out my dream, I was taken aback by the grueling schedule.

Every subsequent year of *The Nutcracker* was slightly different, but every year was also the same. During my early years in the company, my experience with Balanchine's *Nutcracker* was a whirlwind of tinkling music, colorful costume changes, swollen feet, and deli runs in full stage makeup and hair. I always had multiple parts in every show, and after my hundredth Waltz of the Flowers, things began to blur together.

There were, of course, particular shows that stood out. There was the time Michael Jackson came to the performance and appeared backstage at intermission. The dancers were in a frenzy of excitement; the boy dancing the Toy Soldier wore only one glove in Michael's honor. Since it was one of my first seasons, I always had my camera at hand, and I ran down to the stage level determined to get a picture of myself with Michael. I gathered my courage, approached the giant houselike bodyguard, and asked if I could take a photo with the star. I was given permission, and Michael was very nice, gently placing his arm on my shoulders.

Then there was a long, tense moment when my Spanish friend Inma said in her sweetly accented voice, "Oh, Jenny, I can't figure out how to work your camera."

Sweating behind my placid smile, I gritted, "Just push the top button . . ."

There is another performance, however, that will forever be my most memorable *Nutcracker*. In our production, a great number of the young beginning students from the School of American Ballet dance a variety of the children's roles in the ballet. The two plum parts are the little girl who gets to be Marie and the little boy who gets to be the Nephew/Nutcracker Prince. All of these children are rehearsed for months in an almost military fashion. They are taught to do every movement perfectly through repetition and minute correction. Before the show, they are kept down in the basement of the theater, where they run around wildly and eat too many sweets, as children do. But once the curtain goes up, they are little professionals.

On this particular evening, I was warming up backstage during the first scene before putting on my Snowflake costume. There was a sudden commotion in the wings. Apparently the boy playing the Nutcracker Prince wasn't feeling well. He calmly walked to the back of the stage where the Christmas tree was, threw up, and then walked back to the front to continue his starring role.

Now, our tree weighs one ton and eventually grows forty-one feet tall, but during the party scene, most of the tree is hidden down a deep hole in the stage, and a fake carpet covers up the hole. The Nutcracker Prince's vomit was on the carpet. My friend Dena Abergel was playing the Maid that night, and she was the lucky one given a mop and bucket by the stage crew so that she could go out and mop during the performance. She did a good job.

However, during the transition into the battle scene, when the fake carpet was pulled away as usual, it revealed a stubborn blob on center stage that had obviously gotten through the seam. It was on the giant trapdoor that rises out of the hole when the tree grows. Since it was toward the back of the stage, it didn't get in the way of the battle, which was largely fought up front. However, this was bad news for the Snowflakes because we were dancing next, and the blob remained intact.

All sixteen of us stood in the wings with our eyes on the throw-up. It was in a well-danced part of the stage, but we figured if we just kept our eyes on it, we would be able to avoid it. We had forgotten about the paper snow that is part of what makes our snow scene so beautiful. Slowly, magically, to the majestic and surging music of Tchaikovsky, the snow fell. And slowly, inevitably, the puddle on the stage was hidden.

At the beginning of our dance, some of the Snowflakes run in and out of the wings as "flurries" of snow, lightly fluttering our arms as if windblown. I was one of the first flurries. I ran out for my entrance, eyes lifted, face glowing, arms flowing, as my feet flitted across the stage. Then suddenly my feet flitted no more. They slipped out from under me like lightning. I flew through the air and landed with an echoing thud on the trapdoor—in the vomit!

I heard the girls in the wings burst into laughter. I giggled when I went offstage too. I couldn't believe I'd managed to find that one spot in my brief entrance. Then I heard another thud. I peeked out of the wings to see another Snowflake on her knees—someone else had fallen. The slips and skids became periodic, and I'm sure the audience must have wondered what our problem was. At one point, when we all formed a giant swirling snowball toward the end of the dance, one dancer ended up on the floor scrabbling around with her feet and gasping, "I can't get up! I can't get up!"

When we got back to the dressing room, we counted eight complete falls and countless other mishaps. And while we all had a good laugh once we were offstage, I remember looking at the other girls during the performance and noting that although we were dancing in unusual circumstances, everyone was trying to give the best performance she could. From the sick Nutcracker Prince to the slipping Snowflakes to the Maid with the mop, we all knew that every performance was special and deserved our best effort, no matter what.

After the six-week-long run of *The Nutcracker*, the company went directly into eight weeks of mixed repertory, which was the main part of our season. My first year, I thought that *Nutcracker* was hard. But the whirlwind of being in the rep performance season was a different thing altogether.

The days suddenly became very long. We would show up for class at ten thirty and then rehearse from eleven thirty to six, with an hour off somewhere for lunch. Then there were two free hours when the company members would fix their hair and makeup and then warm up again for the performance. As an apprentice, I was allowed only four individual ballets in one season, though I could dance in every performance my particular ballets were on the program, so if I was in a ballet that night, I would join the company members in preparing for the show. If I wasn't involved, or "on," as everyone called it, then I would go home. Apprentices usually had only about two shows a week.

Outside the theater, I didn't have much time for anything. I was still living with my parents, and at the end of a long rehearsal day, I usually just went home and got on the couch with a book, happy to have the weight off my feet. Life seemed extremely full with everything that went on at the theater, and I felt no need to add to it just yet.

That early January of 1990, I was mostly understudying still and would spend my days standing in the back of the studio, trying to pick up what I could. Often it felt tedious, and it was hard for me to concentrate, especially by the fourth and fifth hours of standing on swollen feet squeezed into tight pointe shoes. When the dancers already knew the steps to the ballet they were rehearsing, I just watched. But I still had to stay standing up; it wasn't acceptable for apprentices to sit down during rehearsals.

If the dancers were learning the steps of the ballet for the first time, I perked up because I felt that I could actually do a good job here; I would dance the steps as fully as I could in the back and make sure I knew what I was doing, just in case the company needed me to step in. From time to time a dancer was sick or double scheduled, and the ballet mistress would ask one of the apprentices to step into the empty spot for the rehearsal. There was nothing worse than being asked to join the group only to reveal that you had not been paying attention. If the chance came for me to dance in a rehearsal, I wanted to make a good impression.

There was no guarantee that apprentices would eventually be asked to join the company. No one knew how many dancers City Ballet was looking for, or whether they knew they would eventually take us in or were still debating about us. Company members loved to darkly remind apprentices of the previous ones who hadn't made it into the company and had left the theater with their dreams shattered.

This particular January was an unusually tough one on the company. For whatever reason, a large number of girls were on the injury list and couldn't perform. Another dancer seemed to get injured, or go "out," every day, and casts were shuffled around like crazy all the time to cover the absences. Then one day the injuries directly affected me. Two girls went "out" in the morning, and there was no one left to replace them in that evening's performance of a Balanchine ballet called *Ballo della Regina*.

Rosemary chose Monique and me to step into the girls' spots. The only problem was that this ballet had been in the current rep for a while, and therefore Rosemary hadn't had to teach it that season, but Monique and I didn't know a step of it. The ballet mistress would have to teach us the ballet from scratch during the day, and then we would have to perform it that night.

I was very excited to be chosen. It meant that maybe I'd made a good impression on Rosemary, and that she felt she could trust me with this responsibility. I also thought that this might be my fifth ballet, over the apprentice's limit of four ballets per season, and that I might get my contract out of this. It might mean I was about to become a full member of the New York City Ballet. I wasn't sure, though. What if they took another ballet away from me, so I still had only four? I didn't know how it worked, and I certainly wasn't going to ask. I focused on learning *Ballo*, determined to do a spectacular job, and figured I would find out eventually if I had won my contract or not.

The rehearsal schedule was changed so that Rosemary, Monique, and I had a studio to ourselves for two hours. Then at the end of the day a rehearsal was added that included all of the girls in the corps of *Ballo* so Monique and I could fit ourselves into the formations. After that, it would be up to us to do a good enough job onstage in front of 2,500 people.

It seemed like an impossible task, but we plowed ahead, and with someone as focused as Rosemary, it even began to seem possible that I might learn a complete seventeen-minute ballet in only two hours. At least it wasn't one of our longer, forty-minute ballets. During the first rehearsal with Rosemary, I forced myself to concentrate and be analytical. I used the mental tricks I'd learned when I was memorizing for tests in school, trying to lay down tracks in my memory so that the sequence of the steps would run together properly. We were never taught how to learn choreography at SAB, but I'd discovered some ways that worked for me.

Luckily, Rosemary was a gifted teacher who understood how to teach choreography so that it could be retained. She would teach a sequence of steps and then go back to the beginning and watch us to see if we had it. Then she would teach the next sequence, but again go all the way back to the beginning, so we could link the two together in both our bodies and our minds. She would continue in this manner, sometimes making the parts larger or smaller, until we finally reached the end of the ballet and could run the whole thing through to the end. When the two hours were up, Monique and I had a good idea of the ballet. We could get through it, still with occasional mistakes, but well enough to do a capable job and cover up any errors.

We had a small break before the next rehearsal with all of the girls, and I obsessively went over the steps, feeling as if the sequence were trying desperately to get out of my brain. I felt nervous about the group rehearsal; suddenly the environment would change from the safely empty studio with just Monique, Rosemary, and me to a room filled with older, critical company members.

The rehearsal began at the beginning of the corps section, and we worked our way through the entire ballet. The other corps members— exhausted after a long day of dancing—just marked their steps, making sure they were in their correct positions so that Monique and I could understand where we were supposed to be. We stopped and started as Monique and I made little mistakes or got into incorrect formations, but there was no time to go through the ballet twice. After we had worked our way to the end, Rosemary dismissed the other girls.

"Okay, well, do you have any questions?" she asked.

Monique and I looked at each other and shook our heads. I was thinking, Well, yes, I have many questions, but at this point I'm not sure your answers would do any good.

My head felt as if it might burst from having a whole ballet crammed into it in two and a half hours. Surely ballet steps were trickling out of my ears. I knew that not only would I have to go onstage and remember all the steps and formations correctly, but I also would be expected to dance like the professional I'd become so that the audience, which had come to see one of the world's greatest ballet companies, would never guess that I was a last-minute replacement.

I went to the side of the studio to collect my bag, my feet aching and my muscles stiff from continuous dancing. The masking tape I'd wrapped around my toes to prevent blisters had disintegrated over the long hours, and I thought I might have a blister. I was fatigued but felt wired and knew that I couldn't allow myself to let down until the performance was over. *Ballo* was the first ballet of the evening, so I had two hours to make sure a costume would fit me, put on my makeup, fix my hair, warm up, and then go over the ballet as many times as I could before the curtain went up.

Rosemary walked over to me before I left the room and said, "I just wanted to let you know that this will be your fifth ballet, so you will be getting your contract. You are a company member now."

There it was. All those months—years—of preparation, doubt, agony, hard work. A thrill zinged up my spine upon hearing those words. I was *in*. I was done with the uncertainty of being an apprentice. But I tried to seem self-assured and nodded happily to Rosemary, thanking her and attempting to sound mature and businesslike. Anyway, I needed to focus on this performance. I wanted to be perfect and prove that I was good company-member material.

The performance went well. The ballet was a sunny, fun ballet to dance, and though I was concentrating fiercely on the steps, I managed to have fun during the sections that I felt confident in. And I did do an almost perfect performance, with only one small misstep that I was aware of—I hit one of my poses with the wrong arm up. Monique and I both felt great about our accomplishment. I don't know why it was so important to me to be perfect; no one was expecting us to be flawless with so little rehearsal. But I expected it of myself and wanted to show that I could be relied on. After the performance that night, I felt proud and relieved and fell asleep reminding myself that I was a full company member at last.

I didn't have long to enjoy my new status. That week in mid-January

actually held three milestones for my sixteen-year-old self. I got the official notice that I had graduated from high school half a semester early, I
became a full company member, and I began my first semester as a
freshman in college. Since my whole family and I had always assumed I
would go to college, and since we had thought I would be an apprentice
with a lighter dance schedule for quite a while, my parents had encouraged me to go ahead and enroll right away. I'd heard of other dancers
starting to attend school while they danced, and I figured if I started
young, even if I went part time, I would eventually graduate before I
was finished dancing, whenever that might occur. Fordham University
had a campus right beside Lincoln Center; they had classes that met
once a week and even offered the City Ballet dancers special summer
courses that worked around their touring schedules. Plus, a group of
City Ballet board members led by Robert Lipp had come together to
start a scholarship called Dance On to help City Ballet dancers with tu-
ition. So I started with one course a semester on Mondays, City Ballet's
one guaranteed day off a week. Though I am so glad I went to college
and am grateful for the education, looking back now, I cannot help but
wonder if had perhaps taken on too much all at once.

Now that I was a company member, my life at the theater exploded.
Since I wasn't an apprentice anymore, I could be put into an unlimited
number of ballets. With all of the injuries, new dancers were needed to
take up the slack. And I had a new reputation as a fast learner.

My days were as long as before, but I was no longer stuck in the te-
dium of understudying ballets at the back of the room. I was right in the
center of the room, learning different ballets all day long, dancing full
out from ten thirty in the morning until six at night. And I was performing more and more at night, until I had a full corps member's
schedule of eight shows a week. It was exhausting, but it was all so new
and such a dream come true that I didn't mind.

I loved the performances. I loved the sense of belonging in the company and starting to feel like I had a place there. One of my favorite
times of the day was the two hours before the show, when rehearsals

were done. The crowded girls' dressing room was often filled with joking and laughter as we all started our preperformance hair and makeup rituals. We knew that the work part of the day was over, and all that was left was the reward for our diligence: we were about to get onstage and really dance. The performances for the most part were not stressful for me. I knew the steps, and none of them were difficult. The ballets might be physically taxing, but the steps in my roles as a new corps member were not tricky. I got to go out there and just dance.

On the other hand, I was still learning how to navigate company life. I was making friends with some of the younger dancers and dealing with my fear of the older dancers. The senior members were not mean, but for the most part they didn't have much time for the younger company members. We shared barre space and might dance side by side, but generally the more experienced dancers didn't bother with us first- and second-year corps members. Some of the older women would go out of their way to offer help when we needed it, but most of them rarely cracked a smile in my direction. It wasn't out of dislike or superiority, usually. They were just too busy and focused on their work; a senior corps member worked similar hours to mine but had more difficult parts to dance. A couple of years into the company, I discovered that most of these senior women were very nice, and we became friends. I often jokingly reminded them of how they used to terrify me in my early years.

And then there were the scary principal dancers, the ones who had made it all the way to the top rank of the company and danced lead roles every night. They probably were not scary in reality, but I had no way of knowing. We didn't interact with them much because they were always off rehearsing separately from us. But when they were around, I was very nervous and made sure to stay out of their way. If a principal needed to put resin on her pointe shoes while I was at the resin box, I stepped aside.

I became good friends with the ice bucket. After nine or ten hours of dancing in pointe shoes, my feet and ankles would be swollen and achy when I got home. Though the muscles in other parts of my body might be stiff and sore, I found that my real pain was located from the calf down. One of the girls told me how to do the ice bucket: fill the biggest container I could find with cold water and a large quantity of ice and then put my feet into the liquid for ten minutes.

It sounded easy enough, and the other dancers swore it made a difference in how their feet felt the next day. So I bought a knee-high plastic trash can and put it in my kitchen. After hobbling home from the performance one night, I dumped all of the ice from my freezer into the trash can and poured cold water over everything. I lugged it into my living room and placed it in front of my couch on top of a towel. Then I just stared into the bucket for a while, gathering up my courage.

I put my hand into the water. It was frigid. I looked at my red feet straddling the bucket and saw all the veins sticking out around the hard-worked metatarsals. I picked up my legs and put my toes into the water, immediately jerking them out and putting them back onto the towel. This was going to be horrible.

Finally, promising my feet that they would feel better afterward, I plunged my feet into the bucket, sinking them all the way to the bottom so that the freezing water came up over my calves. My thighs seized up, and I clenched my fists to fight the urge to pull my feet back out of the bucket. The cold water felt like knives. I looked at my clock. One minute had passed. Nine more to go.

After the stinging knives came a dull, achy pain that I had to hold my breath against. I hit my legs with my hands, trying to distract myself from what my feet were going through. I flapped my arms in the air and made weird noises as I tried to breathe normally. I glanced at the clock again. Only a minute more had passed.

I needed a real distraction. I snatched up my remote control and pointed it at the television, flipping the channels just to keep my mind off my legs, which, strangely, now felt like they were on fire. The rest of my body was tense, and my shoulders were pressed up toward my ears. I heard myself humming odd little tunes through my clenched teeth.

Suddenly, around the three-minute mark, my legs went numb. And then, around four minutes, they started to feel pleasantly warm. My body relaxed. Had I given my legs hypothermia? I looked at my feet in the ice water, and they seemed quite intact. I turned my attention back to the television, able to breathe normally again. Finally the clock hit the ten-minute mark, and I took my feet out of the water.

I touched my ankles. The skin was ice cold. Strangely, they felt warm, and they were a bright pink up to the waterline. I sat on the couch a while longer, but when I finally did get up, I happily realized that they felt better than they had before. Perhaps they were just glad to be out of the freezing water. But I did think that the icing had done some good. And the next morning for ballet class, instead of starting off the day with already swollen feet, I felt that I had brand-new, well-working feet.

Soon I grew very accustomed to the ice bucket and actually looked forward to ending the day with my cold friend. I worked out a system where I would make a large dinner of my favorite foods and place the plate on a TV table; then I would make my ice bucket and place it under the table, sit down, turn on the TV, and plunge my feet into the water. And instead of crying out in alarm every time I put my feet into the bucket, I would actually say, "Ahh." Those dinners and that ice bucket were my comfort and reward at the end of days that were often both physically and emotionally difficult. There was constant pressure to prove myself and please the ballet masters in the studio, and every day was different and unpredictable. Much of the time, the one constant in my life was coming home to my TV dinner with the ice bucket.

For my first year in the company, I stayed at home in my parents' apartment. However, we soon learned that they were going to be transferred away again. They would first be going back to Washington, DC, for a year of language training, and then they would be heading off to Europe. My sister and I would stay in New York because we both had our work there.

We thought it might be a good idea for me to move out of my parents' apartment for a while before they moved away so that I could begin to get my footing alone while they were still in town, just in case I needed them. So in 1991, my second year in the company, we started looking for my first apartment. Since my parents were worried about leaving their teenage daughter alone in New York City, they wanted me to have a doorman building in a very safe neighborhood, preferably close to the theater.

Out apartment hunting on our own nickel, with no government subsidies, we discovered what New York City apartments were really like. We quickly learned that if we really wanted to meet all of our criteria, we would have to raise our price and reduce our spatial expectations. But for all of us, safety was our biggest concern, so I ended up getting an overpriced studio apartment in a doorman building one block away from the theater. I could afford it on my salary, but I would not be saving much money every month.

I was ecstatic to have my own apartment. I was eighteen and itching for some independence. I had my own money, and I could decorate however I wanted, buy my own groceries . . . I was a grown-up. I was making a paycheck and paying all of my own bills with my own checking account. No one would be keeping tabs on what I ate or when I slept or what shows were on my television. In reality, my parents didn't really watch me in that way, but just living in the same house with them made my teenage self feel watched. I wanted to be out on my own, with the freedom to make private decisions however I wished.

I decorated my apartment "rustic country" with lots of fishing memorabilia, which my New York friends found hilarious. I made a giant mobile out of baby sand dollars that I'd found on the beach in South Carolina. My refrigerator was mostly empty because I would just buy what I needed day by day; there were two delis within a block of my apartment and a grocery store six blocks away. Two bookcases divided up the apartment and hid my sleeping area. My sister bought me a fish tank with two fat goldfish in it—my first pets.

That second year in the company was even busier than the first. I was now established as a corps member and had a regular rep of the larger ballets that demanded bigger groups of dancers. I rehearsed all day and performed almost every night. I saw my parents regularly but not every day, and my sister was busy with her own life of piano and teaching.

I often didn't make it to church; Sunday was at the end of a long, physically grueling week, and there was still a Sunday matinee and evening performance to get through. My parents put no pressure on me to attend, and I think we had all subconsciously bought into the idea that ballet was a valid reason to miss church. I had access to God everywhere, right? Being a Christian wasn't just about going to a building every Sunday. Ballet was a rare and special thing, something to be pursued and something to sacrifice for. But my priorities were becoming skewed. I was losing out on a Christian community that would have helped me to stay grounded, and my new individual adult life wasn't being founded on patterns that would give me some continuity when work became difficult. I was allowing God to slip away, and it was too easy to let ballet fill the void left behind.

Mondays, my day off, were spent cramming in my homework, getting a massage, and then going to my night college course. My world was narrowing to focus largely on City Ballet alone. Sometimes after the performance I would go out to dinner with my company friends, but much of the time I was just too tired and looked forward to the solitude of my apartment.

I started to get small featured parts during that second year in the company. One of the first was a part in Peter Martins's new choreography that would premiere during the regular repertory season. In addition to being the ballet master in chief, Peter also choreographed regularly, almost one ballet a year, and it was considered an honor to be called to be in one of his ballets. This ballet would eventually be called *Fearful Symmetries*, a twenty-seven-minute work that would be one of Peter's most successful. He had organized the ballet into different groupings: two principal couples, one soloist couple, three demi-soloist boys, four corps couples, and six corps girls. The music by John Adams was fast and driving and the choreography was quick and ate up space, with the dancers rushing on and off the stage. Every part in the ballet was a good one because every part had exciting, visible dancing.

I was originally called to understudy the six girls, but after a couple of days two of the girls pulled out of the ballet. I was one of the girls chosen to replace them, and suddenly I was being choreographed on by the director. Working with Peter was nerve-racking at first but ultimately very exciting.

So far, I hadn't dealt with Peter that much. He occasionally taught company class, giving steps that were often impossibly difficult. He watched every stage rehearsal to make sure he approved of what was going to be seen in performance, sometimes offering corrections and sometimes not saying much at all. During these stage rehearsals he could be moody, and I could rarely figure out why he was in a good or bad mood. But all of the dancers tried to please him no matter what mood he was in.

When he began working on *Fearful Symmetries*, he was upbeat for every rehearsal and seemed inspired by the music and the dancers. He liked to move the rehearsals along quickly and appreciated when his ideas and rhythms were picked up rapidly. The only times he got frustrated were when he couldn't get his ideas across. It was fun for me to see this side of him, involved and energetic, rather than the more removed persona he often adopted for stage rehearsals.

As a new corps member, I knew I had to do every rehearsal full out, no matter who was running the rehearsal at the front of the room. I was still proving myself and couldn't come in and mark rehearsals like some of the more senior dancers did. Marking, I learned, was when dancers saved their bodies by just indicating the steps without actually dancing them to the fullest; senior dancers could do this because they had years of trust built up between them and the ballet masters. I didn't. However, everyone in the room danced at a higher level when Peter was watching, especially when he was choreographing. We all pushed ourselves for the duration of the rehearsals, and I would be red-faced and exhausted after them. It ended up being a very difficult ballet physically; some sections, once we started putting them together and running them, were nearly impossible to get through.

This ballet even included my very first solo on the New York State Theater stage. It was minuscule, only six musical counts long, as I led the progression of six girls onstage for one of our entrances. It only had three ballet steps in it, but I counted it as a solo. It was My Moment, and I was very proud of it.

As we got closer to the premiere, a sense of tension grew in the studio in both the dancers and Peter. The time was coming up when we couldn't laugh at our mistakes and experiment with different solutions for certain technical or choreographic problems. Soon we would be on-stage, performing for an audience, and we would need to appear perfect. And then there was the question: Was it even a good ballet? It was hard to tell because we were all so wrapped up in it.

I remember one rehearsal when we had done a run-through and then taken a five-minute break while Peter talked some things over with Rosemary, the ballet mistress. I was depleted, my legs ached, and I was having trouble with shin splints because of the movement style of the ballet. Peter didn't look happy, and the premiere was the next week. We still had an hour left in the rehearsal, but I was hoping we would just go back and work on a few problem sections. Better yet, perhaps he would let us go, and we would come back tomorrow freshly rested to work on things anew.

"Okay," Peter said from the front of the room. "From the beginning."

There was a moment of silence while all the dancers stayed on the floor, looking at Peter and wondering if they had heard him correctly. Did he mean from the beginning, full out, all the way through to the end? Apparently he did.

A few dancers, thinking quicker than the rest of us, got up into their opening positions, grim-faced and determined. The rest of us scrambled to follow suit. And we did it all over again, disregarding our exhausted bodies. This was the first of many times I would have to grit my teeth and push my hurting, unresponsive body through a rehearsal or performance. It was my first inkling that in this career I would be sacrificing my body, willingly, for the approval of whoever happened to be watching, whether it be a ballet master or an audience. And pushing through pain or "sucking it up" and hiding feelings of tiredness or discomfort was expected and often rewarded. Showing pain or exhaustion was seen as a weakness, and there were plenty of other dancers to take your place if you were not strong enough to handle the workload.

For most young dancers who eventually get promoted, there is suddenly a year when a lot of chances come their way. That was how it happened for me in 1992. I was nineteen and had been in the company for close to three years. At that time, we were still calling in to what we termed "the tape"—a recorded phone message that listed the rehearsals for the day. As I listened to Rosemary read off who would be rehearsing which ballet in which studio at what time, I began to hear my name called for special roles more and more. I got to do some demi-soloist roles in *Nutcracker* and was a Fairy in *Sleeping Beauty*. It was usually a shock for me to hear my name called to a particular role in a ballet; my stomach would flip over, and I would immediately hang up and call the tape again to see if I'd heard correctly. Then I might call it one more time just for the thrill of it.

One of the first featured roles I was selected for was in Jerome Robbins's *Interplay*, a jazzy ballet that depicted youths romping around in the 1950s to an upbeat score by Morton Gould. Jerome Robbins was renowned as a director and choreographer for dance, theater, movies, and television and up until 1990 had shared the title of ballet master in chief with Peter Martins. His ballets made up a large part of the repertory of City Ballet, second only to George Balanchine's. Just being called to rehearse *Interplay* at all was something—it had only four boys and four girls, and was filled with fun and lively dancing. Soloists and senior corps members usually danced it, so it was unusual for me to even be thought of as an understudy. But when I got to the studio for rehearsal the next day, I found out that I was to be learning the Pink Girl, the more romantic of the four girls in the ballet, who gets to dance a bluesy pas de deux in the third movement. It was the part I'd hoped for but hadn't dared let myself expect. The only bad thing about the rehearsal was that I also learned that my best friend in the company, Yvonne Borree, would also be learning the part, and we were to switch off over the next weeks until the ballet master made his decision about who would go onstage when the performance season started.

Yvonne and I had become friends my second year in the company. She was also in the corps but was one or two years ahead of me in seniority. One day I saw her doing something funny to make the other girls laugh and thought, I want to be her friend. She was the kind of girl I could be myself with, both serious and silly, and though she was also very talented and obviously an up-and-comer, we were never competitive with each other. We had a rich friendship outside of our company life and should have felt joyful to be sharing the same part. However, I felt uncomfortable with the situation we found ourselves in during the *Interplay* rehearsals; we both wanted to dance the part but we cared for each other and did not want the other to be hurt or disappointed. All we could do was dance our best and see what happened. Obviously, in a big ballet company there is going to be competition for roles, but I'd never been confronted with the situation of being pitted against a close friend.

After almost two weeks of rehearsals, we finally came to the moment when the ballet master had to make his decision. He chose me to perform it with the first cast, or group of dancers, and Yvonne with the second cast. Now, though every performance is equally important and every performance is before roughly 2,500 people in the audience, there is still the feeling with many in the company that the first cast is the more prestigious because it gets the most attention and reviews.

I couldn't really feel that happy about being chosen first at the time because I was worried about Yvonne. In a wonderful demonstration of her ladylike character, Yvonne came directly over to me, hugged me sideways, and put her head on my shoulder. We stood there a little while until it was time to dance. She taught me a lot that day about how to handle certain aspects of our company life with grace and poise. There were plenty of times when our situations were reversed and I was second cast to her; indeed, she went on to be promoted to soloist long before me, but we continued to be each other's friend and supporter throughout our careers and our friendship was never affected by the whims of the company.

A short while after the *Interplay* experience, I called the tape one night from home and heard something that sent a lightning bolt through me. I was to learn the balcony pas de deux from *Romeo and Juliet*. After calling the tape four more times, I ran around my apartment just to get some energy out. Not only was it a nine-minute pas de deux, with just one man and one woman, a part that only principal dancers performed, but it was also my dream role. Some girls dream of dancing the Swan Queen or Princess Aurora. Not me. I'd always wanted to be Juliet. At the time, City Ballet didn't have a full-length *Romeo and Juliet* in its repertory, though now it does. All we had back then was this simple and, to my mind, all too brief pas de deux. It had been choreographed by Sean Lavery, the former City Ballet principal dancer who was now a ballet master for the company.

I was called to dance with Peter Boal, one of the most beautiful principal dancers in the company. I don't think I had said much more to him than a passing greeting up to then, so I was terrified before my first rehearsal. He couldn't have been nicer, though, and must have realized how nervous I was. Both he and Sean were very patient while teaching me the steps. Ballet is already a different language, but pas de deux work is yet another. A man and woman can speak to each other silently just in the way they give and take their weight or the direction they move their hands. Placement of the partners' clasped hands can make the difference between staying on balance and falling over. It is very subtle, takes a long time to learn, and requires trust and consistency from both dancers. I was still acquiring the skills to partner well, and Sean's choreography was difficult in places, but I slowly learned how to do it. Most difficult for me were the partnered turns in which I had to change my leg position from the front of my body to the back. I had a hard time controlling the force and speed of my turns as the balance of my body changed, and I didn't know how to use Peter's help to make the step work. Sean kept telling me, "Let Peter do all the work. He's got you."

At the end of the scene, there was a kiss before Juliet went back up the stairs, but since Peter was such a gentleman, we never did it in the studio, much to my relief. I was nineteen and had never had any real kisses—just some toddler smooches in preschool. I had no idea what to do.

Our stage rehearsal proved to be a little rocky. Suddenly confronted by sets, lights, and costumes, I felt as if all of my preparations had gone out the window. A giant winding staircase led up to my balcony, with no handrails. As the curtain went up, I was supposed to be hiding behind the balcony wall, but there was only a very narrow space that barely fit my feet and then dropped off nine feet to the stage below. Again, no handrails. The lighting was dark and dappled, surely a lovely effect from the audience, but it made me feel as if I were on a tilt. After peeking out from the balcony, I was supposed to glide down the stairs, looking passionately into Peter's eyes and not at the dark, twisty steps. This all took several tries with much nervous laughter on my part; I just couldn't stop picturing myself as a befuddled Juliet bumping down the stairs on my bottom during the performance.

Before Peter exited at the end of the scene, I was supposed to wrap his thick velvet cape around his shoulders and lovingly send him on his way. My first try, I put it over his face. The next one, I strangled him. The next, it hit his stomach in a ball. I later got my first fan letter from a member of the New York City Ballet Guild who had been allowed to watch our stage rehearsal—a long explanation of how she had never laughed so hard during a rehearsal as when I was trying to get the cape right. Either I finally was able to do it or we just ran out of time, but eventually the rehearsal was over. Ironically, the rest of that day I had other rehearsals for other corps ballets that I was learning. That was just the way things were for young corps members; there were always five or six hours of rehearsals, no matter what you were performing that night. It was a good thing in a way, though. It kept the mental image of my tragic plummet from the balcony before a shocked audience of 2,500 people from repeatedly running through my mind.

I was incredibly nervous the night I performed that first *Romeo and Juliet*, but incredibly joyful as well. The thought of dancing to Sergei Prokofiev's stunning music was a thrill. Even though I was a lowly corps member, Peter Boal very sweetly gave me a single rose for a *merde* gift. I remember that first performance of the pas de deux as amazing—I felt like a figurehead on the prow of a ship. It wasn't perfect—I think some things went wrong, but Peter and I were able to cover them up and give a good performance. I didn't fall off the balcony, I didn't bump down the steps, and I didn't kill Peter with the cape. I had a blast. And there on the State Theater stage, at the age of nineteen, I had my first kiss.

Chapter Four

✥

Darkling

⟨During the years of 1992 and 1993, the parts kept coming. I was just turning twenty, and though I was still only in the corps, I was getting featured roles in a variety of ballets by our three dominant choreographers: Jerome Robbins, the late George Balanchine, and Peter Martins. I was also being noticed by new choreographers and was given lead roles in two of the ballets for New York City Ballet's inaugural Diamond Project, a festival for new choreography. My sister was still in the city, finishing up her master's degree at the Manhattan School of Music, and my parents were leaving Washington for their new post in Europe.

During this time, something about my eating was a little off. For some reason, I began to enjoy trying to eat as little as possible. I'm not sure what motivated me; I don't believe I was trying to be thinner at that point. I think I was trying to have some control over my life, and one of the few areas in which I had full control over myself was in what food I put into my body.

In some ways, appearance is everything in ballet. Dancers spend all day long in front of a mirror, never admiring but always looking for things that are wrong and need correcting. It is only natural that a dancer's critical eye will turn not only to her balletic line but also to her physical body as well. We're supposed to be thin, fit, honed. Some would argue that ballerinas should be painfully thin and actually bony, something associated with the Balanchine "look." I was told by Dr. Linda Hamilton, a former City Ballet dancer herself, that a professional ballet dancer actually falls below the ideal weight for height recommended for a healthy person. In scientific terms, a ballet dancer's body is that of an anorexic, unless she happens to be among the 4 percent of the population who are genetically programmed to be at this low weight without eating disorders. And in the ballet world, very few directors care how a dancer maintains her weight—as long as it looks good, the means justify the end.

Discussions about health and wellness have begun to try to help young dancers traverse this demanding ballet world and retain a normalized view of themselves. When I started out, there was a silence about eating and weight; there was even a popular joke in the company where dancers got the nickname Anna for anorexic and claimed that they would have only a grape for dinner. Everyone would laugh, but there was a disquieting sense of approval of anyone who garnered the name Anna.

In the early 1990s I was reaching a new peak in my career, but because of my demanding schedule at the company, my time was not my own. I woke up, danced all day, danced all night, went to sleep, and then did it all again. Often I was learning new and stressful parts during the day and dancing completely different featured parts at night. My body often hurt. I was thrilled with the progress I was making in the company, but unprepared for the pressures of performing new parts at a high level of excellence daily. Rather than gaining confidence, I began to feel more and more insecure. I couldn't tell whether I was meeting up to everyone's expectations, no matter how much positive attention I received. We got notes from the choreographers and reviews from the critics, bad and good, but the only comments that stuck in my head were the negative, critical ones, and those seemed to blot out any positive reinforcement that came my way.

Reflecting now, I wonder whether if I'd stayed in a healthy Christian community I might have avoided all of the problems I went through. Around my family and Christian friends, I was Christian Jenny, but at the theater, I was Dancer Jenny, and everything I thought and felt about myself and the world was seen through a ballet-centric lens. My family was busy with their own lives, and I rarely saw my Christian friends because I thought I was too busy for church. My faith in God was emotional; it had always been easy for me to believe. Therefore, while I was young I just had a "warm fuzzy" with God and never developed the more intellectual thought processes that might have helped me cope with the pressures of the dance world. My entire identity was starting to be wrapped up in ballet.

My way of responding to all of these confusing emotions was to limit my eating. Despite my grueling schedule and the huge number of calories I burned up in a day, I remember sometimes having just an apple for breakfast, an apple and yogurt for lunch, and then just some vegetables for dinner. Or sometimes I would eat nothing all day and then have a big, regular meal. I remember my friends marveling at my metabolism because we would go out to dinner and I would eat a large plate of pasta. But I never told them that I'd had nothing else to eat that day.

I began to lose weight, and I grew very thin. Some fellow dancers spoke to me with concern. Stacey Calvert, a senior corps dancer who eventually became a soloist, took me aside during a *Serenade* rehearsal.

"Jenny, you are looking awfully thin. I just wanted to make sure everything was all right," she said, looking at me kindly.

"Yes, I'm fine," I responded brightly. "I'm just working so hard right now."

"Okay, but just be careful and try not to lose any more weight, all right?" she replied, with a pat on my arm.

Her words made me feel good, however, instead of serving as a warning. Besides, management seemed very pleased with my appearance, and I was getting nothing but professional encouragement. They said nothing about my weight, but ballet masters seemed friendlier than usual, and I was constantly getting cast in better and better roles. The only thing different about me was my weight.

In July 1993 I flew overseas with my mother as she joined my dad at his new post. Both of my parents would be working for the government overseas. I hadn't spent much time with them since they'd left New York, and now I passed a couple of weeks with them. Since they were waiting to move into their new house, they were living in a very small temporary apartment, and I was allowed to use the one right next to them while I was visiting. I was on vacation, but I exercised every day and ate even less than I had before. I was losing more weight all the time and ate hardly anything, but my parents didn't notice. They were working during the day and only saw me for dinner every night, and they were stressed with their own life transitions; they probably thought my very low weight was just a result of my job. I certainly didn't tell them about my eating.

We used to have twelve-week layoffs in the late summer and early fall. When I got back to New York I spent the time taking ballet class, working on my Fordham summer course, and hanging out in the city. I knew that I'd been acting strangely with food, and with the pressures of professional ballet life relieved, I felt myself striving toward saner, safer ground. My eating normalized, and I regained some weight. The fall started up with another college course and rehearsals for City Ballet's winter season.

During the 1993 winter performance season, I began feeling uncomfortable in my body. I'd gained back all the weight I'd lost in my starvation period, and I didn't like it. My curves were back, and they felt wrong. The ideal at City Ballet at the time seemed to be very thin, boyishly athletic bodies with not much evidence of a feminine shape. Now, looking back at images of myself during this time, I realize that I was actually at a very good dancing weight. But I'd gotten used to myself as a waif-thin anorexic, so I saw only an overweight dancer in the mirror. My self-image was skewed, and I didn't look realistically at my body. I was beginning to identify myself as a pretty dancer who had areas of her body that were bigger than they should be. I focused too much on the parts of myself that I was dissatisfied with: my thighs and my hips.

Two of the ballets I premiered at this time were ballets in which the costume was basically just a leotard and tights—no long, thick skirts for any excess flesh to hide beneath. The first was Jerome Robbins's *Moves*, a ballet that has no music at all. It is a brilliant exercise of choreography in silence, where the movements of the dancers create the rhythms from which more dance emerges. It is largely an ensemble piece, but individuals are singled out in different sections. In my section, I had a brief pas de deux in which I portrayed an angry woman stamping her foot while her partner tried to soothe her.

I was excited to do the ballet and loved all of the rehearsals, but when I was confronted with the costume rehearsal onstage, I was suddenly miserable and self-conscious. I remember standing in my leotard on one side of the stage, arms crossed over my body, silently wishing for a skirt or leg warmers or anything that might cover up the parts of my body I was unhappy with.

A senior corps member who was also in the ballet, Sean Savoye, must have noticed something off in my demeanor. He came up to me and looked me in the eyes for a moment.

"I know what you are thinking," he said quietly, "and I want you to know that you look great. You look beautiful, and you have nothing to feel bad about."

Then he walked away. I was shocked that he had been able to read me so easily, and very touched by his sensitivity. And he did give me the courage to go through with the rehearsals and performances. I thought, Maybe I'm imagining things. Maybe I actually am all right.

The second ballet with a minimal costume was George Balanchine's *Ivesiana*, choreographed in 1954 and set to the sometimes disconcerting music of Charles Ives. This ballet is divided into dramatic sections like acts, and is almost more of a theater piece, or an imaginative exploration of different dream states through dance, than it is a fully choreographed ballet. I portrayed a woman, seemingly blind, who wanders through a forest and then is attacked by a stranger. My costume was a leotard with a short, sheer skirt, and we were reusing costumes previous dancers had worn years ago. When we got to the stage rehearsal, we discovered that the skirt was too short for my long-waisted body; it didn't even cover the bottom of my rear.

I had to go out and do the rehearsal anyway, feeling exposed and knowing that the costume was horribly unflattering. Peter came on-stage, obviously displeased with the costume, and questioned the costume mistress about it. Her response was that the costume was what it was, and nothing could be done about it at this late notice. The performance was that night. Peter was angry, and I couldn't tell if it was because of the costume or because of how I looked in the costume. I immediately assumed that it was because of my body and felt terrible.

I tried to solve the problem of my body with a classic cycle of binge and starve. I fell into a pattern where I would eat very little for days and then suddenly let go like a snapped rubber band and eat whatever I wanted. My weight began to fluctuate subtly, going up and down depending on what I ate and how hard I was dancing. Nothing was right. I constantly felt insecure about how I looked and danced. I couldn't remain confident in myself for long, and my eating was about to have a terrible effect not just on my psyche but on my career.

I believe that it was during this year that I got my first gentle suggestion that I lose weight. I don't even remember who said it or what was said to me, but the realization that the company wasn't pleased with my appearance dramatically changed the way I thought. No longer was I just afraid that management might be unhappy with me; now I *knew* that they were not happy with how I looked, and my insecurity changed into shame and self-hatred. How could I, the perfect, straight-A, always smiling and well-spoken daughter of the South have allowed myself to be chastised for something as simple to control as my weight? My solution: I stopped eating again.

There was no one I wanted to turn to for help. I could admit my failure to no one. Throughout my whole life, I'd been able to find guidance and strength in prayer, but God was not in my life at this point. I'd stopped going to church. I just didn't have the time or the energy. Religion seemed to have no place in my new world; I still prayed, but only in moments of extreme need. It was as if God were up on my shelf and I would pull Him down when I needed His help, only to put Him right back into His spot again when I felt strong enough to get going on my own.

All during the season of 1994 I was given more and more demanding corps roles, along with bigger featured parts. I didn't get any more of those "hints" from the company, but my eating was still wacky and out of control, veering between under- and overeating. For the most part, I managed to stay slim enough that I figured I was on safe ground—or at least could get away with my erratic habits. I was getting noticed in the press and did my first Sugar Plum Fairy in December of 1994, with Peter Boal as my cavalier. I was singled out for principal roles both in the regular repertory and when new choreographers came to work with the company. Peter even used me as the soloist girl in his new work that season. I was overworked and overtired and overstressed, thrilled with how my career was going but underneath still unsure of myself. I had no self-confidence but relied solely on others' approval to feel that I was doing okay. An approving comment would only last me a short time before I was in need of another one. If only I was promoted to soloist— the rank in between corps and principal—then I would be happy, I thought. Soloists are set apart from the corps and given the company's official stamp of approval. Even better, they get a pay raise. If the company made me a soloist, I would know that I was okay. Then I could relax. Then I would be normal.

In January 1995 we were putting the Balanchine ballet *Harlequinade* onstage. I was an understudy for the soloist girl, the character of Pirouette. I hadn't been cast to dance it that season, but I knew the part cold because I'd been there when they were teaching the steps to Yvonne, who would be dancing the role. Even though it was understood that understudies should watch the stage rehearsals to make sure nothing went wrong, I was feeling exhausted and burned out, and I went back to my apartment to rest instead.

A few hours later, I got a phone call from Peter Martins. This wasn't normal, and I knew something was up. Had I royally screwed up by not going to the stage rehearsal? It was probably one of the few times I had ever not followed the rules, and it would be ironic if I ended up getting in trouble for it.

"Hello, Jenny," he said.

"Hi," I said, cautiously.

"Weren't you supposed to be understudying *Harlequinade*?"

I stammered something about being tired and knowing it really well and not thinking it would matter if I was at the stage rehearsal or not.

"Well, I was looking for you," Peter said.

"Oh . . . ," I replied, feeling awkward.

"I wanted to tell you I was promoting you to soloist."

And that was that. In a very anticlimactic way, I had gotten the promotion I was longing for. I gushed my thanks and didn't really know what else to say. We got off the phone fairly quickly, and I was left alone in my apartment, thrilled but oddly at loose ends as to what to do with myself or even how to feel. This was the moment a switch was supposed to go off, turning me into a happy and confident person who was no longer obsessed with compulsive eating. But I was still the same person, with the same fears—and the same solution. I went out that night and bought a box of cookies and a pint of ice cream and ate all of it.

Over the next year I dug myself further into my hole. I defined the binge-and-purge mentality; I would grossly overeat at times, and then not eat at all for a period. I never threw up, though I tried, so I would take extra ballet classes to compensate for my overeating. I couldn't seem to achieve a normal way of putting nutrition into my body. But like most people with compulsive eating problems, I worked extra hard at keeping it all a giant secret, locked away inside my own apartment and my own head. I was determined to present a perfect façade; I assumed that if I told no one my problem, then no one would ever know. When I went grocery shopping, it was furtively and with shame, hoping that no one would see the items I put in my basket.

Meanwhile, my career was going wonderfully. This of course only accelerated my quest to hide my disorders behind a happy, beautiful shell. At the beginning of the year I was working closely with Jerome Robbins on his hilarious spoof ballet *The Concert* as well as the debut City Ballet cast of *2 and 3 Part Inventions*, which Jerry had originally choreographed on students from SAB. I was sought after by new choreographers and featured in articles in *Time* magazine and the *New York Times*.

Despite all the accolades, my self-confidence fell lower every time I looked in the mirror—and in the ballet world, there are mirrors everywhere. I constantly felt like my body was horrible, and was particularly ashamed of my thighs. I remember a stage rehearsal for a new Kevin O'Day ballet called *Huoah* where I sobbed in the wings. The costume was a short skirt with no tights, and the two other women in the piece were Wendy Whelan and Stacey Calvert, two ladies who were all beautiful muscles and angles. I looked at my own softer body and felt completely inadequate.

I stood in the wings, gasping and sniffing as I tried not to cry.

Wendy took my shoulder. "Jenny, what's wrong?"

"I . . . I just feel awful in this costume," I choked out.

"Why, girl?" asked Stacey, adopting a lighter tone to try to cheer me up.

"I just . . . I just don't think my . . . my body looks good in it. It's not right for it," I finally managed.

"No, Jenny. You look beautiful," said Wendy.

"Seriously, Jenny," added Stacey. "You have such a wonderful feminine body. You should be proud of it. Lots of us wish we had a body like yours!"

But I couldn't or wouldn't let myself believe it. Much of my dancing began to take on a frantic edge; I simply wasn't comfortable in my own skin.

On another occasion, during a second performance of Peter Martins's *Sinfonia*, everything seemed to go wrong for my three fellow dancers and me. We were young and inexperienced to have principal roles, especially those with such tricky partnering as a Martins ballet,

and we didn't realize that if a week or two passed in between performances of a certain ballet, we needed to take it upon ourselves to rehearse with each other, even if a ballet master didn't call a rehearsal.
Several key partnering moves went badly, and the timing between the
four of us was way off. After the performance, Peter was furious with
us and told us we were irresponsible. It was terribly upsetting to be
chastised by the artistic director, but what I secretly believed was that
he was actually unhappy with how I'd looked in the short white
costume, and upset with me because of my weight. I completely ignored the fact that I'd indeed made a mistake by not maintaining the
ballet with extra rehearsals. I couldn't seem to stop obsessing about my
appearance.

Gradually my behavior unraveled to the point where I was no longer
cycling between eating and starving. I was almost continually overeating, and I started to gain weight. In a desperate effort to head off the
pounds, I joined a gym and would do long, intense workouts every day
in addition to my regular dancing schedule to compensate for the
amount of food I consumed every night. I told no one about my struggles. When I went food shopping, I would go to different stores so the
cashiers wouldn't see the quantity of foods I was buying every day. If I
saw someone I knew in a store or deli, I would run out before they could
see me. If I saw someone on my way home from the store, I would try to
hide the contents of my bags so they wouldn't see the cookies and cheese
and ice cream in my shopping bags.

In 1996 I was selected to be part of a new cast of *The Waltz Project*, a
ballet by Peter Martins for four couples dancing to music by a variety of
American composers. It was a jazzy, sexy ballet, and despite my personal struggles, I was excited about being called, especially when I
learned I would be doing the part of the girl who dances the funny
"Sneaker Pas." In the middle of the ballet, I would actually change into
running shoes for one of my dances. My partner was to be James Fayette, a corps dancer whom I enjoyed dancing with and who I knew was
a great partner.

Despite the desperate emotions inside me, I did manage to enjoy a lot of the rehearsals for the ballet. The ballet mistress for *The Waltz Project* was Suzy Hendl, my favorite coach to work with. She knew how to bring the "ballerina" out of a dancer and could always inspire me to dance better. It was wonderful to work with her, and I loved dancing with James. Since he was such a good partner, I always felt secure and knew I didn't have to worry about things going wrong. However, despite how strong he was, I didn't like to practice the lifts with him; I felt that I was too heavy and maybe hard to lift. I kept trying to avoid the lifts, or at least avoid doing them repeatedly. After another day of me saying, "You don't have to do this lift," James stopped the rehearsal.

"Stop saying that. I want to do this lift. It's easy with you. You are a piece of cake. Don't worry about it," he said.

He made me feel better, and I stopped asking him not to lift me, but I still had anxiety about my body. Peter came in for a couple of studio rehearsals, since we were a new cast. He is great to work with in the studio and gets very excited when new dancers are learning the choreography for the first time. He was also known as one of the best partners in the world while he was dancing, so he is particularly good at coaching difficult pas de deux work. Since his choreography for *The Waltz Project* contains a lot of difficult partnering, we definitely needed him for some of the moves.

Our rehearsal for Peter was going great until he decided to actually do a lift with me in order to show James how to do it. Mortified, I tried desperately to get out of it.

"Come and show me what position you are in," Peter said to me.

I indicated the position loosely, not close enough that Peter could actually get a good grip on me. I was hoping Peter would just show James how to place his hands properly.

But Peter stepped closer. I just stood there, not preparing to jump as I would have if I were actually going to be lifted.

Peter met my eyes in the mirror. "Go on," he said. "Do it."

Cringing inside, I did it. Peter had to pick me up and flip me completely around head over heels before putting me back on the ground. After he had done it, I felt myself blushing and couldn't think straight the rest of the rehearsal.

I wondered, Had I felt heavy? Did my body seem squishy? Did he suddenly and magically know I was overeating every night with no self-control? It was almost as if I had entered a paranoid state where I thought he could read my mind and see my shameful acts. Obviously, in my mind, I'd given him way too much power over me. I ran home after rehearsal and binged again.

The rehearsal weeks went by, and then, right before casting was due to go up, I saw a strange rehearsal on the schedule. I was called, by myself, for a rehearsal from six to six thirty in the Practice Room, our smaller studio. The rehearsal was strange for a couple of reasons. I never rehearsed *The Waltz Project* by myself; since I hardly danced a step in my part alone, I always needed my partner with me. And the company rarely rehearsed after six unless there was an emergency. I got a sinking feeling in my stomach.

That night, Suzy called me. Her tone was kind, and she seemed reluctant to say what she had to say. "Peter wants you to come to the rehearsal in costume. He is concerned you are going to be too heavy and not look your best if he casts you."

I was devastated. I had been stressing about the costume already. It was just a unitard and a skirt, and I knew I was going to feel very exposed. But I didn't think my weight was at the point where such an extreme measure needed to be taken. This was the first time my weight was directly affecting my casting. It felt humiliating. I knew the entire company must know that something was going on with me due to the weird rehearsal on the schedule.

I started crying and refused. It was just too mortifying to think of walking through the theater with my costume on just to be examined and judged.

"Suzy," I said finally, "I would rather not do the ballet at all than have to show myself in the Practice Room like that." We ended the call.

I'm not sure what transpired after that. Perhaps they relented. Maybe they decided to take a chance on me. But casting went up, and my name was on it to dance in *The Waltz Project*. This sent me into a frenzy of working out, and I tried desperately to stop eating. I would starve myself for a day or two and then fall apart and binge. I would go to the gym for hours on end and then dance a full day of rehearsals. I prayed, but I did not feel like God was listening.

I felt stiff and worried during the stage rehearsal one week later and wondered if everyone was staring in horror at my body. Afterward, I went home and frantically went through Pilates exercises in my living room. I felt something grab in my back, but kept going. I thought maybe some exercise would miraculously thin out my legs before that night's show.

When I finally got out onstage to perform *The Waltz Project*, I felt like two people. There was the smaller, much diminished side of me that was enjoying the performance, loving dancing on the stage in a fun ballet with a great partner. The larger, monstrous side of me was consumed with anxiety about what my body looked like, what angle would be the best to present to the audience so that I would look the thinnest, and what I could do to look skinny to the dancers watching from the wings. Ultimately, during the finale of the ballet, my back grabbed again, but this time the pain couldn't be ignored. I made it through the rest of the finale, but could hardly do the bows. It hurt to bend forward in a curtsy.

Waiting at the elevator to the dressing rooms with James, I pressed my back flat against the wall and bent my knees. I was scared. I looked at James.

"I think I hurt my back," I said calmly. I couldn't let the fear show.

"Oh, I'm sorry. You should ice it," he replied, not very concerned because I hadn't sounded worried.

I walked slowly to my dressing room and removed my makeup. I told Yvonne that I thought something was wrong with my back. When I went to put on my coat to go home, I froze with one arm in the sleeve. Yvonne met my eyes.

"Do you need help?" she asked with growing concern. She helped me put my coat on. I took a cab home and ate dinner lying down. The next morning, I couldn't walk.

I'd had injuries on my feet before—breaks and sprains—but had never hurt my back. For all dancers and athletes, a back injury stirs up a primal fear, maybe because the primitive part of our brain knows that the spinal cord is crucial. I felt very afraid when I called the physical therapist to ask if she could see me. But overwhelming that fear was a sense of relief. I'd been given a break, and a reprieve. I didn't have to go back into the theater and face my problems. At least not for a while.

I stayed in the city for a few months after my back injury, what the therapists called a back sprain, splitting my time between going to physical therapy and hiding in my apartment and eating. My back wasn't getting better, and I was gaining more and more weight. It was easy to isolate myself. I never went into the theater and was not asked to; an injured dancer isn't very useful to the company. My friends were too busy with their performing lives to see me, which I preferred. My sister was still in the city, and we did see each other often, which was probably the only thing that kept me from completely imploding. But I did not share my shameful eating even with her, my best friend.

One of the physical therapists encouraged me to go on a mail-order macrobiotic cleansing diet. She said she was worried about how heavy I was. I tried it for two days and then gave up, telling her that I was still on it.

In the spring, my parents asked me to come stay with them in Washington, DC, where they were staying while in between European postings. They were very worried about me and tried to help me in several ways once I arrived at their home.

My mother quickly took charge of me; she couldn't bear to see me hurting. She knew something was terribly wrong, but I refused to talk to her about anything except the practicalities of a back injury. Mom found me a physical therapist who incidentally also knew about weight-loss techniques. She found some local ballet studios where I could take class anonymously when I was ready. My mother also started talking to me about quitting.

She sat down with me one day in the living room of their house and was quiet for a while. I knew she wanted to talk about something important, something that had to do with my situation, and I felt myself building a defensive wall against her, despite the love I saw in her eyes.

"Jenny," she said carefully. "Do you think you would ever want to stop dancing?"

"No, Mom. I can't just stop."

"But why not?" she asked. "You could come and stay with us, maybe enroll at William and Mary College. . . ."

"I'm not going to do that." Silence. "I'm just not." I can see now how worried my mother was, and how much she was hurting because she could see how much pain her dear daughter was in. But at the time, I could only see myself, and I shut her out.

Despite the darkness I felt, I couldn't even conceive of quitting ballet. I was angry with my mother for even suggesting it. In my mind, I had to be perfect: pretty, smart, talented, kind, funny—and a ballerina. That's who I was, who I had to be. I was not a quitter, and I was not someone who failed. I got straight A's. I got promoted. I went to college while I danced professionally and did both extremely well. While the fact remained that I was failing, that I was now ugly in the eyes of the ballet world, that making jokes couldn't cover up the fact that I was falling apart, still I couldn't admit my failure to myself. I kept thinking that I just needed to discover the trick, the secret, the key to ending my addiction to food, and that once I did, I would fix all of my problems and be happy again and no one besides me would ever know my disgusting secret. I couldn't just give up and stop dancing, because then I felt everyone would finally see the truth: that I was not, in fact, perfect.

I didn't open up to my parents about my eating disorders. I was too ashamed, despite the safe environment they provided for me. It was impossible to believe that even these two people, who loved me unconditionally, could still love and understand me if I revealed to them what I felt was such a horrible behavior. But of course I didn't have to tell them; my mother knew exactly what was going on without our ever talking about it. The problem was, she was as much at a loss as I was about how to deal with it. When my mom hesitantly approached me with the suggestion that I try out an Overeaters Anonymous meeting, not even saying outright that she thought I had a problem, I rejected the idea and felt angry and encroached upon. But the more I thought about it, the more I thought it was something I should try. It was terrifying to think of attending a meeting of strangers and publicly admitting that I had this shameful problem. But I had no other ideas. Finally I decided to go, just once.

It was a revelation to me. The meeting was close to my parents' home in Virginia, just outside DC, and close to a Metro station. It was held very early in the morning so that the people who attended the meeting could get to their jobs on time. My parents dropped me off on their own way to work, and then I would get on the Metro afterward. There were only about eight or nine people in the meeting, and everyone sat at an oval table in some office's conference room.

I mostly sat silently while the others talked, but everyone was encouraged to share something in this meeting, particularly because there were so few people there. Also, this group knew that there was something healing in the sharing of stories, whether they are stories of failure or triumph. No one commented on another's stories or offered advice; the telling was enough. They went around the table, everyone opening up their time to speak with the phrase "My name is _____, and I am a compulsive overeater." Stunned, I listened while these individuals around me matter-of-factly talked about their abnormal eating habits and their struggles to find normalcy in healthy ways. They spoke of the twelve steps and how those steps helped them out in different situations. They spoke of taking it moment by moment and relying on a higher power. They spoke of failure and frustration and success and forgiveness.

I looked around the table at the small group and saw very normal people, some thin, some heavy, some young, and some old, all of whom admitted to living daily with abnormal attitudes toward food. They talked about their feelings and emotions, even if those feelings and emotions were unattractive. They spoke of how they used food in order not to feel the more difficult emotions of everyday life.

I listened to those courageous people, and learned that I wasn't alone and that what I was going through was not so strange.

I looked around the table and saw my heroes.

When the sharing made its way around the circle to me, everyone looked at me with gentle expectation. I didn't feel a sense of pressure from them and probably could have just passed, but once again, I needed to "do well" and rise to the occasion, even here where my need to be perfect meant that I had to admit to strangers that I had a problem.

I hesitated, my throat closing up.

"My name is Jenny," I finally said, "and"—I swallowed—"I am a compulsive overeater."

I blushed bright red, feeling a wave of shame soak me in self-hate. I said no more.

The people at the table nodded politely, greeted me with the ritual response of "Hi, Jenny," and then moved on to the next person. That was it. They accepted me. And all they knew about me was the absolute worst thing about myself.

So I sat there, silent and stunned, listening to these very regular people talking about their eating disorders, and knew I was going to be coming to the meetings. Over the weeks I stayed with my parents, I regularly attended the group, and eventually I began to open up during the sharing time. For those brief months, I became friends with those wonderful people, and felt a connection with each one of them, young or old or male or female. And they treated me as just another member of the group, someone working to escape an addiction but normal nevertheless—not a weak failure with no self-control, as I had felt at

City Ballet. Here I was accepted and surrounded by those who were winning their battles against food addictions. It was amazing.

Unfortunately, despite what I was learning from the group and my internal revelations, my eating disorder continued at full force. I was gaining an understanding as to why I was behaving the way I was, but I was unable to stop it.

As I look back now upon my twenty-three-year-old self, I see a stranger who was absolutely incapable of coping with difficulty. Up until this juncture of my life, things had always come easily for me, and I'd had a degree of success with almost everything I attempted. Growing up in the South, I learned that a good southern girl was pretty, polite, gracious, and friendly. She was always pleasant and avoided ugly topics or feelings, at least in public. She was well put together and always had her hair fixed, her makeup on, and her smile ready. I could be this perfect southern girl really well.

I was rarely allowed to feel unhappy for long, neither by society nor by my parents. I don't blame my parents—they loved me and wanted to protect me from being hurt. But they did always fix my problems, and we never let on to anyone outside the family if we were sad or hurt or disappointed. I learned that negative feelings were to be ignored or hidden or taken care of by someone else. I didn't learn any tools for dealing with pressure or difficulty or hardship. And I didn't learn that it was in my weaknesses and my failures that I needed to rely on God the most.

Perhaps if I'd finished high school and gone to college at the regular ages, I would have matured and learned how to manage adult problems in a healthy way with the help of experience. But I threw myself into the ballet world, becoming a professional at the age of sixteen. I was barely a teenager when I found myself dealing with high pressure, exhaustion, and physical pain; I was slow to realize that the reality of a job as a ballet dancer was very different from the glowing dream version that I was determined to see instead.

In my family, we used to always celebrate special occasions with food:

we would go out to a nice restaurant; we would get a certain dessert; we would be allowed a candy bar at the grocery store. There is nothing wrong with that, of course, but I associated some of my happiest memories with special foods. Since my mom was often concerned with her own diet, we rarely had sweets in the house because she did not want to tempt herself. But once I had an apartment of my own, I suddenly realized I could eat whatever I wanted whenever I wanted. I could celebrate with food, yes. But I could also make myself feel better with food. Or I could just somehow *not* feel with food.

It had come to the point where success in the ballet world was my only measure of happiness, but even when I was successful, I wasn't happy. As I began to realize that not only was I imperfect but this dream life I was living was also not as beautiful as I thought it would be, I started to turn to food for some modicum of control over my life and my feelings. I might not get my ten-hour rehearsal schedule until eleven o'clock the night before, but I could know what I was going to eat that day. I might be anxious about a part I was hoping to dance in a week, but I could make that anxiety disappear by eating a large bowl of pasta and reading a science fiction book. If I was still feeling anxious and out of control after dinner, I could watch TV and eat more food, even if I wasn't hungry. And no one would ever know, because I ate alone, in secret.

After my time with my parents, I went back home to New York City to check in with the physical therapists there. My PT was concerned about my weight and told me about some diets I could try while I used the summer to get back into shape for City Ballet's winter season. I thanked her and actually tried the diet, thinking that I would do it, lose my weight quickly over the summer, and return to the company in the fall as if I had never had a problem. But the diet was dramatically limiting, and after two days of very little food, I binged and was right back into my destructive eating cycle. I looked for OA groups in the city, but they were huge and crowded and intimidating. I found a sponsor whom I could call and talk to, but I started to close up on her and eventually stopped trying to contact her.

That summer of 1996, at my sister's wedding, I reached my highest weight; I was probably forty pounds over my dancing weight. I couldn't fit into the bridesmaid dress I'd bought and had to buy another in the wrong color. My sister of course said she didn't care—she just wanted me to feel beautiful—but I felt I'd let her down on her special day.

In the fall I returned to City Ballet, officially reporting for work. My back had healed, and I was taking ballet class and had even lost some weight—but it wasn't enough. As I waited for rehearsals to begin, something became clear to me: there was a very important component missing from my routine. I realized how much I needed to make God a part of my life in New York again. Since becoming a professional dancer, I'd put God aside. But while visiting with my parents in DC, I'd attended church regularly and we had prayed together as a family. I'd received counseling from a pastor at their church and had even danced in a service, something I hadn't done in years. It had felt wonderful to be part of a Christian community again and to have my thoughts turned regularly to the bigger picture of faith in life. But once back at home in New York, my focus narrowed to ballet again, and I'd fallen back into my old patterns. I felt that I was suffocating, and I realized I was missing an essential part of my life by not attending church and not having Christian friends I could talk to. I also felt instinctively that I would not become a full, realized adult, able to face life frankly and fearlessly, until I addressed my relationship with God and recommitted my life to Him. I needed to be able to stand on my own two feet, but with those feet firmly cemented in God's steady foundation.

I started attending All Angels' Church regularly once again and was immediately welcomed back into the community. It was a new experience to be attending on my own as an adult rather than as the teenage daughter of Doug and Scharlene. My heart was filled to bursting the first Sunday I returned and participated in the wonderful worship songs and prayers. I wanted to kick myself for letting my faith go, for pushing my beautiful Savior off to the side as if He were of no consequence.

I joined a House Church, one of several small fellowship groups that studied the Bible and prayed together in one of the member's apartments. At first I was wary of attending: what if these Christians were . . . weird? What if they were too touchy-feely, or invasive, or socially awkward, or more-pious-than-thou? After all, they didn't go to church only on Sundays. They also went to this middle-of-the-week Bible study and who knows what else. What if they asked me to open up and show my true self by sharing my problems? What if they wanted me to do scary things like help other people? The dangers were endless.

You may not be surprised to hear that I learned this group was friendly, down-to-earth, and hilariously funny. In addition to earnestly studying the Bible together, we laughed a lot and shared our lives in an empathetic and supportive environment. After several weeks, I gathered up my courage and revealed my eating disorder to my small prayer group. I thought it might be my last day with them: surely they would be horrified and disgusted when they discovered my lack of self-control. But no one judged me; they heard my prayer request, went on to hear everyone else's prayer requests, and then we prayed. They asked God for help and healing on my behalf. We parted with hugs and the promise to see each other the next week.

I soon felt more comfortable with my friends at House Church than I did with my friends at the theater. At House Church I was completely myself, knowing that everyone there loved me for the person I was and not for what I looked like or what I could do for them. In contrast, my theater friends backed away from my difficulties and couldn't relate to me if I wasn't thin enough to successfully perform. They didn't do it maliciously or even on purpose; my situation confused them and made them uncomfortable. Plus, they were all overwhelmed with their own busy dancing schedules. They still loved me, just from a distance. At the theater, ballet was everything—ballet was god—and few there could understand someone who had been a part of the ballet world but was now operating on the outskirts of it. And from artistic management, all I received were grim looks and stony silence.

At church, I became more and more involved in activities beyond regular services and House Church, participating in and eventually assistant-leading a weekly program for people questioning the Christian faith. God was slowly peeling back my layers, enabling me to discover and adjust to who I was as a Daughter of Christ as He worked on my heart to heal me.

At the company, however, things were quickly deteriorating. Although I'd recovered from my back injury and could dance, I wasn't being cast for performances because of my weight. I felt like an utter failure and an outcast; just walking into the theater felt like entering a dark prison. I dreaded going into that windowless concrete building and felt like I could breathe only when I was outside again.

I was still called to rehearsals, but always as an understudy, and I only stood in the back and watched other people dance parts I'd once performed. I remember a brief conversation with Rosemary during which I begged to be allowed to perform something. I needed something to shoot for, something to look forward to. We met in the girl's locker room.

"Why can't I dance in *Suite No. 3*?" I asked. "It has a long dress and is behind a scrim."

"You are too heavy even for that," she replied. "It would not be fair to the other in-shape and ready-to-go dancers if we cast you right now."

"What about *Firebird* princesses? That is just a corps part, and they have long sleeves and long skirts."

"You would stand out too much. It wouldn't be a good example. You just need to lose the weight. You can do it quickly if you want to."

I sat there and cried but accepted it. And went home and ate until my stomach hurt.

It seems strange when you think about it, given how prevalent eating disorders are in the ballet world, but at the time it was one big scary undiscussed secret. There was only silence. The other dancers and ballet masters didn't know how to interact with me. Some just ignored my weight and the obvious problems it was causing and talked to me about other things. Many ignored me altogether, avoiding eye contact. These same ballet masters had been extremely friendly when I was thin. Sometimes I found people staring at my body, and when they realized I was looking at them, they would quickly look away.

Some did try to intervene: a few of the ballet masters took me aside to talk to me, trying to gently help me or inspire me to lose the weight and get back on the right track. Others seemed angry and disappointed when they talked to me about how heavy I had become. I was never commended, however, when I lost weight. Despite the revelations in my inner spiritual life, I was still in the binge-and-purge cycle, eating practically nothing for a while, losing weight significantly, until something broke and I started binging again. I was so self-absorbed that even an imagined critical look would send me to the deli for ice cream. But management only spoke to me when the news they wanted to give me was bad. The assumption at the company was that no news was always good news.

I had conversations with Peter during which he was very frustrated and couldn't understand why I couldn't get my act together. He was seeing my weight fluctuate wildly from week to week.

"I gained weight once. I just had to stop eating cheesecake," he told me.

If only I could just *stop*, I thought. If only it were that easy.

Other meetings with him revealed his anger at me. He felt I had severely let him down. I don't remember what exactly was said, frankly. I do remember him throwing a magazine at the wall. And I remember sitting on his office's red leather couch and just crying.

I saw Jerome Robbins backstage during this time, and he said, "Come on. You just need to get the weight off. Just do it. We need you."

The conversations varied, but their effect didn't: after each one, I went home and bought a pint of ice cream and consumed it in front of the television.

It wasn't that I'd given up trying to lose weight. I tried weird diets where I was supposed to only eat green vegetables or have just fruit before noon or have minuscule little meals mailed to me. The diets would last for a day or two until I felt weak and headachy and sick and would finally buy a whole bunch of food and eat to the point of discomfort. I did give up on OA—I couldn't make a connection in the big loud meetings in New York. And though I went to a wonderful nutritionist, I lied to her about what I ate, telling her I couldn't figure out why I wasn't losing weight because I was following her program almost perfectly.

I worked out frantically at the gym for hours. But when I came home, there was only me and my obsession with food and failure. To prevent myself from thinking about the disaster of my life, I turned repeatedly to books and television—and always food. Though I had God back in my life and in my head, my heart was still broken. Something in me still needed to be fixed, and God was the only one to do it. But though I was praying, God was not answering my prayer in the way that I wanted. To me, it seemed He was not working at all. Unfortunately, I was still trying to be my own fixer, which meant ultimately that nothing was getting better. And the company wasn't seeing any improvement.

In December of 1996 another ballet master, Russell Kaiser, asked me to come in for a talk. Russell and I had danced together before he retired, and he now worked very closely with Peter. He gently told me that he was worried that if I didn't lose the weight, I was going to be let go. Here it was: my worst fear and the ultimate failure. If I were fired, then the whole world would know that I was worthless. I was so wrapped up in my inner world that I thought I was still fooling everyone. I told outsiders that I was fixing things and that eventually I would be back onstage. I put on a smile at work and pretended I was on the road to recovery, even at church. But if they actually fired me, I would be caught in my lie. Everyone would know that I had no self-control and couldn't overcome my addiction to food. Russell was kind and understanding during our meeting, but it was too late and not enough.

In February 1997 I had a meeting with Peter before the regular contractual deadline, when the company must inform dancers whether or not they were going to be reengaged. There wasn't much to say.

"Well, we have said it all before," he told me, no longer angry, just resigned. "It has been too long now. We're going to have to let you go. But we need you here, onstage. Your contract lasts until the end of our Saratoga season. You have your job through July, and if you can lose the weight by then, I can rehire you and no one has to ever know that you were fired. I really hope you can do it."

And that was it. As in all of our meetings, I didn't say much. I accepted. I cannot remember if I cried during the meeting or not. I cried so often in that office that it is hard to keep track.

After leaving Peter's office, I headed to a restaurant where I was meeting my parents, who were in town visiting—the last thing I wanted to do at that point. I broke down sobbing right there, unable to wait to cry until I wasn't in a public place. I couldn't keep the news from them. But I told no one else. Still a coward and still trying to keep up some kind of strong public image, I hoped to fix things by the end of Saratoga so that no one else would know that I'd been fired.

My mother came to stay with me and lived in my apartment for almost a month. She was so worried about me and didn't know what to do to help. Unfortunately, as I went through the daily paces of ballet class and gym workouts, I felt like I was encased in rock around my mother. For some reason I couldn't open up to her, nor could I accept or welcome her advice. Perhaps I felt that her presence was too threatening in the sense that she would cause me to show my vulnerability; if I opened up a crack, I knew I would crumble. I shut her firmly out of my inner world and almost ignored her the entire time she was with me. I regret terribly how much I must have hurt her, and I'm sure she was distraught over my behavior. But I couldn't let her in; she knew me too well, and it felt too dangerous to allow her access to my thoughts and feelings. I wanted to shield myself and be alone.

Finally she went home, and I felt relieved. But things didn't get better. I tried to go to some OA meetings again but still couldn't make a connection. I became inconsistent at House Church. The theater felt like a trap—I was unwanted and unuseful and seemed to make everyone uncomfortable. I went there as little as possible. When I did have to go, it felt as if I were going into a dark place that required all of my energy just to protect myself and survive.

I tried frantically to lose weight, to fix myself quickly so I could keep my job. I tried not eating at all but couldn't maintain it. I worked out at the gym and ran in Central Park until I couldn't walk the next day. I thought about taking up smoking so that I would have something else to do with my mouth besides eat, but I hated cigarette smoke. I considered drugs: didn't people on cocaine get really skinny? Maybe I should try that, I thought. But I didn't know how to buy drugs or know anyone I felt comfortable asking about it.

I began seeing a Christian counselor. I was very resistant to going at first. It was my parents' suggestion, first of all, which made me particularly unreceptive. Additionally, I mistakenly thought only weak, crazy people went to counseling—not strong, perfect Christian southern girls. I had the wherewithal, though, to take a look at myself and realize that I really needed help and I would take it from just about anyone—even someone my parents had suggested. So I went to counseling.

It was helpful. The therapist was a stranger who had no previous knowledge of who I was or even what the ballet world was like. When I first sat across from her in her office, I had no idea how to even begin to talk to her. But she asked a couple of questions and then just sat back and listened, looking small and kindly in a Mrs. Claus kind of way. I started to dispassionately tell her my history and why I was there. I heard myself being completely honest with her, as I'd never been with anyone before. I had nothing to lose at this point. After each horrible revelation, she just nodded and waited. I laid myself bare, and it was a relief. There was no need to pretend with her. Finally I was really talking to someone.

Two other women I was completely honest with were Fay Fondiller and Kathy Mihok, friends of my mother's from All Angels' Church. They knew I was having trouble because my mom had asked them to pray for me. So they came and offered to meet with me for prayer. They were lovely Christian women, gentle in spirit and loving in demeanor, who felt called to pray for people who were in need. I know now that God obviously put them in my life as instruments for His healing. They would meet me once a week in a small room at the church. The two of them would ask me how my week was and what I needed prayer for, and then they would spend forty-five minutes praying for me, holding my hands. They would assure me of God's love for me and encourage me to accept His love, despite the repeated failures and ugliness that I felt I carried around on my back everywhere I went.

Their prayers slid like water over the shell I'd created around myself, wearing away at the hardness. No great, sudden changes were occurring in me to the outward eye, and I often felt that nothing good at all was coming as a result of the counseling and the prayers, but I know now that God was working and a light was being nurtured back to life within me. At the time, however, I could not see it. I was still so lost in the darkness.

The spring season went by with no real change in my weight. I was allowed to dance in some corps roles with big dresses, but really, I was unusable. The company went to its summer home in Saratoga Springs, and I went too, knowing secretly that this was going to be my last season with City Ballet. I started hinting to my friends that I might want to stop and go to college full time, still maintaining the image that I was in control. None of them talked too much to me about it. I'd effectively shut them out long before.

I hoped I would not have to talk to Peter again; I would rather have just slunk away. No such luck. The air was heavy with resignation and disappointment during our final meeting. I'd been given chance after chance and hadn't been able to conquer my weight. I was done.

Directly from Saratoga I had a gig, or freelance performance, with James Fayette and other dancers from City Ballet in Vermont and Nantucket. Often during our layoffs dancers would take performing opportunities outside the company for the experience and the extra money. James had asked me to be his partner on this gig months before, and I'd accepted. Much to my surprise, I relished the dancing for the first time in a long time; it was my first solid, challenging dancing in months, and I knew it might be my last. When I got home, my life would completely drop off a cliff.

There were two performances, and I danced a pas de trois by an up-and-coming choreographer at the time, Christopher Wheeldon, as well as the pas de deux from Balanchine's *Stars and Stripes*. Though the other dancers on the gig were some of my oldest friends, dancers I had gone to the School of American Ballet with, I told none of them I was fired or even leaving the company. I kept things superficial.

Finally I returned home and had to face the facts: it was all over. What had been my life, in essence my god, had been ripped away. The weeks after that gig were probably the darkest of my life. I was twenty-four years old, and I felt utterly worthless. I had failed at everything that had been important to me my entire life. I was supposed to be perfect and successful: I had been fired. I was supposed to be beautiful: I was overweight and gross. I was supposed to be smart and in control: I couldn't eat a meal without overeating until I felt sick. I was supposed to be funny and friendly and loving and generous: I'd shut out all of my friends and family. I was supposed to be a Christian: I still hadn't made God the priority of my life.

I don't remember much about how I passed the time during those weeks. I holed myself up in my apartment with my favorite compulsive foods and movies and books. If I went out to shop, I wore baggy clothes and a baseball cap to cover my face. I played every sad song I owned over and over, crying on my living room floor, grieving over a song because I couldn't grieve over my own losses and sadness. It came to me also that I never danced in my apartment anymore—a heavy stillness in my body permeated my days. Even great music couldn't inspire me to sway just a little when I was home. Whatever had been in me, inspiring me to dance even just for the enjoyment of it, was gone.

Looking back, I realize how completely self-absorbed I was. I'd blown my situation way out of proportion; people around the world were suffering terribly and had much worse things to deal with than weight problems and job loss. But I had allowed my psyche to be twisted by the ballet world until I believed that a successful career in ballet was the only road to happiness and self-worth. Wrapped up in my failure, I couldn't see out of it. Despite everything that had happened to me, I still believed that I could only find meaning and joy in ballet, almost as if I suffered from Stockholm syndrome and City Ballet was my captor.

One night during those six or so weeks, I sat in my bed sobbing and talking to God. I cried out in anguish to Him, asking Him why this was happening to me. I told Him I was worthless and repulsive. It didn't occur to me to ask for help or forgiveness—I was too repellent even for God. I told Him I didn't know what to do or where to go. I didn't think I could ever crawl out of the deep abyss in which I was trapped.

Then I grew calm, and I realized that there was really no point to a life like this one. It benefited no one and was a torture to me. Why was I staying in it? There was no reason. Perhaps I should just . . . kill myself. It would be the ultimate escape—an escape that no book or food could ever provide. I could even escape from my bondage to food.

If I were to end my life, how would I do it? I contemplated methods of suicide. In a clinical, dispassionate way, I thought about which techniques would be plausible. I settled on one, and in my mind's eye I played the scenario out, watching myself do it, trying to imagine what I would feel during the act and then its aftermath, when I would leave my unbearable existence.

And then I thought about what would happen next. I saw my parents and my sister at the moment during which they learned what I'd done. I saw their terrible grief and the way my action would ravage their lives. I realized that I could never do anything so horrible to these three people whom I loved so very much. I couldn't be so selfish as to wound their hearts so irreparably. I started crying again, knowing I needed to keep moving forward if not for myself, then for them. I would have to figure out a way to make a new life for myself, one dark night at a time.

I didn't reach a resolution with God that night. But God was all I had left. I was spent and empty, and I knew that God was faithful. I'd been told of His faithfulness, had seen it in my life and in the lives of those close to me, and had read about it in books and in the Bible. Somehow, He is always faithful. I had to trust that even in these circumstances, God was working for me. He had a plan. Eventually maybe I would see where exactly He was leading me. Finally that night, I just laid my head down and fell asleep.

I devised a strategy of sorts over the next few days. There was no City Ballet schedule for me to call anymore to tell me what to do; I had to figure out a plan for myself while I waited for God's plan to take shape. I had very few credits left to earn at school and knew that if I went full time for one semester, I could finally graduate with a BA in English. Indeed, in true perfectionist fashion, I did end up graduating summa cum laude. My parents wanted me to move in with them, but I stubbornly insisted on staying in New York; it was where I'd become an adult, and it was my home. They told me they would pay for my college but not for my rent. They were trying to be responsible parents and didn't want to fund an easy existence for me in New York City. I would have to find a way to pay rent on my own.

I had some sources of income: there was some severance pay from City Ballet, and I could collect unemployment insurance for a time. Also, a former City Ballet dancer, Rebecca Metzger, whom I'd danced with before she retired, ran the company's New York City Ballet Workout program, which was taught all over the city in New York Sports Clubs. She certified me in the program, and through her efforts, I soon taught several regular workout classes at gyms around the city. I not only earned a bit of money but also regained a little self-esteem.

Rebecca also talked to me about weight and emotional eating and gave me some tools to battle my eating disorders. She took me to live with her in her apartment for a week to model healthy eating and exercise habits, and otherwise tried to help me out of my depression. She offered me lively, intelligent conversation and an understanding ear and could speak to me as one who had gone through the rigors of the professional ballet world and was now living successfully and happily outside it. Just spending time with her and being accepted and taught by her meant more to me than I could express at the time.

I also tried to find work at a temp agency, but when I interviewed, I was told that I had no business skills and was pretty much useless. The woman I met with told me to take some courses and come back later when I had something worthwhile to offer.

In the late summer of 1997 I learned that All Angels' needed a receptionist. I asked if they would hire me part time. I could work in the afternoons, which would give me time to go to school and teach the workout classes I'd scheduled. I was hired. I would need to answer the phone, do some simple data entry, and man the front door when visitors came.

I loved the job. In many ways it was, of course, tedious. I would finish my assigned tasks rapidly and end up with a lot of free time on my hands. I remember creating a huge rubber-band ball out of the large quantity flopping around in every drawer of the receptionist's desk. But I was in a great environment, surrounded by Christians doing meaningful work, and felt that I was contributing to something good. And there were no mirrors anywhere.

There was one day when the Xerox machine in my little desk area broke down. We needed to print the programs for the weekend's church services right away. I stared at the monster with its blinking lights and decided that I would fix it. I took the entire thing apart, opening every compartment one by one until I found a wad of papers clogging one of the moving parts. After I removed every last one of the papers, I closed it all back up, pressed print, and suddenly the machine was a whirling box of productivity again.

Maybe it sounds silly, but that was a huge moment of triumph for me. Perhaps I wasn't going to be a dancer anymore, but I could learn to function in this other, nondancing world. I wasn't completely without skills or hope. I had the ability to learn, and things to offer.

Throughout that fall I did what I could. I attended college courses, taught the ballet workout, and worked at All Angels'. I tried my hand at writing children's stories, a secret dream of mine, and sent some of them out to publishers. I prayed regularly with Kathy and Fay, and slowly, slowly, my food cravings and disorders began to ebb away. My depression began to lift. I was weaning myself off my therapist, feeling stronger without her. I returned full force to House Church. I began to have a normal relationship with food for the first time in a long while, and was starting to feel like I had a regular life: I had nondancing jobs, was going to school, and had nondancing Christian friends. No one cared what I looked like or ate or how much I weighed. I was valued for the kind of person I was, not how I appeared on a stage. In my head I had quit dancing completely and was looking forward to starting a new life. I was thinking about joining a master's program in psychology.

One day I happened to bump into my ballet teacher from Steps, a public dance studio on Broadway and Seventy-fourth Street where anyone can take classes. Many professionals take classes there when they find a teacher who particularly helps them to grow as dancers. My favorite teacher there was Nancy Bielski; I'd taken classes from her since my first summer course in the city when I was fourteen.

Nancy had never judged me based on my weight and had always focused on teaching me to dance, caring about me as a dancer and a person but never basing her approval on my professional success. When we saw each other on the sidewalk, I was happy to talk to her and tell her what I was up to.

She looked at me there on the street and said, "You should come back to class."

"I don't know, Nancy. I think I'm done with that. I don't think I would feel comfortable anyway," I replied.

"You should come back just for you. Not to dance professionally or anything. I think it would be good for you to just dance and move to music. I don't care how you dance or what you look like, and you can take classes for free as my guest. Just come back."

I gave Nancy a noncommittal answer, but over the next couple of days I couldn't get the idea out of my head. Maybe it would feel good to dance again with no one pressuring me to do it. I would just be going to dance for myself, to make my body feel good, and to do exercises that I'd been doing since I was a child. Since I was no longer a part of a company, I didn't have to worry about my appearance. My body was now my own, and I could enjoy dancing without being anxious about what I looked like as I danced. Lots of people took dance class for fun. Why couldn't I?

A few days later, I walked into Nancy's classroom at Steps. I was suddenly terrified to enter the studio and had to talk myself into actually going through with the class. I had to remind myself that I was free from anyone else's judgment, that I was a Daughter of the Lord, and that I was just going in to take a ballet class for the fun of it, for me. Nancy greeted me with an encouraging smile, but I still had the remnants of the shame I'd been dancing with prior to having been fired; I wore a giant T-shirt and large "garbage bag" shorts that obscured my shape. And I was relieved that no one from City Ballet was in the class that day.

The class was like a renewing rain. From the first chords the pianist played for the plié combination, I felt a sense of happiness and familiarity. Nancy's class had a rhythm I was comfortable with, and it felt good to be doing the barre exercises that I'd done in one way or another since I was ten years old. My body moved into the ballet combinations as a train travels down the tracks: the path my limbs traced in the air seemed inevitable.

Even the center work felt good, even though I was out of shape and couldn't dance anything very well. It was simply wonderful to dance to music again, and I found a freedom in the familiar structure of a ballet class. Nancy gave me corrections as if I'd never stopped and treated me as simply another student.

The one thing I did find was that I couldn't look at myself in the mirror. As comfortable as I was growing in my new regular life, I couldn't see my reflection in a ballet setting without hearing the old voices of disgust and condemnation ringing through my head. My solution was to simply not look so that I could enjoy dancing again.

After a few days of this, I had a moment in the middle of Nancy's class that was a culmination of all the healing that had slowly been taking place in my life for the past few months. Everything seemed to come together: the prayers, the conversations, the new friendships and new jobs, the new, daily reliance on a personal God. As Nancy was giving the adagio combination in the center, I was in the middle of a group of dancers trying to learn the sequence. The dancers in front of me shifted just enough so that I could see myself in the mirror; I locked eyes with my reflection.

I stared at myself for an uncomfortable moment or two, immediately going into self-hating dancer mode. From the beginning, we ballerinas are taught to look at ourselves in the mirror to find out what is *wrong* or *bad* or *ugly*. We try to perfect the shapes and lines our body is making and feel unsatisfied if our feet aren't arched enough or our legs aren't high enough or our arms aren't well shaped. I know some dancers who were told, ridiculously, that their necks were too short. They would wear their hair high to try to disguise the "problem," but I'm sure that most of the time when they look in the mirror, they think, "short neck." Me, I stared at my hips and thighs and arms and waist, disgusted by them and ashamed that I'd even walked into a ballet class.

But then, like a golden light, a thought fell over me: *You are beautiful just the way you are, like this, right now.* It was not my thought. It must have come from God. But I saw the truth in it, because I realized that my beauty came not from my body but from the fact that I was a Child of God, redeemed and forgiven. My appearance wasn't important. I could allow myself to be in this body, exactly the way it was, and feel beautiful and loved by my Savior who pursued me—He had sought after me, lost though I was, even with all the things about myself that I hated. I could accept God's forgiveness and also forgive myself for falling and failing and self-destroying.

I realized that I looked fine, just the way I was, and if I stayed at the weight I was right then for the rest of my life, it was all right. I did not need to be a professional dancer. I didn't need to constantly wish I was thinner. I accepted myself for who I was, inside and out, and allowed myself to picture my life moving forward with me at this weight; I saw myself happy and free and able to function in and contribute to the world. I was not perfect and was still very broken in many ways, but it was that very brokenness that was enabling me to lean on God and invite Him ever deeper into my life. My very failures had become the things that God was using to heal me so that He could use me to His purposes, whatever those might be. I went through the rest of class with no one being the wiser that my world had changed. Outwardly, no apparent change had occurred or would occur for months, but I knew that something was different, and I clung to it.

Chapter Five

❧

Dawning

I never had a boyfriend. Actually, scratch that. I had lots of boyfriends, up until the age of ten. In preschool, I loved this sweet little dark-headed boy. He and I would run the length of the front yard when preschool was done for the day, get behind the large sign that proclaimed our school to the road passing in front of the building, and kiss until our mothers decided it was time to go home.

During kindergarten, my neighbor John soulfully sang seventies love songs to me while we played hide-and-seek in the empty grass lot by my house.

In the first grade, there was a quiet redheaded boy named Lenny. When I went through a string of viruses and missed a lot of consecutive days of school, Lenny and his father came to my house with a gift for me. Inside the little box that I shyly unwrapped was a chain bearing a golden key.

"It's the key to my heart," Lenny solemnly declared. After that I skipped second grade and went to third, and Lenny and I lost touch.

In the fifth grade there was a tall boy named Tim. We used to hold hands while we walked around the track during recess. He instructed me on how to properly hold hands.

"Why is your hand so relaxed?" he would ask, pressing my fingers around his. "You have to actually *hold* my hand."

I was not very nice to Tim and suddenly decided I liked another boy named Chris instead. Tim and I had a bad breakup, and I made Tim feel sad, which I later felt very bad about. But it was too late to go back, and now Chris and I were an item, slow-dancing at the fifth-grade gym dance with our ten-year-old tummies pressed against each other.

And then, after Chris, there was nothing. I had lots of crushes on boys but never had the gumption to assert myself, and my reticence made them leery of approaching me. Ballet began to take up all of my after-school time and left little room for other social activities. I was a hopeless romantic, however, and loved reading books with a love story in them. In fact, if there was no love story, or if, when I read the end of the book in advance (yes, I'm one of those people), I discovered the love story didn't work out, I would put the book down and search for another. Around the age of ten I even prayed for my future husband. I asked God to watch over my future spouse and to develop him and make him and me both ready for each other at the right time. I made a list of things I was hoping for in a husband, which I prayed for and then put away in a drawer; the only things I remember now from that list are that I wanted a gentleman, a hero, and a good dancer.

God would one day answer that prayer in every way, but in the meantime I had several misfires. There was a horrible incident in the ninth grade when I was sweet on a handsome boy named Gary from my Spanish class. I was hopelessly in love with him, but he was in the popular crowd and had no idea I even existed. My two friends and I formed a very small, quiet group that went largely unnoticed by the other kids. Every time Gary walked by my desk or glanced at me, I would feel my face flush and grow hot. I must have talked about him a lot at home because my mother hatched a scheme to try to get his attention, much to my dismay.

"Why don't you call him and ask him what the Spanish homework is?" she asked. I thought about the idea, tempted but also appalled.

"I could *never* do that. He would *know*. It would be *so* embarrassing!"

Besides, everyone knew I was a straight-A student and a "good girl," and it would be ridiculous to pretend I didn't know what we had been assigned for homework.

My mother and I went back and forth for a while until I found myself with my finger on his number in the phone book, sitting by our telephone. I have no idea how she managed to convince me. I ordered my mom out of the room so that I could have some privacy and rehearsed what I was going to say. I picked up the phone and then hung it up. I dialed his number and then quickly hung up again before the phone rang. I took a moment to giggle uncontrollably. Finally I plunged in and did it.

The phone rang. "Hello?" It was his mother.

"May I speak to Gary, please?"

"Who's calling?"

"It's Jenny from Spanish class."

There was an agonizing pause while Gary was fetched. I wanted to hang up, but it was too late!

"Hello?" His voice sounded weird on the phone.

"Hi, it's Jenny from Spanish class."

"Hi."

Silence.

"Um, I forgot what the homework was. Can you tell me?"

Now, as I said this, I remembered that not only was I known as a good student but my only two friends, Susan and Erica, were also in my Spanish class. He must have been wondering why I didn't call them, if I'd indeed forgotten about the homework. Soon he would figure out that I'd called him because I *liked* him.

"Uh, let me go check."

Gary put the phone down while I writhed in embarrassed agony on the other end. He came back to the phone and told me the page numbers and assignments.

"Oh, thanks," I said into the awkward silence.

Then, "Okay," I said rapidly. "See you tomorrow!" I hung up the phone, moaning. I was going to kill my mother. How could she have done this to me? How did I ever let her talk me into it?

Gary continued to ignore me at school, as did the rest of his friends, so

I didn't, at least to my knowledge, become the class joke. But I also never went out with him.

For the rest of my high school life in Virginia, I nearly always left school early for dance and got to know very few of my classmates. There were hardly any boys at Washington Ballet for me to spend time with either. During my last two years of high school in New York City, I attended the Professional Children's School and was rarely in class; the same was true of the rest of the students there. My friends from the School of American Ballet also attended PCS, so we stuck together.

There was a large male class at SAB, but I didn't really get to know any of them very well. Their classes were separate from ours except for the pas de deux class, and I wasn't outgoing enough to make friends with them. I had my three main girlfriends, and we did everything together; I suppose we were the nerdy ones and were not really invited to parties. There was certainly a popular crowd, and anywhere there are teenagers, there are always wild and crazy parties, but we never saw them. We would make homemade pizza together or, if we were feeling really crazy, go and get ice-cream cones in the middle of February.

I loved pas de deux class despite my awkwardness around the boys. There were always the sweet quiet ones who would come and ask me to be their partners. Once I began taking the class regularly, I gained confidence in my abilities as a partner and in my ability to ask someone to dance with me. It was still very challenging, but a lot of the challenge was just being a teenage girl in a room full of teenage boys and wanting to impress them and not embarrass myself. I developed regular partnerships with the boys who didn't scare me too much.

After I got into the company I went on a couple of dates, usually blind dates set up by friends, but I was never interested enough to try to sustain a relationship beyond three dates. Ballet just took too much of my mental, emotional, and physical energy. On my free days I was attending Fordham University and doing homework or getting massages or doing Pilates. I had plenty of friends and a fat, loving cat. What more could a girl need?

I used to force myself to go on dates because my friends and family told me it was good for me. If the first date with a guy wasn't a winner, I would still go on at least one more to give him a good try. But one day I realized that if I had to force myself to go out with someone, I obviously must not be interested in him. Why was I wasting my time? I held on to my hopes for romantic love and nurtured dreams of a hero who would appear from on high to sweep me off my feet. In the meantime, I just had a lot of guy friends, nothing more.

One guy had been on my radar since I was fifteen: James Fayette. At SAB he was in the cooler, more rebellious crowd. He wore clumpy Timberland boots and a puffy jeans jacket with the collar turned up. He would stub out his cigarette and slouch into the ballet school with a wink at the girls, telling some guy-joke to make his friends laugh. One of the most muscular boys at SAB, he was the strongest partner and the one every girl wished she could dance with because he could do all the hard lifts. James and I knew each other, but we rarely interacted because we didn't partner together and kept to our separate crowds.

I got into the company one year before James did, and even after he joined the corps, we maintained a strictly professional relationship. Some of my best friends were close to him, but I always found him a little intimidating, so I kept my distance. Professionally, however, we were soon thrown together and found ourselves frequent partners. James had a steady girlfriend to whom he was faithful, even though he could be flirtatious and flippant; knowing that his playful comments and winking were harmless, I found that I enjoyed dancing with him and trusted him completely as a partner. It was fun for me to flirt when I knew nothing serious would come of it. And when it came to doing his job, James was very serious; I knew that if he was the one responsible for holding me up, I would be in good hands.

Now James claims that sometime after he and his longtime girlfriend broke up he asked me out several times. I have no recollection of this. James swears that he asked me out with groups, in a casual way, so that we could get to know each other better. He asserts that he had been interested in me since our SAB days. I was completely oblivious to this and, inexperienced as I was, don't remember James asking me out even as part of a group. James says that I would always say yes and then fink out at the last minute, leaving him disappointed.

That, unfortunately, does sound like me. I tended to enjoy my alone time and often found too much socializing to be draining. Most of the time I was happy to be home reading a good sci-fi or fantasy or romance novel, curled up in my pajamas. The thought of having to go out and see people was exhausting. The only person whose company never tired me out was my sister, Becky, because she always let me just be myself, with no judgments or expectations. Our relationship was balanced and reciprocal. But I do remember agreeing to social engagements in the moment, because I had a hard time saying no, and then coming up with an excuse later so that I didn't have to go out.

When I began to struggle with weight in the company, I became even more of a loner. I would take long walks at night through the city, often ending up at a bookstore where I could sit on the floor and read for hours. I would stay at home and rent old musicals. One day, however, I discovered Denim and Diamonds, the line-dancing country music bar on Lexington Avenue and Forty-eighth Street.

Ever since I was a little girl growing up in the South, country music had been the background sound track of my life. My father would blast Willie Nelson on our pickup truck radio, singing off-key, to my sister's groans. My mom recorded me mournfully singing "Rhinestone Cowboy" as a child with the thick twang of coastal Carolina in my voice. But I didn't fully love and embrace country music, ironically, until I moved to New York.

My clock radio just happened to be tuned to the one Manhattan country music station when I set it up in my bedroom after my family and I moved into our new apartment. Since I didn't know any of the other stations, I left it there until I could find the popular rock station. After listening to one song by the Judds, I was hooked and gave up my search for popular, cooler New York rock. I loved Garth Brooks and

Clint Black and Dolly Parton and Willie Nelson, and the Judds and Mary Chapin Carpenter were particular favorites. Their songs were sweet and funny and filled with bluegrass-tinged harmony to which I would try to sing along, mostly unsuccessfully. I thought if I could live my life all over again, I would do it as a country singer.

When I found Denim and Diamonds, I discovered a little oasis in the city. It was across town from me and had a large white horse rearing up on the awning outside. On the ground floor there was a regular bar, but downstairs was a large space with tables and cowhide chairs surrounding a sunken dance floor glittering beneath a rhinestone disco saddle. Country music blared from the speakers, and I was in heaven.

I began to visit regularly by myself, usually once or twice a week. There were two free dance lessons early in the evening, followed by line dancing and couples dances, and there was no drink minimum, perfect for me, since I was alone and didn't want to drink. I would go for the dance lessons and then stick around, ordering water from the disgruntled bartender, having a great time for just the cost it took me to get over to the East Side on the bus. Because of my dance training, the lessons were easy, and I could pick up the regular line dances I didn't know throughout the rest of the evening just by watching a couple of repetitions. I would spend hours on the dance floor having fun all by myself— it wasn't a "pickup" place because most people came with their dance partners. This meant that I was left happily alone unless some of my friends had come along.

One night around 1995, James joined a group of friends and me at Denim and Diamonds. I was surprised to see him there because I didn't think him the type of guy who could tolerate country music. But word had gotten out at NYCB about Denim and Diamonds, and when a group of dancers came, we usually had a blast and practically took over the dance floor. He ended up line dancing beside me, and though he managed to turn the fairly tame line dances into wilder versions of themselves, I started to think he might be all right. During breaks between dances, he always seemed to be near me, and we talked about inconsequential things, shouting over the music of Brooks & Dunn. I didn't find James as threatening as I had before and was noticing changes within myself; I was nurturing new and different aspects of my personality as I searched for an identity outside ballet. I was having fun with a guy and realized I might be . . . interested.

But then on the cab ride home with James and some others, he suddenly said that he was meeting a friend and had to get out of the cab early. It was late at night, and I enviously assumed he was meeting a woman. Disappointed, I realized that he was operating in a different world from mine with different values, and I put him out of my mind.

Another moment during that same year when my heart thawed a little toward James was during a rehearsal for a non–City Ballet gig. Christopher Wheeldon, a fellow dancer and budding choreographer, had asked us to perform in a ballet he had made for two couples that was to be danced uptown at Riverside Church. Chris made James and me partners. During a pause in the rehearsal one day, we were all grouped around the video screen so that we could learn our next steps. Out of the blue, James suddenly did a very silly imitation of Steve Martin in *The Jerk*. Surprised, I laughed out loud and wondered again if there was more to this guy than a bad-boy attitude.

While I was having my difficulties over the next few years, James was going through his own period of struggle and growth. He began to run his own gigs, taking out small groups of dancers to perform outside City Ballet's regular work. He joined the dancers' committee for the union, helping to negotiate the dancers' contracts and becoming an advocate for the dancers and a liaison with management. And at the age of twenty-five, James began to confront his ideas about God and truth, and to explore what kind of life he really wanted to live. Though he had been raised Catholic, religion had dropped away from his daily life, and he came to realize he needed more of God. So he was changing as much as I was, though we were on separate journeys at the time.

I told no one, not even my closest friends, that I'd been fired from the company in February 1997. My family members were the only ones who

knew, although it was clear to everyone else that I was having some issues. I kept dancing, always hoping that my problem would soon somehow be fixed. Despite my obvious troubles, James invited me to perform
in some performances he had organized in Vermont and Massachusetts
that would take place after the company's summer season in Saratoga
Springs. I agreed, hungry for any performance opportunity, particularly
away from the judgmental eyes of the company. Knowing it could be
my last chance to get out onstage, I traveled to Vermont with the group
directly from Saratoga, where I believed I'd just danced my last season
with the New York City Ballet.

The gig was a blessing for me in many ways. The other six people on
the trip were some of my best friends and favorite people in the
company. I felt only acceptance and warmth when I was around them.
We were dancing fun ballets, one of which was a ballet for three dancers that Christopher Wheeldon had created during a previous choreography workshop. In Saratoga, Chris choreographed a new solo just
for me that somehow managed to tap into everything I was feeling
and fighting at the time. The solo started out with my arms
crossed behind my back as I struggled to free myself from invisible
bonds; the music built until I was able to break free and dance fully in
the space of the stage. The other ballet I was dancing was the pas
de deux from Balanchine's *Stars and Stripes*. My partner for that ballet
was James.

We all spent a week together performing, and the best part of the
week was the last leg of our tour in Nantucket. None of us had been to
the island before, and during our free time we explored as much as we
could. We were hosted by families on the island and stayed in their
houses as their guests. James and I started to spend a lot of our free time
together, just as friends, but I realized that I was developing a crush on
him. On one of our free afternoons, some of us rented scooters to go to
the beach, and I ended up riding on the back of James's. For me, it was a
very daring thing to do; two of my girlfriends opted to go back to the
house and rest, and normally I would have been right there with them.

But I wanted to have some fun with this boy that I was starting to like, so I went.

It was a great afternoon. I remember particularly the moment when our group arrived at the beach and everyone ran into the water. I purposefully stayed behind, wanting to be last so that no one would look at me in my bathing suit. Somehow, though, no matter how slowly I moved, James was still there talking to me, waiting to go into the water with me.

Finally, there was nothing else for me to do but head toward the ocean. James still lingered.

"Aren't you going in?" I asked, hoping he would run ahead of me.

"I wanted to watch you go first," he replied flirtatiously.

"I'm embarrassed," I finally said, horrified that I was admitting this to him.

"Why?" he asked casually. "Jen, you are gorgeous." But he spared me the moment and ran ahead of me, daring me to catch up with him. He had no idea how much his words meant to me.

That night, I couldn't sleep and didn't feel like staying inside the house with the other girls. James was in the backyard talking to the guys, but I didn't feel like being part of that group either, so I walked around to the front of the house and sat on the hood of one of the cars, lying back to look at the stars. It felt nice to be alone with my thoughts and contemplate the beauty of the night sky; stargazing had been a favorite pastime for my father and me since I was a child. But I was also yearning to talk to James, and as the night wore on I finally realized I might have to take the initiative and go talk to him myself. Just as I was about to go around to the back of the house, James came to find me.

He hopped up beside me on the hood of the car, and we just talked like two good friends. I felt so happy sitting there, talking to him about nothing in particular. I wanted the night to last forever, but since we had a performance the following day, James finally suggested we go in and get some sleep. We were both reluctant.

The performance was a blur but for the feelings of both freedom and sadness as I danced; this was probably my farewell to the stage. For all of my friends, this was just a fun gig, a chance to dance something new and make a little money. But for me, it was my good-bye to ballet and the beginning of a big unknown.

After the performance, we went directly to the ferry that would take us to the mainland. There our group split up into two cars for the drive through the night back to New York City. I got myself into the car James was driving along with my two good friends Elizabeth Walker and Dena Abergel. We all settled in for the long car ride, knowing we wouldn't get back to the city until around 4:00 a.m.

I taught the girls my family's car song, a complicated tune with two separate parts that my mother had learned at summer camp when she was a child and then passed on to my sister and me. It takes a lot of practice and repetition to get the two parts coordinated, and we sang it over and over, trying to perfect it, until James begged us to take a break. Then James was in charge of the conversation, and true to his nature he decided to ask a difficult, thought-provoking question to get a discussion going.

"So, Jen," he asked me. "What are you looking for in a husband?"

I was flabbergasted. Dena and Elizabeth looked at me with raised eyebrows, laughing a little. I wondered: Did he have an ulterior motive, or was he just being flippant?

I decided to give James a serious answer, so I had to think. What was the most important characteristic I was looking for in a husband? Was it the hero, the prince I'd prayed for as a child, writing down lists of my future husband's qualities and then hiding them in my drawer? I realized that what actually mattered the most to me was that my husband be a Christian man. I wanted to be able to share my faith with him. Obviously I wanted friendship and attraction and humor and faithfulness, but the main thing I wanted—needed—was to be able to walk beside my husband in faith and to raise our children together to walk with Christ.

But I paused—I was afraid to reveal my answer. What if I told this to James, and it turned him off to me? We hadn't talked about religion yet, so I didn't know where he stood. I had no idea about his faith at all. I liked him so much, but I really couldn't tell yet if he was looking at me romantically. I decided to take a chance and lay all of my cards on the table. That way, if he was really interested in me, he would know what he was getting into before we even started. And if my faith scared him off, then neither one of us would have wasted our time on something doomed to fail.

"Well, I suppose the most important thing to me would be that my husband is a Christian," I said, not sounding very confident.

"Really," he said, sounding surprised. I think everyone in the car was a little surprised, actually. They probably imagined I would answer more lightly than that. But I had a real crush on James, and it was worth it to me to be totally honest, just to see how he would react and whether he was thinking of asking me out.

My revelation kept the little car occupied for a while. As can only happen among close friends stuck together in a small space in the middle of the night, we ended up talking intensely about every subject imaginable. We discussed religion endlessly. Elizabeth was a Protestant from the South like me, Dena was a devout Jew, and James was a lapsed Catholic. We talked about marriage and relationships: Dena was married, Elizabeth had a boyfriend, I'd never had a boyfriend, and James was at loose ends. All of this led to my second bombshell that night.

"Actually, I don't want to have sex until I get married," I said timidly. I knew that in the world I inhabited, this assertion could make me seem really uncool.

Silence. For several long moments, no one spoke. Then soon no one could *stop* speaking. James had a lot of questions for me, some of which were uncomfortable because I'd never discussed my opinions on these subjects before outside my family. I have never been vocal on controversial subjects, always content to let others do the talking when it comes to difficult topics. But here I was with two of my oldest friends and the man I had a crush on, so I figured now was the time to speak up, if ever. When James asked me difficult questions, such as "But what if you really love each other?" I answered them as honestly and humbly as I could, offering my opinions and hiding nothing. I figured that in the end, it would be best that way. James respected my opinion and seemed very interested and thoughtful.

We finally arrived in Manhattan around 4:30 a.m. The darkness of another humid summer night was punctuated by stoplights and walk signals as we neared my apartment building on Eighty-fifth Street. We were all exhausted and had grown silent.

James pulled up in front of my building, and I gave quick hugs to Dena and Elizabeth.

"Thank you so much for bringing me on the gig, James. I had a great time," I said.

"I'll walk you to the door," James replied.

"Oh, you don't have to," I said, even though his offer pleased me. "I'm fine. You can see me through the window."

He ignored me and got out of the car to get my luggage, carrying it up the stairs in the little entrance that led to the locked door of my lobby. He set my suitcase down, looking tired from the long drive.

"Well, thank you again," I said as we looked at each other.

He leaned forward, and we did that very New York kiss on the cheek that friends give each other to say hello and good-bye. I hadn't done it growing up in the South, but by now I was a pro at it. Then I turned, unlocked the door, waved, and went inside. As I watched James go back to the car, I realized that I felt sad already, and wistful. It occurred to me that I might never see James again. But I thought there was a connection, and I went inside and fell asleep, hoping that James had felt it too, and that he would call me soon so that we could see each other again.

He didn't call. As I floundered in the darkness of that summer, I figured I'd misunderstood things, and I let my crush on him fall away along with my love for dance.

Three months later, in October 1997, I was in a much different place emotionally. I had jobs, was finishing up college, and was starting to take ballet class again. I was still fragile but was beginning to figure things out. I was relishing my rediscovery of God and felt certain that even if I didn't know in what direction He was taking me, *He* knew, and He had a plan.

Then one day I got a phone call. I screened it, as I always did at that time. I never knew when it would be an uncomfortable call, so why not choose whether or not to deal with it?

I stood in my bedroom with my giant cat, Storm, purring on the bed and watched my answering machine, waiting to see who it was. My breath caught when I heard James's voice. Butterflies rushed through my stomach, and I had to calm myself to actually listen to what he was saying.

"Hey, Jen, it's James. I was just calling about that *Nutcracker* gig we were going to do up in New Paltz for Peter Naumann. It is in early December, so I wanted to see when we should get together to rehearse. Give me a call when you get the chance. Okay, bye."

I was shocked for two reasons. First of all, no one from the company had called me since I'd left. I don't believe it was on purpose—the schedule of City Ballet can be so overwhelming that they probably hadn't had the time or energy. Also, I'd been very successful at closing myself off from my friends.

Secondly, he was calling me to *dance* with him?

I was horrified. What *Nutcracker* gig? When had I agreed to do it? We must have discussed it a long time ago, and maybe I'd just said yes, hoping or assuming he would forget. I certainly had forgotten! There was no way I could do the performances with him, I thought. I was too heavy and too out of shape, even though I was taking some ballet. I was taking for fun, not to be ready to perform. I would be terrible, and it would be embarrassing.

I worried all day, wondering what I would say to James. A thousand lies and excuses came to mind, ways that I could avoid the truth and save face. But the more I thought about it and prayed about it, the more

I realized that I needed to take a step as the real me and not hide behind a persona of false perfection, as the old Jenny would have done. James was a good guy and a friend, and despite my summer crush on him, I didn't have to hide from him. I would tell him the truth.

I returned his call that night after a long, nervous day. I was actually hoping that he would not answer so I could just leave it all on his machine, but of course he did.

"Hello?"

"Hi, James, it's Jenny."

"Oh, hey!" He sounded excited. We chatted a bit. Then I took a deep breath and plunged in.

"Look," I said, "I don't think I should do that gig with you. I wish I could, but I'm really out of shape."

"There's tons of time for you to get in shape," said James. "And we can rehearse a lot too, which will help."

I realized I would have to be more explicit. I'd never come right out and called myself overweight to a fellow dancer; I'd always avoided the word, using phrases like "out of shape" or "bigger than usual." But I was going to have to do it this time. I felt myself blushing and held my clenched fist over my stomach.

"The truth is, James, I'm . . . I'm really heavy right now. I'm overweight. I don't think you are going to want to dance with me. I think you should just get someone else. But I so appreciate you asking me to do it, and I really thank you."

There was a pause that I hoped would lead to the end of the conversation so that I could get off the phone as quickly as possible. Then James spoke.

"Jen, I don't care about your weight. I just want to dance with you. Let's do the gig. I really think it would be fun."

I was stunned by his response. And touched. No one from the City Ballet world had ever told me that my weight didn't matter to them. No one else had been able to get past the fact that I was heavy. Feeling both confused and pleased, I agreed to give it a try and meet with James to rehearse.

I was extremely nervous for our first rehearsal. Now that there was a prospect of performing again, I realized how much I wanted to be back onstage. What if James saw me and changed his mind? I was at least twenty pounds overweight for a ballet dancer. I wasn't sure how much I actually weighed because I'd thrown my scale away in an effort to become less obsessed with it. But I knew I was heavy. I told myself that I would be all right if James wanted to do the gig with someone else. I was stronger now and would not fall apart if James decided to go with another dancer. I faced my fears and gave it a chance.

The rehearsal went surprisingly well. James seemed pleased to see me and had almost no trouble in the partnering sections. He never once gave my body a second look. I honestly don't remember many details from that rehearsal or any of the subsequent ones because I think I was in a very strange emotional state for them; I was anxious and excited and battling all of my habitual insecurities with the new weapons of God-centered identity that I was acquiring. The only choreographic concession we had to make to my weight was during the sustained *grand jeté* lifts, where the Cavalier holds the Sugar Plum aloft for three slow counts of music. James, though one of the strongest male partners in City Ballet, couldn't keep me in the air for that long, and we changed it to a quick throw of a lift that lasted only one count. We would then run into an arabesque and continue into the regular dip that followed.

I was slightly mortified by this, but not surprised. In fact, I was relieved that we changed the step a little so that I didn't have to feel guilty about James struggling to hold me in the air.

Later, James told me that he believes God gave him a different way of seeing me. To James, I hardly appeared overweight, and he just saw a pretty girl with whom he liked to dance. He thought that the reason we couldn't do the proper *grand jeté* lifts was that he was a little out of shape and not as strong as usual. He always prided himself on his strength and his ability to lift any girl over his head; he figured that since it was the beginning of the season, he was just a little weaker than normal.

James and I fit rehearsals in wherever we could between our two conflicting schedules. I was really enjoying the process and was having fun spending time with James again. But reality hit when James told me that I needed to get a tutu. Somehow I'd completely forgotten the important detail that I would need a costume. That meant I would have to approach City Ballet's costume department to ask for a rental.

I worked up my courage and called Dorothy Cummings, the ladies' wardrobe mistress. She and her assistant, Norma Atrides, were warm, motherly women who took on the task of making sure the women of City Ballet were properly attired for the stage. They also handled costume rentals when dancers went out on independent gigs. Dotty was happy to hear from me, and we set up an appointment to meet at the theater and find me a tutu.

I hadn't been to the theater since the end of the spring season, and it was strange to go in knowing that I no longer worked there. The building still seemed oppressive to me, but I reminded myself that I was there for my own purposes and that I was no longer subject to the company's judgment.

Dotty greeted me with a warm hug and twinkles in her big brown eyes.

"Let's get you fixed up, all righty?" she said in her cheerful British accent.

I followed Dotty to "the pit" where they kept the costumes for rent. We tried on tutu after tutu. None of them fit me. Some would not go past my hips, but those that did were too tight around my torso. I was soon close to tears.

Dotty stayed calm and matter-of-fact. "There is one last costume we can try," she said. "It isn't a tutu but has a romantic tulle skirt that comes down to your knees. I think it could be very pretty. And everything on the bodice is made of stretchy material."

I agreed to try it on, not knowing what I would do if this one didn't fit me either. I imagined the phone call I would make to James, telling him that he would have to get a different partner after all. Blessedly, this costume fit me, and the mirror showed that it was even somewhat flattering. Dotty was encouraging and said she thought it was lovely.

Grateful for her gentleness, I hugged Dotty. I couldn't tell her how much her kindness meant to me; no words would come out. I accepted the costume and went home, hoping that I would still look enough like a Sugar Plum Fairy to satisfy both James and the owners of the school we were performing with.

After a few more days of rehearsing, all too soon it was time to travel up to New Paltz, New York, for our gig. James and I would be taking the train together and were getting there the night before our first performance, which was an early-morning school performance. During the train ride James and I chatted and teased each other intermittently while I did some homework; I was taking a drawing elective at Fordham and had brought my sketchpad so that I could meet the course requirement of drawings for the semester, which ended the next week. I did self-portraits using my reflection in the train window and even convinced James to let me do his profile. James made up a silly train song and serenaded me from time to time.

We arrived in New Paltz and Peter Naumann, co-owner of the New Paltz School of Ballet along with his wife, Lisa, picked us up. Peter and Lisa were former City Ballet dancers who had moved upstate with their children when they retired from dance; they had opened the ballet school in a studio attached to their home. James and I would be staying with them and their two young boys for the weekend.

Peter and Lisa were both very laid back and friendly and welcomed James and me into their home as if we were family. James had probably told them that I'd left the company, but they didn't even appear to notice my weight, and happily gave us a tour of the town before showing us around their house. It was the typical home of a family with young children: decorated for adults but with random toys poking out of every crevice. There was a black Labrador named Chance that rang some bells with his nose when he wanted to go outside. There was a new gray kitten plopping and sliding on the slippery hardwood floors. And in young Trevor's and Carl's rooms, where James and I would be sleeping, the boys' personal pets resided. I was given the choice of whether I would sleep with the snake or the iguana. I chose the iguana.

After James and I got settled, we went back out into the living room to chat with Peter and Lisa. They told us hilarious stories of their days in City Ballet, which had overlapped with our own early years in the company, and we stayed up much later than we should have, given that we had an early-morning performance the next day. Then somehow the conversations shifted to the costume I'd brought to wear in the performance.

"Could we see the tutu you brought for the shows?" Peter gently asked. "James said it was a little different."

"Sure," I replied, feeling dread drop into my stomach. I was already here, and there was nothing anyone could do at this point, but how awful would it be if I had to do the next six shows knowing that Peter and Lisa were disappointed.

I went into the Iguana Room, as I'd begun to think of it, found my costume, and brought it back out into the living room. Peter and Lisa looked at it seriously, and I could tell they were not thrilled with it. What is a Sugar Plum Fairy without a real tutu?

"Jenny," Lisa said with a little smile, "when we first came out here and opened our studio, I danced the Sugar Plum Fairy for our production. I was pregnant with Trevor at the time. My mother, who makes beautiful costumes, made me a tutu and it is really pretty. Would you feel like trying it on, just to see if it would work?"

Of course I said yes. There was nothing else to say. But inside I was mortified. They were asking me to wear a tutu that a pregnant woman had danced in because I couldn't fit into one that a real dancer would wear. I was so embarrassed. What must they think of me? And why did this have to happen in front of James? At the same time, Peter and Lisa were so considerate in the way they were approaching me. They were looking at me not with disgust but with understanding.

They were treating me as a human being who had value to them outside of being their Sugar Plum Fairy. And I wanted them to be happy.

Lisa retrieved the tutu, and it really was beautiful. I took it back to my room to try it on, hoping fervently that it would fit. How terrible it would be if I were even too big for that one! I put it on, and like a miracle, it fit perfectly.

As I looked into the mirror, I forgot that I was wearing a maternity tutu. The tutu was dark pink, professionally made, flattering, and pretty, with beautiful small details. I felt comfortable in it because it fit me so well, and I felt beautiful. I felt like a ballerina. I realized that this was something only God could have done. How else would a perfectly fitting tutu have been waiting for me here in New Paltz, ready to be worn tomorrow with no alterations? God was taking me on some kind of journey, not revealing the whole path, but showing His love for me in tiny steps along the way. I felt a little bit of healing slip into my soul in the Iguana Room that night.

I went back out into the living room, feeling shy about showing myself in the tutu and trying not to look too happy about it. It occurred to me that even if I thought I looked beautiful in it, they might not, and they might still want me to wear the other costume. But when I entered the room, Peter gave me a jovial smile, and Lisa laughed and clapped with happiness.

James, looking at me with a quiet smile on his face, allowed Peter and Lisa to exclaim their delight before he looked me seriously in the eyes and said, "Jen, you look beautiful."

I didn't sleep well that night. Part of the reason was nerves and excitement for the school performance in the morning. The other reason was the iguana. I couldn't figure out how to turn the light out in his aquarium, and he stared at me with at least one eye all night long. From time to time he would suddenly spasm his body in his cage, changing his position so that he could focus his head on me from a different angle. It was disconcerting, and when I did sleep, I had weird dreams. I wondered how any child could possibly sleep in that room.

The next morning, we awoke to a blizzard. It was not yet dawn, but the windows showed drifts of white deepening inexorably with the snow falling from the sky. Peter and Lisa were on the phone trying to figure out what this might mean for our school performances; they finally just turned on the local news to watch for school cancellations.

The house was in the state of chaos that is normal in a household of two busy parents with young children. The boys were running around in their pajamas with their hair sticking up in funny directions. Lisa was making them breakfast while Peter drank from a mug of coffee, holding the phone to his ear. Chance was picking the kitten up in his mouth and then slinging it down the hallway, an activity that apparently agreed with the kitten. It made an impression on me to see two people from the ballet world living such a normal, love-filled life.

James and I drank coffee and waited to see what the day would hold for us. James was looking a little grumpy, probably due to the fact that I'd opened his bedroom door to wake him up, letting the dog run in and give James a very enthusiastic greeting. I really wanted to play with the kitten, so I went to find it. Chance had just bowled him down the hallway again, so I walked over to the sprawled-out bundle of gray fur and picked him up.

His fur was stiff and matted, and when I brought him closer to my face, I realized he was covered in feces. I made a face and abruptly put him down, heading for the bathroom to wash my hands. Peter saw me.

"Aw, no, is he covered in poop again?" he asked. Then he yelled, "Chance! Outside!"

Apparently Chance liked to eat from the kitten's litter box. The resulting slobber, which now covered the kitten's fur, was pretty gross.

James looked at me darkly from the kitchen. "Yeah, Chance licked me this morning when you woke me up. Thanks." Ah, that explained his grumpiness.

Soon we learned that school had been canceled. Due to the storm, there would be no performances that day, and so we had a whole day to ourselves. One day stretched into two, as the storm didn't slow down. James and I spent the whole time together.

We spent part of these days in the ballet studio connected to the Naumanns' house, giving ourselves a ballet class and then rehearsing *Nutcracker* to keep up our stamina. But mostly we just messed around. We watched movies on television. We played with Carl and Trevor. Peter and Lisa took us up to a lodge on the top of Mohonk Mountain for dinner one night with the boys. I drew every living creature in the house for my art class. James laughed in disbelief at my regular clumsiness, learning as my family already knew that I was one of those walking oxymorons called Klutzy Ballerinas. We listened to more City Ballet stories from Peter and Lisa. We talked.

I remember one conversation in particular. I was doing some homework in my room when James came in. After a couple of minutes of casual conversation, James started asking some curiously personal questions.

"So, how old are you now?" he asked.

"Twenty-four."

"When do you see yourself getting married?"

What? Well, actually I'd always thought I would be married by the age of twenty-four, but I didn't want to tell him that.

"I suppose before I turn thirty," I said.

"Do you think you want to have kids?" James asked. The iguana cocked its head at me, as if he, too, were wondering why James was grilling me about marriage and children.

"Yes, I would like to have children," I told James cautiously.

"Would you ever date a dancer?" he then asked. Many dancers have rules about whether or not they would go out with another dancer.

"Well," I said, wanting to be truthful, "I used to swear I would never date a dancer." My life had already been consumed by ballet—I didn't want to also have my date talking ballet nonstop. "But now," I said, "I'm open to it."

After every question, James would nod and then go to the next one, continuing in this vein for a while. I knew there was something on the line, but couldn't tell exactly what it was. During all of the rehearsals for these *Nutcracker* performances, I'd realized my crush on him was back full force, but it was still difficult for me to tell how he felt about me. I felt a tension in the air though, and even wondered if he might try to kiss me right there in the Iguana Room.

"I've been thinking a lot about things," James told me. "I'm twenty-seven now, and I'm thinking I want to get married before I turn thirty. My other goal is to keep my hair until I'm forty," he added, laughing.

The conversation moved on to other subjects, and finally James left, saying he knew I had homework to do. I gazed at the iguana and the iguana gazed back. No wisdom from him anyway. I had no idea whether the conversation meant nothing or a great deal. Confused but a little hopeful, I decided not to put too much thought into it and just enjoy the weekend.

Because of the blizzard, even our regular performances were at risk of being canceled. But we finally got the go-ahead and drove to the theater for our first matinee. I was almost sorry to be returning to the "work" aspect of the weekend. I'd been having such a good time with James and the Naumanns that it felt strange to have to get down to the business of performing. And this would be my first time back onstage since the gig right after I was let go.

James and I didn't go onstage until the second act of *The Nutcracker*, so we put on our stage makeup and warmed our bodies up during the first act. We were in a very quaint old theater that was supposedly the "oldest hemp house in New York." A hemp house is a theater where scenery is hung on hemp ropes that the stage crew can pull on and tie off, much like sailors, to raise and lower scenery for different acts. Since the theater was so small, James and I shared a dressing room underneath the stage, going into the bathroom when we needed to change.

At intermission, I put on my tutu and went up onto the stage to warm up some more in my pointe shoes. I felt self-conscious and nervous and worried not only about how I looked but also about how the performance itself would go.

But then two things happened. First, I remembered that God had a plan for me and that I was doing these performances for a reason. There was no need for me to be afraid; I should accept this opportunity as a gift. I might never dance onstage again, and this weekend was like a little last blessing and a way to find some positive closure to my dancing career.

The second thing that happened was that the children performing from the ballet school arrived onstage to prepare for their entrances.

"Oh, it's the Sugar Plum Fairy!" they gasped with delight.

They surrounded me, exclaiming over my tutu and asking me a million questions. It came to me then that this performance was not about me at all; it was about the children and the audience and bringing the magical beauty of ballet to life for the watchers' imaginations. I put aside my self-centered worries and told myself to just enjoy giving a gift of dance to these children and their parents.

The second act began, and it was time for me to go onstage for my first entrance, a solo. Somewhere in the middle of that solo, I felt those old, negative thoughts falling away from me. *You are disgusting.* I dropped the thought on the stage. *Everyone watching you is horrified by your appearance.* I let that thought fall off too. I felt beautiful. I was dancing for God, and I knew He was pleased. God had given me a gift, and I was using it. I felt joyful and free. I was really dancing, really performing, and really loving it in a purer way than I had in a long time.

After the weekend was over, I felt such a sense of accomplishment. I was proud of how I'd danced and proud of how I'd overcome, with God's miraculous grace, certain emotional mountains I hadn't even realized I would have to scale. I was sad the performances were over. I'd enjoyed the company of James and Peter and Lisa, and I'd enjoyed feeling like a dancer. Then, to my surprise, after the last performance had ended, James asked me to dance with him at the World Financial Center downtown on New Year's Eve. This weekend was not, after all, the last time in my life I would get to perform.

The train ride back to the city felt short as James and I talked and enjoyed each other's company. By this point, we were very comfortable with each other, and he felt like a close friend. I'd never felt this kind of friendship with a man before. We got on the subway from Penn Station, and suddenly, as we approached the Seventy-second Street stop, I realized that James's stop was before mine. He would be getting off the subway. Our weekend was really over.

The subway began to slow, and I hardly thought before blurting out: "I'll miss you!" Panicked by my honesty, and afraid of how he would react, I tried to turn it into a joke by batting my eyelashes and looking wistfully at him.

James gathered up his stuff and turned toward the sliding doors.

"Don't worry. I'll be calling you. We have to rehearse for New Year's Eve! How about next Thursday?" And with a wink, he was gone. The doors closed, and I sighed.

Soon enough, it was Wednesday. James called to make plans for the next day.

"So," James said, "I'll pick you up around seven."

My breath caught. Seven o'clock? That seemed late for a rehearsal. And why was he picking me up?

"Okay, sounds good," I said calmly, trying to be cool.

"All right, see you tomorrow," James said, and we hung up. That was it.

I stood in my bedroom, staring wide-eyed at my phone. This wasn't a rehearsal. This was an actual *date*! I immediately called my sister, my go-to person for anything important or interesting that happened to me.

I started talking the moment she answered the phone.

"I think I'm going on a date with James!" I exclaimed, trying not to squeal. Becky gasped. She knew me better than anyone, and she knew that I'd never shown any real interest in a man before. James was the first guy I'd actually wanted to ask me out on a date since Gary from Spanish class back in high school.

"I think you are going to marry him!" she exulted.

"I think I am!" I replied, not caring that I was getting ahead of myself.

And Thursday, December 18, was indeed a real date. I had no idea what to wear. James picked me up at my building right on time. I was so happy to see him that I felt jittery when he smiled at me. He didn't tell me where we were going, but struck off immediately in the direction of Central Park. Since it was winter, it was already dark, and I wondered why we were going to the park after sundown. Wasn't that a no-no?

Was James taking me to Central Park to murder me? No, I told my imagination. This was a date, and it was going to be fine. We walked through the park, which was actually well lit and surprisingly crowded, until we came to Wollman Rink, the ice-skating rink.

"I thought we would go ice-skating," said James, turning to me. Surprised and delighted, I agreed, even though, from the evidence of my only previous attempt, I couldn't ice-skate at all.

After we survived on the ice with much laughter and flailing on my part, James led me out of the park on the East Side so that we could walk along Fifth Avenue and see the Rockefeller Center Christmas tree and the famous Christmas windows in Saks and Bergdorf's. My clumsiness chose this moment to rear its head, probably because I was so excited to be on a date with James, and I kept tripping and bumping into things. Finally, after my tenth near face-plant, James grabbed my hand with a laugh.

"I think I need to hold on to you," he said. And we held hands the rest of the night. It felt perfectly natural.

We fought our way through the tourist crowd for a while, stopping when something interesting caught our eye. After a while James asked if I was hungry. Since by now it was around nine, I was starving.

"I want to take you to one of my favorite restaurants, but it's a subway ride away. Is that okay?"

I would have been okay with anything he suggested, I was so glad to be with him, and I happily agreed. We got on the subway and rode down to the Fulton Street stop. When we came up out of the station, we walked toward South Street Seaport, which I assumed was our destination. But at the seaport, James turned left and we walked across the darkened cobblestone streets of an older New York to a tiny restaurant under the Brooklyn Bridge called Bridge Café. It was late but we were shown a table immediately and had a great dinner of fresh seafood.

After dinner we took the subway home. We both got out at Seventy-second Street, but I was still thirteen blocks from my apartment. James was going to walk me home, since by now it was almost one in the morning.

We were laughing hilariously at something—I think my gum had shot out of my mouth, my awkwardness at work again—when James stopped suddenly and looked at me.

"Do you want to go somewhere and get a drink?" he asked.

Of course I did. I never wanted this night to end. We went to a favorite haunt of City Ballet dancers at the time, a little pub called the Emerald Inn that was a few blocks from the subway stop. It was smoky and full of people, but not so crowded that we couldn't get two stools at the bar, and no one from City Ballet was there that night. The people in the bar were in a festive holiday mood, and everyone was talking to everyone else as if we were all long-lost friends.

There was a portly man in the corner of the bar holding a glass of whiskey with his eyes half closed. From time to time he would take a sip of his drink, place it carefully on the bar, and then sing parts of beautiful arias and Christmas hymns with a surprising professionalism for an Irish bar crowd. We soon learned that he was a singer for the Metropolitan Opera.

James glanced at me teasingly and said, "You should sing something, Jen." I'd sung the role of Rosalia in City Ballet's production of *West Side Story*.

I refused, saying the only Christmas song I knew was "The Little Drummer Boy."

Someone called out, "Sing it!"

And there was enough craziness in me that night that I did. I started to sing "Drummer Boy" loud enough for the entire bar to hear me, and soon the patrons around me joined in for the *pa rum-pum-pum-pums*, beating their glasses on the bar in time to the music. When I continued on to the second and third verses, they looked at me with consternation for a moment but then went back to their jobs of *rum-pum-pum-pumming* with seriousness and dedication. We all finished loudly and triumphantly. Someone began another Chrismas carol, and we were off again.

Finally, it was past 3:00 a.m., and James and I reluctantly headed for my apartment. It had been a wonderful night. James walked me all the way home, holding my hand. I thrilled in the moment, never having felt this way about anyone. I wondered if he would kiss me at the door.

He didn't. He told me he had had a great time and that he would call me soon to rehearse for New Year's Eve. And then he smiled and left.

I thought I might go crazy. And I did drive myself crazy for a little while, going over the night and wondering what it all meant and WHY he hadn't kissed me, but finally I just had to let it go and see what would happen. I did my best not to be a "freaky chick," as I'd heard James refer to girls who were too clingy and desperate. I tried to be patient and play it cool; I didn't want to make the next move. Eventually James called me a couple of times just to talk, and I knew that I would be seeing him again very soon for our next performance.

We didn't have any more dates before our New Year's Eve gig. James had a busy schedule with City Ballet's *Nutcracker*, and when we did get together, it was to rehearse the pas de deux from Balanchine's *Stars and Stripes* for our performance. *Stars* is one of those ballets that is challenging but fun, with music by John Philip Sousa, and James and I had already performed it together in Vermont. It was relatively easy for us to put it together. During our rehearsals we were flirty but professional, needing to use our available time together to make sure we would dance well.

New Year's Eve arrived, and we went to the Winter Garden at the World Financial Center, which was located very near the Twin Towers.

We were performing as part of First Night and were just one of many acts. After our performance, we headed to a restaurant across the city where we were to meet James's sister Deena and her friends. We quickly changed and jumped into a cab so that we could make it there before midnight. I was eagerly anticipating twelve o'clock—surely I would get a kiss from James then, even if it was obligatory!

We were still a few blocks away from the restaurant when I glanced at the taxicab's dash clock. It read 12:04! We had missed it.

"Well," I said to James, a little deflated, "Happy New Year."

"Happy New Year," he replied. Then he said, "Can I give you a kiss?"

Finally! I tried to say "Yes" like a sophisticated New Yorker would, but I'm not sure it came out that way. After that night, when the year turned 1998, my heart was taken and I never looked back.

Chapter Six

❧

Dancing Through

James and I continued dating throughout January and February. My life was settling into something of a routine; I took ballet class with Nancy Bielski in the mornings and worked at All Angels' in the afternoons. I taught regular New York City Ballet Workout classes at various New York Sports Club locations. I was no longer in therapy and had finished all of my course requirements at Fordham; I would be graduating in May. James popped up in every area of my life—he visited House Church, picked me up after work, took my Workout classes, and came to All Angels' with me on the alternating Sundays when we were not visiting his Catholic church. Since he was making such an effort to come to me on my turf, I also wanted to make an effort to share in his traditions.

I was also working as a dancer again. James had asked me to be the Juliet to his Romeo in Francis Patrelle's production of *Romeo and Juliet* at the Sylvia and Danny Kaye Playhouse. I was thrilled to be asked, since I had always dreamed of doing a full-length *Romeo and Juliet*. Francis had founded his own company, Dances Patrelle, in 1988 on the East Side of Manhattan and specialized in dramatic dance. He wanted to see me before agreeing to cast me, since we had never met, and after I'd taken a class with him, he told me that he would like for me to be his Juliet. He said that he would love it if I lost some weight, but even if I remained at the weight I was, he would enjoy working with me. Francis was extremely kind to let me be in his production after my history, and was the first person from the New York professional dance world to take a chance on me after my "disappearance," for which I'll always be grateful.

Indeed, I was still overweight for a dancer, but I'd made so much progress with my weight loss and, more important, my general relationship with food. Somehow, through all the many different areas of my life in which I was changing and growing, God was slowly healing me of my eating disorders. My compulsive episodes were dwindling, and I was beginning to feel that I could handle whatever life threw at me with God's help, not with food's help. I knew where my identity and true worth lay, with Christ, and I had a rich life with good work to do and good friends to laugh with. Plus, for the first time in my life, I had a boyfriend.

James was fun and smart and gentlemanly, full of integrity and honor. We spent time together both as two normal people in love and as dancers working on the various gigs James found for us. Though he was Catholic and I was Protestant, we went to church together, and many of our discussions revolved around God and our faiths.

One of our favorite places to spend time together was Riverside Park. Both of our apartments were closer to the Hudson River than to Central Park, and I'd always loved walking by the river whenever I could. I found something peaceful and healing in looking out at a large body of water, especially when coming from the hard cacophony of the city. James would call me and tell me that he was leaving his apartment on Seventieth Street, and I would then leave mine on Eighty-fifth. We would both start walking through Riverside Park along the river, James heading uptown and me heading downtown, meeting somewhere close to the Seventy-ninth Street Boat Basin. Then we would see where our fancy would take us.

I knew that James was the one for me when I realized that I never got tired of his presence. With other people, my introverted nature would eventually take over, and I would need some alone time to recharge my batteries. No matter how much I liked someone, I always needed to get away for a little while, or else I became cranky. My sister was an exception to this rule; with Becky, I could always be myself and never required a respite. It dawned on me one day that I could be completely myself with James as well, and that being in his company never tired me out.

I tried to communicate this to him. To me, I was paying him the highest compliment I possibly could. I took his hands and looked at him tenderly, letting him know that I was about to say something meaningful.

"Jim, being with you is even better than being alone," I told him earnestly.

James didn't take this well. He blinked at me and said, "What?" sounding a little miffed.

"Being with you is better than being alone—I don't need to get away from you. You don't wear me out."

I wasn't making things better with my explanations. James continued to be slightly offended—to him, it was obvious that being with good company was better than being alone. Didn't that just make him like any other guy? But to me, he was unique in the world; when I was with him, I was as comfortable as if I were alone. The more I talked, though, trying to make him understand, the more he just started laughing. I still today cannot get him to fully comprehend the huge compliment I pay him when I tell him this truth. He just shakes his head and looks at me, exasperated.

By the fall of 1998 I was back to full dancing strength, and almost back to a good dancing weight. I'd spent the summer doing gigs with James and had rediscovered my love for dance. My eating was normalized, I was dancing well, and I felt that I was standing on solid ground, basing my worth on things other than ballet and not needing outside affirmation to feel valued or valuable. I felt that I needed to give dancing professionally one more shot, this time as an adult fully aware of what she was getting herself into. Though I knew that City Ballet might not take me back, with James's encouragement I began to think about trying to rejoin the company. It seemed important that I try to conquer this area of my life that had so thoroughly defeated me. As James pointed out, no matter what the outcome, it was vital that I at least confront the scary beast that the ballet world had become for me.

James offered to approach Peter on my behalf, and I took him up on the suggestion, still feeling a little anxious about making the initial contact. Peter said that I could come and take a company class that he was teaching so he could take a look at me. The day arrived, and I felt as if I were gearing up for battle as I walked down the sidewalk from my apartment. I was certainly afraid to go; I knew I was going to be stared at and assessed by everyone in the studio, from the dancers to the ballet masters. I'd lost almost all of the weight I needed to lose, but I still had five pounds to go before I was really ballerina weight. From all of my experiences, I knew that the last bit of weight would not come off in a healthy way unless I was dancing a ballerina's schedule. So I would have to see if Peter was willing to take yet one more chance on me.

There were many people praying for me, and I had studied Bible stories about various courageous individuals, such us Daniel and David, who had relied on God's strength to get them through difficult periods. I had a strong sense that God wanted me to take this class and stand up to my general fear of the condemnation of those from City Ballet. I didn't know whether it was going to be God's will that I actually dance there again.

The morning of the class, I vacillated between fear and peace. For me, I was about to face the monster that had warped and twisted my spirit until I was almost destroyed. As I walked down the sidewalk to the studios at the Rose Building, near Lincoln Center, I imagined a legion of angels accompanying me, ready to fight for me and bolster me up if I needed them. I did feel confident and proud of my growth and progress, but I knew that I would be reentering a world very different from the one I'd inhabited the past year. Whereas I'd been in charge of my days and surrounded by Christian friends, I was now going into a secular environment where ballet was god and individuals were often sacrificed or destroyed in the pursuit of an indefinable and subjective ideal of art and beauty.

Perhaps the most difficult part of the day was the long walk I had to make across the ballet studio from the doorway to a spot at the barre on the other side of the room. I had to pass by all of the company members, most of whom I hadn't seen or talked to in a year. I was greeted warmly by many dancers, just stared at by others, and ignored by still others while they murmured to the dancers around them. But everyone seemed to take a moment to look at my body, and they certainly made their opinions very quickly. I knew I'd already been judged by all the dancers, but I reminded myself that I was a Child of God, and no matter what anyone thought of my appearance, my true worth was unchangeable.

Once I'd found a comfortable, low-key spot at the barre somewhere in the middle of the room, I felt more relaxed. I moved through the normal dancer's routine of stretches and warm-up exercises while I waited for the class to start. Finally Peter walked into the studio, and my stomach did a little flip. I took a breath, got into first position, and started pliés with the rest of the dancers.

The class was anticlimactic in that it felt completely normal, just like all my other Peter classes over the years. Peter greeted me with a smile the first time he walked by my barre. After class, I was due to meet Peter and Rosemary in the ballet masters' dressing room. I was happy that at least we were not meeting in Peter's office, where I'd had so many unhappy conversations.

I waited outside the door while Peter and Rosemary talked; then they called me in. There was a bit of awkwardness as we all found a place to settle inside the small room, and then we looked at one another for a moment.

"Well, how are you?" Rosemary asked with a smile. I understood that this was my pitch to make, that the burden of convincing them fell completely on me.

I took a breath and thought back on all I'd been through in the year since I'd been fired. I looked at these two people who'd had so much control over how I thought and felt about myself. I'd given them the power over whether I loved or hated myself, but I realized that now I was free. I was no longer under their control but instead empowered as a Daughter of the Lord to use the gifts He had given me in whatever way He saw fit. I was sitting across from two regular people who happened to be experts at what they did, and were therefore in high positions, but if I chose to put myself back under their authority, they would be my bosses and nothing more. They would not determine how I felt about myself—not anymore.

So I exhaled and began.

"I'm good, really good. I've had an amazing year and have completely changed. I've obviously lost a lot of weight, and I've been dancing and feel strong and ready to perform again. I feel like I've conquered a lot of the things that were holding me back, and can move forward in a much better way. I know that I'm not all the way back to a perfect ballet weight, but I feel like I can only get there if I'm rehearsing and performing a full schedule again. I'm happy to do every demi-soloist role in *Nutcracker* for the entire six-week run if you want me to—I just want to come back and dance again. And I know you will be pleased with my progress."

I finally stopped the rush of words, rather amazed by my own confidence, especially when I remembered all the other weepy meetings I'd had with Peter and Rosemary, where I'd mostly cried and agreed that I was failing. Rosemary and Peter also seemed a little stunned, staring at me in surprise for a moment or two. They looked at each other and then asked me to give them a moment while they discussed it between themselves.

I left the room and waited outside in the hallway, already feeling triumphant but not knowing what their decision would be. When James and I had discussed this day, he had encouraged me to try for City Ballet but reminded me that there were many great companies to dance in, and that if it didn't happen with City Ballet, I could go somewhere else. He also wanted me to feel that I had closure at City Ballet and that I could leave my experience there with my chin up, not slinking away in defeat. Further, he was adamant that if City Ballet took me back, it would be a chance for *me* to assess whether I actually wanted to stay there; he suggested I try it for a season and then decide if dancing in this particular company with these particular people was something I really wanted to do.

All of these thoughts raced through my head as I waited. I prayed that God's will would be done, even as I hoped that Peter and Rosemary would say yes. But I didn't feel ashamed or worthless or apologetic. God had truly changed me in unbelievable ways. I already had conquered a great darkness in my life.

The door opened, and they invited me back inside.

"We see a lot of progress, and we're very happy about that," Peter said. "We would obviously be happy to have you back, but we're thinking of hiring you on a temporary contract just to see how it goes. We will hire you for *Nutcracker*, just through to the beginning of January. What do you think of that?"

I took it. I was thrilled. I was stepping back into the dance world, but this time it would be on my own terms as a new and changed person.

It was strange to be back with the company again. Life there had continued in the same vein as always while I was returning as someone completely different on the inside. I fell easily back into the rhythm of things, all the while knowing that I might only be there for a month or two. I approached each rehearsal and class a little cautiously, feeling a bit precarious in my newfound confidence and convictions. What if something happened that set me going downhill again? On the other hand, I loved the jokey camaraderie with the other dancers and the feeling that I was doing something I was really good at. No one spoke to me about my "year away"; everyone just picked up where I'd left off. There was a new crop of apprentices I didn't know, but everyone else there had been my coworkers and friends for seven years.

The day of my first performance back with the company arrived. It was the opening night of *Nutcracker*, and it was like every other opening day that I'd experienced since I first joined the company at age sixteen. I'd spent all day at the theater, setting up my dressing room, taking class, and then doing the stage rehearsals for the night's performance. After the last rehearsal, I left the theater for some food and fresh air.

With my bag of food from the deli in my hands, I sat down outside the stage door for a couple of minutes. Perhaps it was the very sameness of all of these rituals that was making the day feel surreal to me. Here I was, about to perform at the New York State Theater again, when a year ago I thought I'd quit dancing forever. I was about to dance on-stage, and instead of the feelings of dread I'd become accustomed to, I was excited about it.

I grabbed my bag and went into the theater to my dressing room. Would I remember how to do stage makeup? I gave myself extra time, but it wasn't necessary—apparently applying stage makeup is like riding a bike. I saw my made-up face in the mirror, unnaturally pale from the base makeup and powder, with dramatic eyes and huge eyelashes. That face was so familiar, but so foreign. Behind that makeup, any thought or feeling could be disguised, but I was hiding nothing now, and I felt great. Even beneath the makeup, with my frizzy hair slicked back into a bun and a giant flower on my head, I felt like myself.

The butterflies kicked in when I stood up to put on my warm-up clothes. I was dancing one of the two Demi Flowers, a part that I'd done more times than I could count, and normally it would not faze me. But this time was, of course, different. I put on sweatshirt, sweatpants, and leg warmers and went down to the stage level to warm up.

I've always preferred to warm up backstage so that I can look into the wings and watch what is happening on the stage. That night I followed my normal routine and entered the backstage area while the party scene was just ending. I found a spot at the barre and watched the dancers playing the Party Parents exit the stage, laughing softly with each other and heading briskly to their next costume change. The men would become Mice in the battle scene. The ladies would turn into Snowflakes.

As always, I stopped my barre work to peek through the wings and watch my favorite parts of the ballet. Our production of the *Nutcracker* is so magical, filled with moments that enchant watchers of every age. The first such moment is the transformation of our Christmas tree—as it rises to its towering height on the stage, it gets applause every time. The next moment is when the Nutcracker Prince changes, in the blink of an eye, into a real prince who then places a crown on little Marie's head. Then the snow forest comes alive and the Snowflakes enter, bringing in the first extended dancing of the production. One of my best friends, Elizabeth, was always the first Snowflake onstage, and I took great joy in once again waving to her across the wings before she entered and danced the brief solo that begins the dance of the Snowflakes.

My warm-up complete and intermission quickly approaching, I returned to my dressing room. This was the time for makeup and hair check, last bathroom break, quick taping of the toes with masking tape to prevent blisters, and getting into tights, trunks, and robe. Then I looked into the mirror once more, and a smile broke out on my face. I grabbed my pointe shoes and went down to the girls' costume room offstage.

Just as my body remembered my old routines, so did my brain: What if I looked fat in my costume? What if everyone was looking at me in secret disgust? What if I looked different from everyone else? I shook my head and pushed the thoughts aside. I would not tolerate those thoughts anymore. I was here, I had changed, and I was proud of who I was. My body looked great, even if I did still hope to lose a couple more pounds. I had a right to be here and a right to dance. I felt great, and I'd been healed from so many things. I was a whole person now. And besides, I told myself, it wasn't all about *me*! I needed to remember the bigger picture, stop focusing on myself, and be grateful I was here. God had given me a gift, not for myself, but to share with others in whatever way I could.

I changed into my costume, leaving my leg warmers on underneath. I carried my pointe shoes to the offstage workstation and did a last check to make sure no threads or elastics were loose. After they were securely and comfortably on my feet, I half-jogged onto the stage to get my heart rate up.

Dancers from the other divertissements were already there, the backstage area filled with living Hot Chocolates, Candy Canes, Teas, and Marzipans. Some were warming up, some were chatting and laughing with friends. I bounced around and joked with people, exchanging wishes of "merde." Then the little girls playing the Angels appeared, signaling that it was almost time to start act 2. We moved offstage to prepare for our entrance.

I removed my leg warmers and felt another surge of butterflies, tensing up when the orchestra started playing. But I reminded myself that it was my choice to be back here, and that this was indeed something I loved. It was a miracle that I was again in this theater and able to perform on this stage. And I wasn't going to waste time being nervous. I was going to enjoy this.

Finally it was time for the Waltz of the Flowers. I stood in the front wing and waved at Pascale Van Kipnis, my opposite Demi Flower for this performance. Our music began, and then suddenly we were taking two steps onto the stage and holding a brief arabesque balance. We ran to our first pose, and I got an initial glimpse of the audience, lit by the warm glow of the jewels that surround the rings of the theater. It looked like home. Then came four beats of the waltz, and suddenly we were really dancing. I felt a surge of joy. I was dancing, and I was free.

During that *Nutcracker*, I was cast in a busy schedule of Demi Flowers and Lead Spanish, just as I'd hoped. Slowly, over the course of the six-week run, I was able to get down to an acceptable ballet weight. The company offered me a full contract in January at my old rank of soloist, and I gradually returned to my old parts. In the spring of 1999 I was even cast in the lead role of the Waltz Girl in *Serenade*, a gift I'd never expected to receive. Dancing in that ballet again, after all that had passed, and with James dancing opposite me as the Dark Angel boy, was an experience I'll always treasure.

I never returned to the almost-too-skinny weight of my late teens, but

I was at a great dancing weight, fit and healthy and strong. I was thin, but I had thighs and a figure. My eating was normal, and, determined never again to succumb to disordered eating, I refused to go on strict diets. Therefore my weight did fluctuate, based on how much I was dancing; at the beginning of a rehearsal period after a layoff, I had a couple of pounds to lose. At the end of a very busy performance period, friends would tell me I was too thin. It was important for me to be normal in my outside life and stay away from the craziness of restrictive eating during layoffs, when I wasn't as active as I was in performance seasons. I couldn't constantly force myself into the ballet mold when I knew it would alter my priorities again toward a ballet-centric life, and eventually drive me crazy. I felt I could never sustain that kind of pressure on myself, so I strove for health and normalcy during every phase of the elliptical schedule of a dancer's life. And it worked for me.

One day in the summer of 1999, James planned a whole day for us as a surprise for me. We were on our summer layoff from City Ballet, looking at twelve weeks away from work. James took me on a ferry to Fire Island for a day at the beach. Then he brought me home and told me to change and meet him at our midway point in Riverside Park. He promised me a bottle of wine and a beautiful sunset.

I met him on a quiet bench a little way uptown from the Boat Basin. We drank some wine from plastic cups and gazed at the sun setting over the New Jersey skyline. James got suddenly quiet. Then he set his wine on the ground and pulled a box out of his pocket. He somehow got halfway off the bench and then leaned close to my cheek and said in a slightly choked voice, "Will you . . ."

He didn't seem to be able to finish. I quickly said, "Yes! Yes!" and we were engaged. I remember feeling so different that night with his ring on my finger. I'd known that he loved me, but it was altogether different to have a symbol on my hand that said that someone wanted me enough to tell anyone who looked at me that I was taken. He not only loved me, but he also wanted us to belong to each other for the rest of our lives. It was an extraordinary feeling.

Six months later, another January had come around, and I'd been back dancing with the company for a year. I'd just had a stage rehearsal for Jerome Robbins's *Fancy Free*, a ballet about three sailors on leave in the big city, and was in my dressing room changing out of costume when I was called back to the stage over the intercom. I put on my terry-cloth bathrobe and fuzzy slippers and went backstage to find Peter waiting for me. He had a little smile on his face.

"So," he said slowly, looking at me as if he had a secret. "I was thinking that it was time to promote you and make you a principal dancer."

He watched my face while I digested the news. I hardly knew how to react. I was thrilled and surprised and in slight disbelief. I stammered out something like, "Wow, thank you," and after we stood there for a moment we both simultaneously figured a hug was in order. The group of dancers rehearsing onstage seemed to have been in on the secret, and when they saw Peter and me hug, they broke out into applause and cheers.

After that everyone was just standing there and smiling at me, so after uttering more thanks and looking around idiotically for a bit, I escaped back to my dressing room.

It felt pretty unbelievable, even though I'd been doing major principal roles for the past season and was about to make my debut as Aurora in *The Sleeping Beauty* in a couple of weeks. To be promoted to principal, the highest rank a dancer could attain in the company, after all I'd been through, was astonishing and a testament to how far God had taken me in my life. I sat in my dressing room for a time, taking it all in and not quite sure how to handle the momentous news. I reminded myself that *this* was not where my true happiness lay, nor was it where my identity was stored. I said a prayer of thanks, and then went to call James and my family.

Chapter Seven

∽

Intermission

I've been a professional dancer for almost twenty-five years now; the rules, rituals, and methods of this lifestyle are as comfortable to me as a favorite pair of shoes. But I realize that the ballet world is unique, and many of my daily routines probably seem exotic. Each dancer develops his or her own way of preparing for the stage, and that preparation is very detailed and time-consuming.

I've discovered that it generally takes me about two hours to prepare for a performance. Backstage, a sheet is posted on one of the many bulletin boards with the timings for each show. The sheet lists each ballet for the night and displays when that ballet starts, how long it is, and what time it will end. It also tells us if there are just three-minute pauses in between the ballets or full twenty-minute intermissions. When planning when I want to start getting ready for a performance, I go to the time sheet, find my ballet, and figure out what time it starts so that I can determine when I need to be in my dressing room to start my preperformance routines.

I enjoy getting ready for a show. I follow the same ritual almost every time, and the sameness is soothing. My dressing room is one of four located on the stage level. These are set aside for the more senior principal women, and each one houses two ballerinas. My dressing-room mate has been Maria Kowroski for over ten years and when we're in the room together we're likely to be chatting and laughing most of the time, unless one of us is feeling particularly tired or nervous. We almost always have music on, and I let Maria choose what we listen to, since I never want to force too much country music on my friends. But when I'm alone, I blast Willie and Dolly and the Dixie Chicks.

Upon arriving at the theater for a performance, I immediately change into some comfortable and baggy warm-up clothes and put fuzzy socks on my feet. If I've been rehearsing all day, I take a quick shower and have a snack before changing so that it almost feels like I'm starting a new day. Then I settle down in my chair at my dressing table to start my makeup.

The large mirror in front of my chair is surrounded by lightbulbs encased in metal safety cages. From the cages I hang a variety of objects such as a water squirt bottle, barrettes, safety pins, and even little shiny disco-ball ornaments for decoration. On the walls beside the mirror, I have pictures of my family, a schedule of the current performance season we're dancing, and Post-it notes reminding me what I need to pick up at the drugstore. On the shelf on top of the mirror, I have boxes of various makeup and hair supplies as well as some paintings and pictures that I brought in to make my corner of the dressing room feel homey.

During the day when I'm not performing, I like to keep the table in front of the mirror clear so that I can more easily sew pointe shoes; yes, we all have to maintain and repair our own shoes, even the principal dancers. I've gotten my shoe-sewing time down to an efficient seven minutes—ribbons, elastics, and all—after so many years of practice. Sometimes I read or even pull out a computer during my downtime. But when I'm getting ready for a performance, I pull down the containers of makeup and hair stuff so that everything will be in easy reach once I finally sit down in front of the mirror.

I always start with my stage makeup, and if I'm going at my usual leisurely pace, it takes me about thirty minutes to accomplish it all. First I apply a concealer stick over my entire face. This helps my base stay on when I start sweating. After the concealer comes a thick stage base that is a shade lighter than my normal skin tone. Our makeup adviser told me that this helps me to look ethereal and otherworldly, not my usual look. The base comes in flat cakes, and I use a wet sponge to get it from the disk and onto my face. I have to apply it fairly thickly because my skin easily flushes, and the second I exert any energy, I get red in the face. No one wants to see a sweaty, red-faced ballerina.

After the base comes some loose powder. I use yellow powder because of my skin tone and because I read in some magazine that movie stars use yellow powder to look younger and more vibrant. I then apply two colors of blush to shade and contour my face and then extend my eyebrows slightly with an eyebrow pencil. I don't have to do anything else to my eyebrows because God blessed me with the Ringer gene for bushy black brows. Next come my eyes. I put a purplish eye shadow in the middle of my eyelid following the line of my eye socket and then extend it out toward my temple about a half inch. I then line the top of my eyelid with a black pencil, blending it up and out at the outer corner, kind of like cat eyes. Then I partially line my bottom lid with a brown pencil, not closing the eye at the outer corner but again extending the line straight out. I put some eye shadow over that lower line to make it look softer.

Next comes the false eyelashes, and at City Ballet we like our lashes huge. I enjoy wearing mine as big as I can without looking ridiculous. We apply them directly to our lashes in order to look as doe-eyed as possible. I always did like to dress up, and stage makeup still gives me the opportunity to look like a serene princess even though underneath the paint my face might show the exhaustion of work or of being up all night with a sick child. Stage makeup serves two purposes: it heightens, glamorizes, and enlarges our features so that audience members at the back of the house can still see our faces under the intensely bright stage lights, and it hides the fact that we're working so hard onstage that our faces are flushed and sweaty.

The last thing I apply is my lipstick, usually something very red unless I'm doing a more muted ballet such as *Dances at a Gathering*. Each ballerina makes her own makeup choices and has her own way of doing her makeup that makes her feel beautiful and confident. And after finishing my makeup, I'm ready to start taming my hair.

My hair and I have been battling since I started wanting to fix my hair myself like a big girl. Though my hair isn't particularly thick, it is somewhere between wavy and curly, and depending on the meteorological circumstances, it can be downright wild and frizzy. It varies in length; I got my first short haircut in the 1980s when I was eleven or twelve, and I remember the enormous quantity of hairspray necessary to make my "wings" stay in place. I used to have to walk with my face constantly pointed into the wind, no matter which way my feet were pointing, because if the wind blew from behind me my wings would stick out like elephant ears.

I had long hair past my shoulders for my first years in the company, but constantly slicking it back into a bun started to do a lot of damage. I began to trim it shorter and shorter until finally one day I chopped it all off to the nape of my neck. I did it at the beginning of a twelve-week layoff so that it would grow back some before I began performing again. Though the only real requirement from the company is that we're able to slick our hair back into a bun somehow, I think management would probably prefer that their ballerinas all have long hair. But I loved the short hair. I think I loved it because it was a small rebellion against the ballerina type. I longed for an identity separate from being a ballerina and didn't want to walk down the sidewalk instantly recognizable as a dancer because of my long, untrimmed locks and turned-out walk. There were so many things I had to conform to as a dancer and so many rules I had to follow. I wanted to be able to control my own hair.

Even when I had long hair, a good stage hairdo was a problem for me. I could make a very nice bun and a beautiful French twist. That wasn't my issue. The trick was getting all of the little frizzies on the sides and top and back of my head to lie down flat and stay there. My willowy ballerina friends with their pliable, cooperative straight hair would brush their hair a bit, bend over to sweep the glossy strands into a ponytail, and then flip back up to reveal a flat, smooth, perfectly executed bun. They would then squirt just a bit of hair spray on, to ensure that nothing moved.

I, on the other hand, would wrestle with my hair until it felt as if all the blood had left my hands and pooled into my elbows, using water, mousse, gel, and hair spray to try to slick down the curly horns that sprang up all around my head. I would use a brush and a comb and my hands and even try to time the hair spray so that it would be slightly dry and sticky before I pressed my hair into place. Ballerinas were supposed to have smooth, perfect hair pulled back into a smooth, perfect bun. And oh, how I aspired to that vision. Often, after I thought I'd successfully wrangled the beast, one horn would suddenly pop out of its confinement, reverberating mockingly as if it had just been released from a spring. At these times, I sat at my mirror and stared at the scissors on my table, wondering how bad it would be if I just cut the darn thing off.

When my hair is short, I scrape it into a tiny little ponytail on the top of my head that looks a little bit like a Hershey's Kiss. Once I've slicked the rest of my hair, I get out my fake ponytails and braids. I love using the fake hair because I can do so much more with it than I can with my own hair. Once I have a nice bun in place, I put in my headpiece for whichever ballet I'm doing that night. Often the principal ballerinas have a lot of freedom when it comes to the headpieces for their costumes, and we can wear them however we feel is the most flattering. I prefer putting my headpieces on asymmetrically and view my head as my own little canvas on which I get to create a shiny piece of art.

Once my hair and makeup are done to my satisfaction, I take out my large sponge and put the same thick base I use on my face on the parts of my arms, chest, and back not covered by my costume. I do this because if I didn't, once I started dancing, my face would stay one light color while my arms and chest would flush red from exertion.

Finally, I put on an extra sweatshirt and my ballet slippers and check to make sure I have everything ready that I'll need for the performance. I look at my pointe shoes. I have a pile of them in various states of use on the floor of my side of the dressing room. Earlier in the day, I've usually decided which ones I'll wear for the show that night. To help me remember, I write something on the bottom of the shoe, such as the first letter of the ballet I'll be dancing. I make sure the ribbons and elastics are still well sewn, with no threads coming loose, and check that the tips and sides of the shoes don't look horribly messy. I get out my tights and anything else I'll need to wear under my costume. I make sure the costume, usually already hung in my room by one of our wonderful dressers, is ready to go and has no problems. Once I feel that all is in order and that I just need to return to my room to get dressed for the performance, I go out to the backstage right area, just around the corner from my dressing room, and start to warm up.

My hair and makeup generally take an hour to an hour and fifteen minutes to finish. When I get backstage, I find a spot at one of the two warm-up barres there and sit down to stretch a bit. Other dancers are usually there as well, and we chat. If I'm warming up before the first ballet of the performance, the backstage lights are on but not the stage lights. Stagehands are starting to prepare the stage for the first ballet of the show: one person is mopping the stage, another is checking the lights, another is making sure the dancers' workstation has all the resin, Band-Aids, sewing needles, and other emergency items that might be required at a moment's notice. The curtain is still up, and from the orchestra pit we might hear the harpist plucking her strings as she tunes her instrument. The audience hasn't been allowed into their seats yet.

If I happen to be in one of the latter ballets of the evening, I watch the performers onstage while I warm up, gaining inspiration from them as they dance their hearts out in that other world that I will soon be entering. I feel that I have the best seats in the house because I'm able to watch my amazing fellow dancers up close as they unfold their artistry on the stage.

A half hour before the performance starts, the backstage area suddenly gets very busy. A stage manager calls into the intercom, "Half hour please! Half hour until the top of the show. Please sign in if you have not already done so!" We're all required to "sign in" by writing our initials onto the company roster highlighted with those performing that night, so the stage managers know that everyone is at the theater and not stuck in the subway or oversleeping. Anyone who forgets to sign in when he or she arrives at the theater—and it happens inevitably—wanders downstage to announce his or her presence. The full contingent of stagehands arrives to finalize the preparations for the first ballet. The curtain is lowered so that the audience can be allowed into the house.

About twenty minutes before I'm due to go onstage, I return to my dressing room to get into costume. I tape my toes and add whatever padding I'll need in my pointe shoes that night. I check my hair and makeup and say a short prayer about the performance, which I added into my preperformance routine as I started incorporating my faith back into my life. This prayer helps remind me that the performance is about something larger than me, and that it points to God and not to myself. I thank God for letting me dance that night, for the opportunity to do something I love that also glorifies Him, and ask that things go well. Most of all, I ask that no matter how it goes, the ballet might move the audience and bring them some joy. I then put on some thick leg warmers, grab my pointe shoes, and head out the door.

Backstage again, I go directly to one of the workstations located on each side of the stage. I dip my heels, clad in their pink ballet tights, in a water bucket and then rub them in the resin box to make them sticky so that the heels of my pointe shoes will not slip off my tights. I tug my pointe shoes on, making sure they are comfortable on and off pointe. I then tie my ribbons in a knot and tuck the ends in, sewing them to the ribbons around my ankles with a couple of stitches so that the ends will not fly out during the performance. Then I take a scraper, a brushlike wooden object whose bristles are actually metal tines, and scrape the leather bottom of my pointe shoe to make it rough. Last I step into the resin box, getting the sticky powder onto the bottom of my shoe and then wiping it over the sides and tips of my pointe shoes with a paper towel.

Pointe shoes fixed to my satisfaction, I head onto the stage, where the curtain is still hiding me from the audience, trotting to get my heart rate up. I practice a couple of steps for the upcoming ballet. If my partner is around and there is something we need to talk about or try, we do it then. The stage is usually filled with other dancers getting ready, and we all try not to bump into each other as we move around. In order to get my first "puff" out of the way, I usually do jumping jacks and a series of big jumps in place so that my heart isn't shocked when I suddenly start dancing hard onstage. I've found that this prevents me from getting out of breath too quickly once the performance starts.

I keep track of the different stage calls so that I can be ready when the curtain goes up. The stage manager calls fifteen minutes, ten minutes, five minutes . . . When I hear "Places, please!" I run offstage to shed my leg warmers and then get ready for the curtain to rise. I usually feel a thrill of butterflies and adrenaline and lift the performance up to God one more time, reminding myself that the show isn't about *me*. Then the conductor walks out to a clatter of applause, the house lights and backstage lights go out, the orchestra sounds its first chords, the curtain rises, and it is finally time to dance.

I'm often asked how we remember all of the steps to the vast repertoire we dance at City Ballet. Corps members might dance twenty ballets in a short six-week season. Principals might dance ten or more, and often we will rehearse three or four ballets during the day and then perform a completely different ballet that night.

I find the music to each ballet to be the key to remembering all of the steps. With choreography as musical as what we're blessed with in my company, someone just has to sing the music to me, and my body will do the steps. Each ballet must have its own little piece of my brain that is reserved just for that ballet, ready to be called up whenever the music is played.

When we're learning a ballet for the first time, whether it's new choreography or one of the famous ones already in the company's repertory, we do it systematically, going forward in chunks and then going back to the beginning to dance the piece through up to the point we have learned. Once we can successfully get from the beginning up to where we stopped learning, we then go forward to learn another chunk before returning to dance it from the beginning again. Layer by layer we train our ear to hear the music and how it matches up to the steps. With enough repetition, the music is inevitably linked by some mysterious connection to our muscle memory so that eventually, we don't have to think about the steps. Our bodies know what to do, leaving our brains free to give flight to our imaginations in performance.

It is certainly easier to learn a ballet if I'm already familiar with the music or have seen the ballet before so that I have a frame of reference for what I'll be dancing. If I have not seen the ballet before, I'll watch a tape if possible so that my brain can have a map in place for where my part in the ballet will go. However, I try not to watch tapes too often if I can help it because it is too easy to find myself mimicking the ballerina dancing the part on the tape; I've always wanted to do parts in my own way, even while I take inspiration and guidance from the wonderful ballerinas who have gone before me. Balanchine and Robbins often made different versions for different dancers, and they wanted their ballerinas to be unique. Though both choreographers have now passed away, their ballet masters try to follow in their spirit as they teach each successive generation of dancers these masterpieces. Though the steps might be mostly the same, artistry is left up to the individual.

And each dancer's artistry is radically different from another's, so that ballets change and evolve according to which dancer is dancing which part. Most of the ballets in the repertory of the New York City Ballet have no story line; there is often drama, but that drama comes from the music and the steps. I've realized that a lack of story line actually gives the dancers more opportunity to place their own personal interpretation into a role.

For example, in the last movement of George Balanchine's *Vienna Waltzes*, a solitary woman dances in a ballroom with a man playing a partner who materializes as if from her imagination. There is a moment when the music comes to a standstill and then starts over, slowly and haltingly. I've never danced the role and have only watched it, but I've always thought that at that moment, the woman's imagination becomes so powerful that she conjures up a real man from her fantasy world. I've seen some ballerinas interpret it this way, and have seen others remain remote, looking at their partners as if they were not quite there.

One day while watching a rehearsal of *Vienna*, I asked my friend and fellow principal dancer Tyler Angle, "Do you think he becomes a real man there?"

Tyler looked at me with interest and said, "You know, I've seen it done both ways. It depends on the ballerina—I've always wanted him to become real. But Jenny, you and I are always searching for a story even when there is none." And he is right about that. I'm one of those dancers who searches for some hint of a story, even in the plotless ballets.

Musicians from the New York City Ballet orchestra have told me that they love to play for our company because of the great music the choreographers have chosen for the ballets we perform. But what may be thrilling for a musician to play can be difficult for a dancer to decipher, and some ballets have more difficult music than others. These I have a harder time learning and assimilating into my body. If I have to rely on counting the music to keep my place in the choreography, I find I have to use a different part of my brain that isn't a natural part of my dancing. These ballets take more focus, and I'm often more nervous for them; sometimes the second I let the performance side of myself take over, I stop counting the music. With these ballets, I have to do a lot more physical repetition and mental dissection of the music before I feel that I really *know* the ballet.

Also, the music we hear from the orchestra is often completely different from what we have been hearing in the studio. We have wonderful rehearsal pianists who play for us during the day, but often the piano accents notes differently than a full orchestra does. The arrangement written for the piano might highlight different sounds and melodies from what we would hear from the orchestra pit during a performance. Also the piano can set a more obvious tempo, whereas sometimes the orchestration is written as more of a wash of sound. There have been plenty of stage rehearsals, particularly of brand-new choreography, that have fallen apart completely because none of the dancers could tell where they were in the music. This is of course incredibly frustrating for the choreographer, and the dancers usually go into a panic as what seemed so certain and comfortable just the day before suddenly becomes an unknown.

This happened to us the first time we had an orchestra rehearsal for a ballet that Peter Martins made called *Naïve and Sentimental Music* to music by John Adams. It used almost every principal dancer on the roster, twenty-six of us either onstage at the same time or just exiting and entering. We were all experienced and used to dancing under every kind of stress, but when we were onstage for our first orchestra rehearsal and suddenly couldn't find a beat or a melody in the music, we just stood around and stared at each other, befuddled. Peter had anticipated the problem and rehearsed us often to a CD of the orchestra version of the music, but somehow the orchestra sounded wildly different from the CD's version of the piece. It was hard for us to find any kind of rhythm or melody to anchor our steps. In group sections where we were supposed to be dancing together, it looked like we were all doing different choreography because we were so out of sync. Peter was obviously very upset, because the premiere was only days away.

We eventually figured out that in every section, there was somebody who could hear where we were supposed to be. Those who were musically lost just found a way to watch that dancer and stay together with his or her movements. We counted for one another and gave one another significant looks. During a section where the women danced in a revolving circle and we couldn't make eye contact with one another, Janie Taylor called out the counts for us. Before a finale step that Jennie Somogyi and I led off, we would look at each other across the stage, nod, and take a large preparatory step so that we started at the same time. At other times, when in doubt, we just watched whoever was in front, and even if we thought she was wrong, we did what she did.

Somehow we pulled it off, but we were all stressed about it. For this ballet, it was not necessarily the dancing that was hard but the musical and mental focus required to do it correctly. I'm not sure I've ever seen that many principal dancers counting music loudly at the same time, both in the wings and onstage, looking questioningly at their opposites and partners to see if they were correct. But in the end, hopefully we looked professional from out front! We tried not to move our lips too much as we counted. . . .

And indeed, despite all of the preparation and repetition of rehearsals, performances are rarely perfect. Actually, performances are never perfect. I've never stepped offstage and thought, There was absolutely nothing wrong with that performance. I find that when I perform, I have many thought processes going on simultaneously. My analytical brain is trying to make sure I do the technique properly; I'm thinking about pointing my toes, straightening my knees, keeping my shoulders down, placing myself in the proper alignment so that I'll stay in balance. I might also be hearing the voice of my ballet master telling me to remember to do something particular at a specific moment. Or I'm counting how many steps I have to do before I take off for a jump into my partner's arms. These are the things that I've practiced and rehearsed over and over again, so they should be mostly in my muscle memory, but I still need to remember them and force myself to execute them properly, especially if I'm tired.

But drowning out that analytical part of myself is the part of me that just *dances.* There is something so different about being onstage. Performance never feels like rehearsal to me. There is a different electricity to the air. I feel a surge of adrenaline as I wait in the wings and hear the music building to the moment when I'll make my entrance. The actual air is usually colder on the stage than in any rehearsal studio because of the air conditioning that flows in from the audience. I can sense a feeling of hushed expectation pressing toward me from the hundreds of people sitting in the dark and watching. Suddenly everything counts, and even if we make mistakes, my partners and I have to make it look good, as if what the audience is seeing right then in that moment was what we fully intended to do all along. We have a responsibility to be our very best, and to transport them to another realm.

In performance, I become primarily consumed with the artistic part of my dancing because all of the rehearsal and repetition gives me the freedom, finally, to just perform. I'm trying to embody and project the feelings the particular choreography evokes within me. It isn't just a matter of counting, or precise balance, or any technical execution of a particular step or combination—it's something less definable. The music suddenly seems more present as I try to interpret it or respond to it exactly as it is sounding that night. I'm also reacting to my partner and what frame of mind he is in for the performance. I may be feeling serene and loving, but if I look at my partner's eyes and he is looking back at me with desperation or sadness, I have to adapt and respond so that we have a silent dialogue going on between us, not only technically but also emotionally, at all times. We may have rehearsed a particular scene in one particular way for weeks, but suddenly, onstage, moods and feelings can change and we have to stay responsive, in the moment. Inspiration or insight can come out of nowhere during a performance, and following that inner quicksilver spark—that something inside that transforms a dancer into an artist—can lead to experiencing the true and honest emotional depths of a ballet. Dancing onstage in front of an audience is the most important part of our day, and it is why we put in so many hours of rehearsal, why we work so hard over the weeks—years, really—to build for ourselves a technical foundation from which we can soar artistically. It is with the freedom of technical assurance that dancers can allow their artistic imaginations to fly unhindered.

One ballerina whom I've always admired for her stage presence is Wendy Whelan. In rehearsals, she works immaculately, fixating on small details as she strives to understand and conquer whatever role she is dancing at the moment. She addresses minute technical issues as well as broad motivations and themes, and at the final stage rehearsal it appears that the part has never been danced better. But then the performance comes, and Wendy somehow takes everything to another level, transporting herself into the role, inhabiting it as only a creature of the stage could. Her way of working yields amazing results and has made her one of the most memorable artists of this generation; I've held her up as an example to follow ever since I first saw her perform.

When dancers step onstage, they see each and every performance as the culmination of years of work and dedication. They are prepared to expend any amount of energy and to sacrifice their bodies in order to make the performance somehow special. The goal is to move and thrill the audience, and to make them feel lifted up and taken beyond the ordinary world.

But as I said, performances are never perfect. Usually the mistakes are minor and are noticed only by the dancers. We might take off for a jump on the wrong leg and have to fix our position midair, or find a new ending position for a pirouette that didn't go as planned. A lift might go badly, and the man may have to carry the woman in an unrehearsed position that the woman then has to find a way to make pretty. Sometimes, however, something goes so wrong that there is no recovery from it or disguising it, and everyone, including the most inexperienced audience member, knows that a big problem has occurred. I've certainly had my share of every kind of mistake.

First of all, I've fallen. Now, at this stage of my career, I know that falling down onstage isn't the end of the world. It is a little embarrassing, but it usually gains the dancer so much sympathy and goodwill that she gets an extra-loud round of applause. But the first time I fell onstage, I was devastated.

It happened when I was still a student at Washington School of Ballet. For the spring student performance, I was given a solo to dance. It was a short solo with quick footwork that ended with a diagonal of very tricky pirouettes; the pirouettes were *en dedans*, or "inside" turns, which I happened to do well. To turn *en dedans*, the dancer stands on the right leg and turns to the right. The other way of turning, *en dehors*, is the "outside" pirouette, where the dancer stands on the left leg and turns to the right. In variations class, I'd been one of the few who had been able to successfully tackle that diagonal of eight *en dedans* pirouettes, which must have been why I was eventually cast. I still even today feel much more comfortable in this type of turn than in the *en dehors*, or "outside," pirouette.

Rehearsals seemed to be going well, but I was still terribly nervous as the performances approached. We had three shows over the weekend, and I felt as if these were the most important days of my fourteen-year-old life. In the first performance, after executing four of the pirouettes, I fell. I was mortified. I got sympathy and reassurances from teachers, students, and parents alike, but it didn't help. And some of the sympathy seemed tinged with a little bit of gladness that something ill had befallen the "girl who got the solo."

The next day was a Saturday and we had our last two shows, a matinee and an evening performance. My dad was with me that day. He and I prayed before the matinee performance, but I still felt very nervous. While I was dancing the opening section, I felt like I was unconnected to the floor, like a deer on ice. Before my solo, I thought butterflies would erupt from my gut. Then the moment came and I made it through all eight pirouettes, but as I started the steps to get into the final pose, I fell again! I couldn't believe it. Now I was given sympathy with sidelong glances; I could tell that people were wondering if I was a "choke artist." Maybe I didn't have the guts to perform under pressure. Maybe I was one of those talents who would end up a flop. Literally.

In between the matinee and the evening, my dad and I went to a fast-food restaurant for something to eat and just to get away from the theater. I cried. We prayed again. And then, oddly, I fell asleep on a bench right in the middle of that busy restaurant. My brain must have needed a break. But I woke up feeling refreshed and ready to tackle the last performance. The worst had happened, twice, so it could only get better.

Mary Day, the head of the school, was backstage for the last show. She looked anxious for me. As I waited in the wings to go out for my solo,

I was nervous but felt a certain grit-your-teeth determination. I was going to get through this, and I was NOT going to fall. Suzanne Erlon, one of my teachers, had suggested not thinking too far ahead of myself, but just counting each turn as "one." It was too easy (and dangerous) to start worrying about the fact that there were eight turns in a row. I decided to try it. This time I felt connected to the stage and like I was dancing as myself, not as someone labeled as "talented" or "going to be something someday" or "has just fallen twice during her eight pirouettes." I danced the solo well, executed all the turns, and finished on my feet. I had done it. I ran into the wings and jumped for joy; I felt I had never jumped so high in my life. Mary Day jumped up with me and hugged me, saying, "I knew you would do it. I just knew it!"

Since those early experiences, I've been able to handle my falls with more grace. Falling in the corps de ballet was always complicated because I had to get up and somehow find my place in both the choreography and the formation without disrupting things too much. Also, while on the floor, there were usually pointed toes and kicking feet to avoid. Sometimes I had to roll or crawl a bit to get out of everyone's way. We don't get in trouble when we fall—everyone knows that it is an accident and that sometimes there is nothing a dancer could do to prevent it. But certainly no one wishes to fall onstage.

Falling during a solo meant that I had to find a way to recover well and pretend nothing had happened, all the while knowing that everyone knew something had happened. Once while doing the Fairy of Generosity solo from *The Sleeping Beauty* in the Saratoga Performing Arts Center, I had a particularly loud fall. SPAC is an outdoor theater, and the performance was a pleasant summer matinee. I was enjoying dancing and being able to see the faces of the audience while dragonflies and butterflies darted over the lawn. About to dance an easy transitional step, I thought, I'm going to do the loveliest *bourrée* right now, looking back at the audience the whole time.

Suddenly I was facedown on the floor like a frog about to be dissected, staring at the stage tape through my fingertips. There was an echoing *brong* kind of sound bouncing through the amphitheater, no doubt caused by my knees and elbows forcefully connecting with the somewhat hollow-sounding stage. The packed audience of almost three thousand gasped a horrified *Oh*. I stood up quickly and went into B-plus, a ballerina's go-to pose where she stands on one leg with the other leg crossed behind her, toe on the floor. I had a couple of bars of music before my next step began, so I simply smiled at the audience and opened my palms toward them in an acknowledgment of what had just happened. We shared a moment. They clapped.

I once had a tumble during Balanchine's *Kammermusik No. 2*, a neo-classical ballet set to difficult Paul Hindemith music and danced by two women with a corps of men. The counts of the steps were intricate and unusual and took all of my focus. Right in the middle of the opening dance, I slipped and fell to my knees. Luckily I was dancing that night with my friend Kathleen Tracey, who always knew what she was doing. When I fell, all the counts with their matching steps flew out of my brain, and I had no idea where I was in the music. I knew I was about to be hopelessly lost for the rest of the section. But without pausing in her own difficult steps, Katey began barking out the counts to me.

"Seventeen, eighteen, nineteen!" I heard her say, and she looked at me on the floor as if to say, "Get up!" I got up with alacrity and was able to join right in with her; she saved the moment. What would we do without generous friends onstage?

Another memorable fall of mine happened during the Winter section of Jerome Robbins's *Four Seasons*, where all the ballerinas zip around the stage, pretending that they are freezing. There is a section that's particularly hard because it's nonstop jumping; it feels like the hardest aerobics class that must be done with pointed toes and a smile. After the solo girl's first entrance, she stays onstage to dance a pas de trois with two boys. At the end of this part, the three dancers do a series of *coupés jetés*, or turning leaps, in a diagonal to a final pose on one knee. During one performance, I slipped and fell during these jumps. Fortuitously, I had so much momentum built up from my previous leaps that I slid like a baseball player all the way across the stage and was able to pop up onto my knee, right in the perfect formation between my two boys, and finish with my arms out on the last count of the music. This fall was beloved by those in the company and reenacted many times. In fact, I found out weeks later that the boys had gotten a copy of the performance tape and played it over and over in slow motion in their dressing room.

Perhaps my favorite fall, however, happened during a *Nutcracker* gig with Charles Askegard in Brooklyn. December can be a lucrative month for dancers because thousands of schools across the country are doing their own productions of *The Nutcracker* and need dancers to come in for the principal parts. I've always loved to do these gigs, which enable me not only to augment my dancer's salary but also to meet and talk to students across America. It is wonderful and refreshing to see their love for dance and their joy in being a part of such special performances.

On one such gig in Brooklyn, Charles and I came onto the stage at intermission to warm up and get acclimated to the space. We discovered that the Snowflakes had gone rogue with the resin box. Dancers use this sticky powdery substance called resin when the floor is slippery; there is usually a box offstage that we can step in so that we can get some of the substance on our shoes. Apparently the Snowflakes had felt that the stage was especially slippery, because they had taken the resin box and dumped the entire contents onto the stage. The stage now felt as if someone had covered it with upside-down duct tape.

Charles and I could hardly dance. We had to pull our feet off the floor with every step we took, resulting in little *tick-tick-tick* sounds as we moved around. Even in my pointe shoes and with Charles's vigorous partnering assistance, I could turn around only twice during the pirouettes of our pas de deux because the tip of my shoe would stay planted on the floor while the rest of my foot and body tried to turn. Before his solo, Charles found some baby powder and sprinkled it on his shoe while he was in the wings, hoping that he could eke out a double pirouette himself, but he made it around only one and a half times and then had to jump the rest of the way. Under normal conditions, Charles usually turned like a top.

Somehow, in the middle of this very sticky situation, I managed to slip and fall. It was right before our big *grand jeté* lifts, and Charles and I had moved to opposite sides of the stage as the choreography built suspense. The music soared, Charles ran majestically toward me, and I wound up on my bottom, feet in the air. Charles just looked at me in consternation and then helped me up gallantly. While he held me over his head in the first lift, he said, "How did you possibly manage to fall?" I will never know.

Another problem that often catches dancers unaware (literally) is what we call "blanking." Sometimes, no matter how hard we have rehearsed or how many times we have repeated the choreography day after day and week after week, we get onstage before the audience and our brain draws a complete blank. It is a disconcerting feeling to be standing in front of over two thousand expectant people and not have a clue as to how to entertain them.

This has happened to me several times, but two instances in particular stand out. The first is when James and I were dancing the lead roles in Francis Patrelle's *Romeo and Juliet*. It was a full-length ballet and we were onstage the majority of the evening, so there were lots of entrances and exits to remember. This is usually not a problem, however. It was, after all, what we had trained ourselves to do for a living. But during one of the shows, the worst happened: both of us blanked out at the same time.

In a pas de deux, when one partner forgets the steps, usually the other remembers what they are supposed to be doing and is able to prompt his or her partner with either physical movements or a whispered verbal cue. But I turned to face James and suddenly had no idea what step to do next. I stopped moving and looked into his eyes. He looked back at me, waiting for me to move so that he could respond and partner me.

Playing at being ballerina at home, about age four.

My grand introduction to the stage: singing a solo in my school's Christmas pageant.

This is from a photo shoot Terry Shields arranged at her ballet studio in South Carolina. I was about eleven.

Trying out a "fish dive" with Dad—my first pas de deux partner—at my grandmother's house.

Grand jeté under the oak tree in my yard in Summerville, South Carolina.

My mother took this photo on the balcony of our New York City apartment in 1988. I was wearing a real New York City Ballet tutu for the first time, for a performance with the School of American Ballet.

Dancing with Arch Higgins during SAB's performance of Balanchine's *Serenade* at the New York State Theater, at the age of fifteen.

In costume for the role of the Maid in my first *Nutcracker* as an apprentice with the New York City Ballet, in 1989.

Waltz of the Flowers costume from *The Nutcracker.*

Hot Chocolate costume from *The Nutcracker* . . . along with a famous visitor. Meeting Michael Jackson was definitely a highlight of my first *Nutcracker*.

The *Waltz Project* performance with James Fayette during which I hurt my back, a serious injury for a dancer.

Dancing in the third movement corps from Balanchine's *Brahms-Schoenberg Quartet,* in the early nineties.

Now a soloist, leaping as the lead in the Winter section of Jerome Robbins's *The Four Seasons*.

Visiting an ailing but still elegant Alexandra Danilova at her apartment.

The dreaded ice bucket.

On tour in Italy with one of James's independent performing groups.

Jerome Robbins's *The Concert* with Russell Kaiser and Ethan Stiefel in the midnineties.

George Balanchine's *Divertimento No. 15*. I remember being very self-conscious of my body in the tutu during these performances.

From my sister's wedding, in the dress I had to buy because I could not fit into the original bridesmaids' dress.

Graduating from Fordham University in the spring of 1998, during my year away from dancing.

Francis Patrelle's *Romeo and Juliet* with James. Not back with City Ballet yet but performing again and on the road to recovery.

Karin von Aroldingen coaching New York City Ballet principal dancer Jenifer Ringer in George Balanchine's *Robert Schumann's "Davidsbündlertänze."*

[Brian Rushton. The George Balanchine Foundation Interpreters Archive]

In the studio with Peter Martins.

Fellow principal dancer Wendy Whelan took this picture of me preparing my pointe shoes during a rehearsal of Robbins's *Dances at a Gathering* while the company was on tour in China.

Le Baiser de la Fée
(original version, 1937),
Maria Tallchief coaching
Jenifer Ringer and Nikolaj
Hübbe, in 2003.

[Brian Rushton. The George
Balanchine Foundation Archive
of Lost Choreography]

"Fish dive" with Philip Neal during the Wedding Scene from Peter
Martins's *The Sleeping Beauty*—just like the photo with my dad!

Dancing the girl in pink from Robbins's *Dances at a Gathering* with Jared Angle as the boy in purple.

Swanilda in Balanchine's *Coppélia* with Damian Woetzel.

Peter Martins's *Thou Swell* with James.

Grand jeté as the Sugar Plum Fairy.
The setting is just a bit different from my backyard under the old oak tree.

From a fashion-meets-dance photo shoot for a cover story of *Dance Magazine*. My costume, for Melissa Barak's *Call Me Ben*, was designed by J. Mendel.

Peter Martins's *Swan Lake*.

In rehearsal with James.

On the way to the church, in the wedding dress that the saints of the NYCB's amazing costume department saved from disaster.

It's July 29, 2000, and we just said, "I do."

From the infamous performance of "Sugar Plumgate" with my wonderful partner, Jared Angle, 2010.

Self-portrait with stage makeup! Now you can see why it takes so long to prepare for a performance . . .

Balanchine's *Serenade* with James and my good friend and dressing-room-mate Maria Kowroski.

I have always been proud of this picture of the Wind Waltz from Robbins's *Dances at a Gathering* because Sébastien Marcovici and I are completely in sync.

Alexei Ratmansky's *Russian Seasons*.

Waving at my daughter in the front row during final bows after Francis Patrelle's *The Yorkville Nutcracker.*

Backstage with Grace after a matinee of Balanchine's *The Nutcracker.*

Our family.

I said one word to him: "Blank!" and watched as panic entered his own eyes when he realized that he didn't know what to do next either.

So I spoke another word. "Spin!" I told James, and I got up *en pointe* and started turning around and around in the middle of the stage, hoping I still looked somewhat tragically in love with my Romeo. After the briefest of pauses, James started to run around me, looking ardent and as if he had intended to passionately run around me all along. Eventually, one of us was able to figure out where we were supposed to be in the choreography, and we resumed the real steps. James still blames me for the entire incident. But as far as I'm concerned, it was a meeting of the mindless . . .

My other favorite blanking memory happened while Peter Boal and I were dancing Twyla Tharp's *Beethoven's Seventh*. Her choreography for us was lightning quick, and the music often rushed us along with its intensity; she had choreographed the ballet on Peter and me, and we knew it inside out. Many of our entrances began in a similar fashion, with Peter carrying me onto the stage in a *grand jeté* lift. After one such entrance, Peter put me down gently on the floor and moved around in front of me to begin our dance. I looked at him and said, "Blank."

Peter stopped and looked at me for a second, and then, never changing facial expression, he went into a wild, spontaneous, fast-moving solo. I stood there watching him for a second and then started my own jiggling improv behind him, giggling uncontrollably. Finally, when it was apparently time for us to leave the stage, Peter mercifully danced around behind me, picked me up, and carried me offstage. Thank goodness he could think on his feet!

Dancers aren't the only ones who blank; sometimes our musicians blank as well. At City Ballet, we're privileged not only to dance to some of the most beautiful music ever composed but also to have some of the finest musicians play that music for us. These artists are dedicated to their craft and will spend hours practicing, obviously because they want to play the music beautifully but for another reason as well: they feel an intense responsibility to support the dancers by playing the music consistently, precisely, and artistically. And the musicians are truly wonderful and rarely make mistakes that affect the dancers.

But every now and then, it happens, because nobody is perfect. During a performance of a Balanchine ballet called *Robert Schumann's "Davidsbündlertänze*," I was dancing a section with three other dancers. Peter Boal was once again my partner. The music is scored for a single piano, and the piano is placed right on the stage with the dancers. The music for this section is slow and contemplative and has many repeats built in. The pianist must have forgotten whether or not he had already played one of the repeats and was trying to make up for it, because he repeated one of the phrases a third time. This was extra music for the dancers, and we had no choreography for it. We all realized what was happening and looked into each other's eyes, wondering who was going to take the lead. We all knew someone had to decide to do something, and no one wanted to be that person. Plus, two dancers could have decided to take control with different solutions, leading to a disaster that would have made the mistake obvious to the audience.

Thankfully, Peter Boal took the initiative, but I wasn't happy with how he chose to fix the problem. He gallantly took my hand, gently turning me to face the audience, and gave me a gentle push forward toward center stage. Then he stepped back, gestured in a way that said, "Please, dance," and looked at me. The other two dancers remained motionless, smiled, and waited for me to dance. So I danced. I'm not sure now what I did, but I managed to fill up the time until the familiar music came on again. Maybe this was Peter's revenge for my blank during Twyla's piece.

We have to be ready to catch whatever is thrown at us when we perform. I had a bit of a challenge once during a performance of Jerome Robbins's *Dances at a Gathering* while we were on tour in Tokyo, Japan. The ballet is done by ten dancers, differentiated only by the soft shades of their costumes. I was dancing the part of the Mauve Girl, and the Green Boy was my primary partner in the piece. However, when I came to the stage level during the intermission before *Dances* to put on my pointe shoes, I discovered Amar Ramasar in the Green Boy's costume. Amar wasn't the dancer I'd been scheduled to perform with in that performance, and Amar looked a little stressed out.

"What happened?" I asked.

"Your partner just pulled his calf and can't do *Dances*. I was here anyway to do *Symphony in Three*, so I'm doing *Dances*," Amar replied.

Well, this was a surprise. But I wasn't that worried about it. Yes, *Dances at a Gathering* is a difficult hour-long ballet, but I'd performed it for years, and Amar and I had danced it many times together. Amar was a great partner, and I knew we would be fine, even without any rehearsals. I told Amar that.

"I know this will be okay," Amar said. "I'm just worried about doing *Symphony in Three* afterwards."

I understood. *Dances* is a challenging piece, and to then turn around and do the pas de deux in Balanchine's *Symphony in Three Movements* would be very hard. I knew now why Amar looked worried.

"Just take it one entrance at a time," I suggested, and Amar nodded.

"Yes. I'll get through it. I just want to do well in both."

By the time I had my pointe shoes on, there were only a couple of minutes before the curtain went up.

"Should we try anything?" Amar asked.

"No, I really think we will be fine," I said. "Let's just dance and enjoy it." Plus, I figured that if we did try some moves and they went badly, it would just make us nervous.

Amar agreed. He gave me a hug and a wink and said, "It's going to be fun."

He was great in the performance, and we had no problems except for the one musical surprise that happened during our mazurka pas de deux. This time, instead of having too much music, we had too little. The pianist mistakenly cut out one of the repeats in the music, and we were suddenly dancing the wrong steps to the wrong music. Amar and I kept doing the choreography in sequence, not sure how to pick up where the music was in a coordinated fashion.

Finally I heard something in the music that sounded like a good place for us to join in, and I turned around and said to Amar, "Flip me."

After the fact, I realized that this was actually a cruel place for me to decide to pick up the choreography. The "flip" was one of the more difficult partnering moves; Amar had to pick me up, toss me into a half turn, and catch me in midair. There were many things I could have chosen that didn't require split-second timing and coordination between the two dancers. And as I went into the preparation for the step, the thought occurred to me that because Amar and I hadn't rehearsed this pas de deux since the last time we had performed it over a year ago, there was a chance that this flip could go very badly.

Luckily Amar knew exactly what he was doing, and the flip went just fine, as if we had rehearsed it that afternoon. Caught up with the music, we continued with the pas de deux, trying to look as if nothing unusual had happened. The pianist felt terrible, but we assured her that all was fine and that everyone makes mistakes. And Amar went on to do a stellar *Symphony in Three Movements*; he was exhausted afterward, but what a story to tell.

Perhaps one of the strangest performances I was a part of took place while I was on a gig in Verona, Italy. Nikolaj Hübbe, a Danish ballet star who had moved over to City Ballet, asked me to dance with him in a string of five performances for Carla Fracci's company. It was a wonderful and thrilling opportunity, especially because it was a difficult period in my life personally; I was discouraged and in the early throes of my struggle with weight. Nikolaj had always been supportive of me and we had danced together often; I think he was trying to give me some inspiration and encouragement.

The pieces we were dancing were way out of my realm of experience. They were from the older, traditionally classical ballet world, not the neoclassical Balanchine world. The first ballet I was performing was the famous *Pas de Quatre*, choreographed in 1845 on the four greatest ballerinas of the time. It was performed at Her Majesty's Theatre in London

only four times by the original cast of ballerinas, who were each wor-
shipped as stars and had tremendous egos; apparently it was a miracle
that they all danced in the same ballet at the same time. The ballet is
laden with history and needs to be danced subtly with proper romantic
port de bras and demure grace. It is romantically classical and not the
kind of modern ballet that dancers from New York City Ballet are
trained to dance.

The other ballet Nikolaj and I were dancing was *Giselle*, another ballet I had no experience with, but at least here we were not doing the entire thing. Three other couples were splitting the pas de deux with us, so
that each couple did a section in turn. Carla Fracci, one of the most
famous ballerinas of her generation, and her partner danced the final
section.

The whole experience was amazing for me. We arrived a week in
advance so that we could rehearse with the other dancers. The costume
shop there made brand-new costumes just for us. I had to learn how to
fix my hair in the old-style bun where the hair drapes in front of the ears
before sweeping to the back. The other dancers tried to help me attain
the proper romantic style and classical body shapes for the ballets, and
Nikolaj was supportive with his big laugh and passion for dance. And
then there was Verona itself, home of Romeo and Juliet, with its pink
streetlights glowing in the misty nights.

The performances were a thrill, and all went well until the last performance. Susan Jaffe, a beautiful principal dancer with American Ballet Theatre, was one of the four ladies in *Pas de Quatre* along with Carla
Fracci, a very young Lucia Lacarra, and me. Right before the performance, Susan hurt her calf. She wasn't going to be able to dance full out,
but she had gotten into costume and was ready to perform the piece in
whatever limited way she could. We had no understudies.

However, because of the insurance policies of the theater, the stage
manager would not allow Susan to perform injured. Suddenly, *Pas de
Quatre* had become a pas de trois. Because of Susan's part in the ballet,
there were several times when she would dance while the rest of us

watched. Just before the curtain went up, she tried to teach Lucia one of those solo parts. And then, with but a brief warning, the curtain suddenly rose.

The three of us popped into the famous opening pose. We were supposed to be peacefully grouped around the center girl, who balanced *en pointe*, like petals of a flower. But I was so flustered that instead of hitting the position with a more romantic style, my body instinctively went into what it knew best: Balanchine style. I was meant to be peering under my arm poetically, but instead I arched my body back, face lifted proudly to the balconies. As I stood there, I realized my mistake and slowly tipped my body over into a more appropriate line. Right away in the first section, we came upon our first moment when Susan was supposed to dance by herself.

I settled gracefully to my knee, thinking that surely this was not going to be my problem. I was the least experienced in this ballet, so no one would expect me to take any initiative. They had already tried to teach Lucia some steps to another part, so perhaps she would take on the responsibility for all of Susan's solos. Furthermore, Carla Fracci was the major star of the evening. If anyone should have extra featured dancing, it should be her, and I was not about to step up when it might offend the important ballerina.

But then, after we had all knelt onstage for a few counts of music with no one dancing, Carla turned those famous giant brown eyes on me, made a grand gesture that in ballet mime means "Get up," and said to me, in a very low commanding voice, "*Move*."

Well, I moved. I stood up immediately and started dancing around, racking my brain for the steps that I'd seen Susan do in previous performances. I knew there was a slow arabesque in there. The trick was to keep myself in the style of the piece and not go on autopilot and look as if a time machine had transplanted a Balanchine dancer into the 1800s. I'm not sure I succeeded, but my efforts seemed to satisfy Carla. During my little impromptu solo, I heard Nikolaj's rumbling chuckle from the wings. He was loving this, especially because since he came from both the classical tradition of the Royal Danish Ballet and the Balanchine style of New York City Ballet, he knew exactly how wrong I was getting it and the reasons why.

The piece progressed, and we made it through to the finale. I thought that the excitement was over, but then before my own entrance I realized there was yet another solo for Susan. A feeling of inevitability came over me even before those huge brown eyes swung in my direction again. I had no idea what Susan did at this point in the ballet; I was usually preparing for my own entrance and not paying that much attention to the other dancers' steps.

What did ballerinas do in these romantic ballets when the music was fast? I only knew what Balanchine or Robbins would do. Didn't those romantic sylphs run around on the tips of their toes a lot? I took a deep breath and plunged onto the stage. I ran *en pointe* from one side of the stage and back again, trying to look like a flitting fairy. I must have run around *en pointe* for about four measures of music. I heard Nikolaj's laugh boom out from the wings. I was trying to look serene and joyful, but I had the feeling that I really just looked harried. Finally Susan's music was over and my own was starting; I could start doing steps that I'd actually rehearsed. With relief I continued the finale as my own self, and the curtain came down.

After the applause was over and the curtain was down for the last time, Nikolaj burst from the wings, running on his tiptoes and laughing in imitation of me. He proceeded to reenact the whole ballet for all of us with great enthusiasm. Little did I know that Nikolaj would continue to relish retelling this story for the rest of the time he was in City Ballet. At least my frantic fish-out-of-water moments had brought him a great amount of lasting joy. And moments like these are what make live performances so exciting. You never know what might happen, bad or good.

Chapter Eight

 ✑

The Other Side

In July 2000 my life was in a completely different place from where it had been two years before. I was now a principal dancer with the New York City Ballet, and I was about to be married. My mother was horrified when I informed her that I wanted to be married in New York City. She didn't think she could ever pull off a New York wedding, and our budget was very limited. But I'd become the person I was in New York City. It was where James and I had met and walked and loved, and no other place felt like home to me. So my mom gamely accepted the challenge, and the two of us started the planning ten months in advance.

James was named after his father, who was from Connecticut; his mother, Benita, was from Spain. His family was Catholic, and though we wanted to be married in a Protestant ceremony, it was important to James and his family that the Catholic Church recognize our marriage. We were able to find a Catholic priest from the church James had attended in the city who was willing to take part in our Protestant wedding, led by a pastor whom I'd known at All Angels', the Reverend Jonathan King. The Catholic priest would be able to give the blessing of the Catholic Church to our marriage. Both priests wanted us to attend premarital counseling with them, and the Catholic Church required us to go to a group couples counseling seminar. Needless to say, we felt very well prepared by the time we got married.

We were married in the Cathedral Church of Saint John the Divine, the largest Protestant cathedral in the world. We chose the cathedral as a nod to James's Catholic family tradition and also because Reverend

King was on staff there. Since we wanted a smaller wedding, with just eighty guests, we decided to have the ceremony in the front choir section of the church, which made that huge space feel very intimate.

Looking back on it now, there are probably things I would change about the events before and after our wedding. But of the ceremony itself, I would change nothing. Little things certainly went wrong during the day: we thought at one point we had run out of wine during the reception, and our car never came to pick James and me up from the reception. But I didn't care about any of it. I was so happy, I felt that nothing could ruin my day once it had finally arrived. I have the dearest memories of this time: my sister quickly marking my leg with a blue magic marker right before I was to walk down the aisle because I'd forgotten the "something blue"; my dad touching my arm as we walked down the aisle and murmuring, "Walk slower, honey"; the happy tears bright in my mother's eyes; James's face looking pale and serious and full of love as I walked toward him; the sniffles of my bridesmaids and beloved friends from the company, Elizabeth and Yvonne, as they sat behind us; watching my friends and family take communion, even those who were not churchgoers, out of a sense of honor and celebration; praying beside James for the first time as man and wife. At the reception, my sister, the matron of honor, played a Gershwin prelude on the piano for our first dance. I felt tremendous joy.

I also felt huge relief because, to my surprise, I was actually wearing a wedding dress. Though a wedding isn't really about The Dress, sometimes it feels like it is, and just days before, it had looked like I might be a bride wearing a sequined prom dress.

I had chosen to wear the dress my mother wore at her own wedding, thirty-three years before. She had bought it off the rack for herself in the 1960s, and it was a beautiful long-sleeved, empire-waisted gown. My sister had worn it when she got married, and I knew I would feel special wearing the same dress my mother and sister had both gotten married in. The problem was, I also really wanted a strapless dress, and I casually thought that it would be easy to alter my mother's dress.

My parents were living in Virginia at this time, and my mom found a seamstress who was willing to convert the dress into the style that I wanted. She seemed to know what she was doing. We had some fittings at Christmastime while I was in Virginia guesting as the Sugar Plum Fairy at a local school's performances of *The Nutcracker*. However, when I returned to her shop in March during City Ballet's spring layoff period, the fitting didn't go so well.

I stepped into her dressing room, eager to see how I looked in the dress in which I was to be married. I slipped it over my ankles and moved it over my hips—where it stuck. It would not move. I tugged. Here we go again, I thought. But this time I knew it wasn't my weight that was the problem; I was at my post-performance-season thinnest and it appeared that the seamstress had just made the dress too small. She promised me that she could fix it and that I didn't need to be worried. I decided to trust her and put it out of my mind. The next time I would see my dress was a couple of days before the wedding, when my parents brought it to New York City with them.

July was a bit of a whirlwind for James and me because the first three weeks of the month were spent in Saratoga Springs performing with the company during their regular summer season there. We were to get married during our week off before the rehearsal period for our summer tour. My parents arrived in the city, and my mom and I ran around doing various last-minute errands for the wedding. My mom was still very nervous about being in charge of a New York City wedding and was driving me a little nutty with her anxiety about everything going perfectly. And since we were trying to save money, we were doing a lot of the small things ourselves. Finally on Wednesday night, three days before the big day, I excitedly tried on my wedding dress alone in my apartment. It was a disaster.

Not only was it still too small, but the seamstress had also created a strange asymmetrical line running down the back of the skirt in her attempt to correct her previous mistake. I was dumbfounded and had no idea what to do. The wedding was on Saturday.

Early the next morning, I placed a frantic call to the costume department of City Ballet and left them a message pleading for their help. Then I dashed off to the restaurant to attend my bridesmaid's brunch. I told no one what was happening because I didn't want the whole brunch to be about my dress. And I really didn't want to tell my mother because she had so much on her mind and I knew it would upset her. But after all the girls had left I took my mom aside.

"Mom," I said, holding her arm. "I have to tell you something. I tried on my dress last night, and it does not fit."

I watched my mom's face go slack and the blood drain away. I saw a look of dismay and pain in her eyes that clearly showed she wasn't worried about the dress or the wedding, she was worried about *my* being disappointed. In that moment I realized that all of the anxiety she had expressed over the wedding was really her fear that I would not have the perfect day for myself.

"It's going to work out," I told her. "I'll either buy a different dress or get this one fixed. Don't you worry about it, because I'm not."

I realized then that I really wasn't worried about it. The wedding was more about marrying the man I loved and celebrating the support of my family and friends than having the perfect dress and the perfect food and the perfect music. My bridesmaids were wearing silver dresses, and I had a silver dress in my closet, left over from a City Ballet gala. I could just wear that if I had to, I thought.

Just in case, I walked home from the brunch and stopped in every dress shop along the way to look for a white dress. The only one I found was tight and mermaid-style and covered with sequins. I thought the silver dress in my closet would be better.

Just as I had given up my search, I got a call from Dottie and Norma, the wonderful ladies from City Ballet's wardrobe department, and they told me to come right over with my dress. I rushed to the theater, and we assessed the situation. Dottie and Norma discovered that the seamstress from Virginia had actually cut material from the dress rather than folding it back as a seam, in case it had to be adjusted. She had tried to cover up the mistake by pulling the material up and tilting the zipper off-center. Basically, it was a complete mess, and they really didn't know if they could fix it.

Dottie and Norma looked at the dress, looked at me, and told me to go away and come back in the morning, and they would see what they could do.

I came back Friday morning, the day before our wedding. Dottie and Norma had performed a miracle. In a bin of discarded fabric they had found some white lacy material and inserted it into the back center of the dress to make a kick pleat. It was actually lovelier than before. I could hardly believe what a beautiful job they had done.

So I was married in my mother's wedding dress after all, thanks to those amazing ladies from the costume department. They were accustomed to working last-minute miracles to make ballerinas look just right onstage; it shouldn't have surprised me that they could work one more miracle to make me look just right on my wedding day. And my mother really was able to give me a wonderful New York City wedding!

James and I enjoyed being married in the same way that any regular couple would; we made dinner together, went for walks in the park, went out to movies or Broadway plays, and took care of each other when we were sick. One real difference for our marriage, though, was that we also worked together, very closely. We were one of the few married couples in the ballet world, and we were partnered often in performances. For five years we danced together as a married couple, and James will forever be my favorite partner onstage.

In 2002, however, James began to think of retiring. He was thirty-two and had been offered a job with the American Guild of Musical Artists, the dancers' union. He had always been an active member of the Dancer's Committee at City Ballet and had caught the attention of Alan Gordon, the head of the union, who asked him to come and work full time as the New York area dance executive. However, just before James was to tell Peter of his decision to stop dancing, Peter surprised James after a performance one night and promoted him to principal dancer. It seemed like a "God thing." James felt that he couldn't turn down the opportunity to be a principal dancer at the New York City Ballet, so he ended up putting off Gordon's invitation and dancing another three years.

Eventually, in 2005, James felt that it was truly time for him to retire. Male ballet dancers tend to retire in their midthirties because of the wear on their bodies; principal women tend to retire around age forty. His body was hurting, and he was weary of a dancer's unpredictable schedule. Plus, he wanted to have a "real" job before we started trying to have a family, something we both hoped for. Since a dancer's career ends so early, he wanted to feel like he had established himself in another job and could support our family before we began trying to get pregnant.

His last performance was in Saratoga Springs, where the company has its annual summer residency at the outdoor Saratoga Performing Arts Center. The new job hadn't been finalized until the spring, so James didn't give anyone very much notice of his retirement. The program for his last show happened to be perfect: he was already scheduled to dance principal roles in both Peter Martins's *Barber Violin Concerto* and Balanchine's *Brahms-Schoenberg Quartet*. The second-movement Intermezzo section of *Brahms-Schoenberg* was a part that James and I had danced together for years, and it was very special to both of us. It is wildly romantic and requires a very strong man to do all the lifts, throws, and dips that the choreography requires. James and I were so coordinated together after years of dancing this movement that we were able to take many of the steps to the extreme. It was very satisfying for both of us and was a part that really showed off James's skill as a partner.

Barber was another ballet that James and I had danced many times together, but only in guest performances outside the company. Unlike James, I had never been cast in this ballet at City Ballet because Peter felt that a taller ballerina should dance the role. James was cast to dance this last performance with Darci Kistler, but we made a special request to Peter that I be allowed to dance the pas de deux with James just this one time. Peter agreed amiably, and Darci as well, so we were allowed to dance both of these pas de deux that had become personally important to us for James's last show.

I will admit to being a little weepy during the performance as I attempted to burn every part of the performance into my memory. James, I think, had decided not to think about the implications of the day until after it was all done. Besides, both of the roles he was dancing were physically very difficult, and male dancers usually do only one of them in any given performance, so he was more concerned with staying strong and dancing well for this, his last show.

Because he had chosen to retire in Saratoga, without any big public announcement, James meant for this to be a low-key private retirement performance. The weather, however, decided that just would not do—perhaps God was giving James a big send-off.

During the first movement of *Brahms*, dark green clouds rolled in across the sky and a strong wind picked up, blowing the curtains of the scenery around the stage of the outdoor theater. The girls' knee-length tulle skirts billowed as they executed Balanchine's already moody, wind-swept movements. As James and I waited in the wings for the upstage curtain to lower during the transition into the second movement, I heard the rumble of thunder and saw bits of leaves and flowers skittering across the stage in sudden gusts. When James and I ran onstage and took our opening pose, I saw that the sky had cracked open to pour torrents of rain on the grassy lawn behind the roof-covered general seating. People were running for cover, a river was running down the aisles of the theater and gushing into the orchestra pit, and some audience members closest to the outside edges of the roof had opened up their umbrellas right there in their seats.

It certainly made the Intermezzo more tempestuous and romantic. It also made James and me relax. We looked at each other, smiled, and knew that we needed to remove the pressure to have a flawless, special last performance together. We should enjoy dancing together and enjoy the performance as a single moment in time, to be lived and treasured just as we had done so many times before.

Throughout our first entrance, lightning and thunder increased in frequency as the storm grew stronger. The climax of the storm came during James's solo, just as he was completing the phrase, which ended in a big double *saut de basque* to the knee. There was a giant, stage-shaking boom of thunder, and the theater suddenly lost electricity.

Now, since it was a matinee performance, we were not plunged into complete darkness as we would have had it been nighttime, but because of the storm it was still very dim and certainly an unusual situation. True to the professionalism of the dancers of City Ballet, the three corps ladies who were onstage dancing at the time kept going as if nothing had happened. Even though the orchestra faltered a bit because their pit lights had gone out, the dancers kept their rhythm and maintained their grace. Then, just before James and I were to return for our final entrance, the generator kicked in and the stage lights came back up.

The rest of the performance took on a dreamlike quality for me as the wind blew the curtains of the set around and I was tossed and turned around the stage by my husband. I felt such a burst of pride for James and his career and a huge sense of gratitude for the times we had danced together both before and after we were married. Dance careers are short, and their end seems sudden, no matter how much thought and preparation may have gone into the decision to retire. For James, this was the end of a career he had pursued since he was a child, something that he had excelled at and a field in which he was an expert. But it was also a beginning; he would be entering the workforce in a whole new way and have a chance to advocate for dancers across the country.

It was certainly an ending for me too. I was deeply sad to be losing James not only as a dancing partner but also, and more importantly, as a companion at the theater. We had been given the opportunity to travel around the world together as dancers of the New York City Ballet, and now I would be traveling without him. I was surprised to discover how much I relied on him for so many small things; perhaps this would be another chance for me to grow some more. I at least had to figure out how to get myself from the hotel to the theater all by myself when I was in a new city.

James's retirement also held the promise of a new beginning for us as a couple; once he had started his new job, we could start planning a family. God had given James a wonderful transition, with no lag time between jobs; he retired from dancing in July and started his new job at AGMA in September. We were ready to begin thinking about babies.

We were still living in a one-bedroom apartment at the time, but the week after James's retirement and right before we were to go away on vacation, we got a postcard informing us that the studio apartment next door to us was up for sale. We realized that this might be our only chance to afford a two-bedroom apartment: we could buy the studio next door and combine it with our apartment. So while on vacation on the Outer Banks, we negotiated the purchase of the studio.

The following year and a half was filled with a great deal of upheaval: James started his new job and dealt with the very difficult transition from dancer to nondancer; we bought the studio, hired an architect, and then moved out to a temporary apartment while our home was completely gutted; I tried to adjust to hardly seeing my husband during the week when I was used to seeing him all day, every day. What was supposed to be three months of renovation ended up taking over six, and we still had to do many of the changes in our apartment ourselves. Renovating in New York City isn't fun, especially on a budget. But ultimately, we found ourselves the proud and exhausted owners of a two-bedroom apartment.

One change in our life that helped us through the stresses of that time was the new church we were attending: Redeemer Presbyterian Church.

After we got married, James and I sought a church where we could have a new beginning and an identity as a couple, and Redeemer was a wonderful fit for us. Though I'd loved All Angels', I knew it was important to find a church that James and I felt equally at home in, and James was drawn to Redeemer. The church had great teaching and a community that was outreach-minded and generously welcoming. Since the Christian walk is never finished, and James and I were very aware of many areas in our lives that still needed healing and grace, we knew we would need to have a consistent Christian community. As we struggled with the changes in our lives, sometimes successfully and sometimes not, we clung to God and the structure we found at Redeemer for stability.

Despite all of this upheaval, the show certainly had to go on, and I was hard at work at City Ballet. I felt more confident in myself as an individual at City Ballet, more grown up. While earlier in my career I'd been silent and subservient toward the ballet masters and Peter in particular, now I felt that I could have real conversations with them about the roles I was to dance and how I was to dance them. I felt assured in the decisions I had to make for myself, even on the rare occasions when they brought me into conflict with the artistic staff. One memory stands out for me: the moment when I realized that no one at the company, not even Peter, had the power to make me lose my sense of self-worth anymore.

We were in a two-week run of Peter Martins's full-length *Swan Lake* shortly after James retired, and I was dancing the Swan Queen in the first week. I was also scheduled to dance one of the divertissements in the third act, a pas de quatre that Peter had choreographed, on some of the shows where I was not the Swan Queen.

The role of the Swan Queen is very difficult, and usually dancers portraying her don't do other parts during a run of the ballet. But I was a new Swan Queen, and they wanted me to remain in my old parts even while I danced the lead. Normally I would have done my best to do this, but this time, I was hurting.

An old injury in my foot was starting to bother me, and I was becoming worried that I would tear my plantar fascia, the muscle that runs along the bottom of the heel, once again. After my first performance as the Swan Queen, I woke up the next morning and could hardly walk. I realized I should pull out of the pas de quatre. I figured this was a logical choice; it was much easier to replace me in the relatively short divertissement, which had multiple casts, than to rehearse my partner with a new Swan Queen for an entire full-length ballet. I had put in six weeks of rehearsals, a great amount of time to City Ballet's way of working, into the role of Swan Queen. I did not want all of that work to be for nothing. Plus, the particular style of steps in the pas de quatre, short, half-skippy mazurka steps, really aggravated my foot.

For a week I'd been warning the ballet master in charge of the pas de quatre that I might not be able to do it, but he avoided me and resisted me and then finally said I would have to talk to Peter. From this, I gathered Peter would not be happy. The old me might have tried to dance through the pain, just to please management and make it easier on everyone, but I asked to see Peter anyway, knowing that it was the right thing to do for my body.

Peter knew why I was coming and greeted me already angry. Now, I know that Peter has a great deal of pressure on him at all times; running a major ballet company isn't at all easy, and there are multiple stresses and problems that bear on every situation. I've had a long and complicated professional history with Peter, and we have had both good and bad moments. His mood could have nothing to do with the people around him at any given time—he might have had a bad board meeting or learned that funding for a certain project needed to be cut. I'm sure the responsibilities he faces are very difficult at times. But for whatever reason, that day our meeting didn't go well.

"Peter," I said, "I think I have to pull out of the pas de quatre. My foot is really bad, and I think if I do all the performances, I'll possibly injure myself and be out for the entire season."

"How can you do that?" he demanded. "Now that you had a great first Swan Queen, you are just going to pull out of the pas de quatre?"

"No," I replied, "it isn't like that at all. The pas de quatre really hurts my old injury, and I just don't think I should add it on top of Swan Queen."

Peter actually pulled me out of his office and into the hallway. I'm not exactly sure why.

"How can you do this? What am I supposed to do?" he berated me loudly. "You are not thinking about me!"

I blinked at him, flabbergasted. Was I supposed to have been thinking about him? Whatever did he mean?

"Peter, if I do the pas de quatre, I'm afraid that I'll be out for the rest of the season," I repeated. "Then you'll have to replace me in all of my ballets." But I also knew there were already alternate casts for the pas de quatre, so I didn't understand what the big deal was.

"I can't believe you would do this to me," Peter said, and stormed into his office. I walked away down the hall, shaken from the encounter, but also knowing that I'd been in the right. And I didn't end up dancing the pas de quatre.

It was really an "aha" moment for me: Peter no longer had any power over me or my sense of self-worth. Because I'd come into the company so young, I had related to Peter as a child would relate to a parental figure. I'd desired to keep him happy and had relied on his positive opinion almost as if we were family members in a dysfunctional relationship. But in reality he was just my boss, and though I had to submit to him as I worked at my job, I could still keep my sense of identity safe from him and relate to him as one professional adult to another. The ballet world is a narcissistic world made up of circles of interlocking insecurities. I could break my own little circle, however, and refuse to feel insecure. I was my own woman, loved by God, and going forward the best I could with integrity and honor. In the past I would have assumed Peter was in the right, and would have taken all of the guilt and pain upon myself; this time I thought, Well, he was in a bad mood. And that was not something I needed to absorb into myself.

————

The arrival of the spring of 2006 meant that it was time for the bian-
nual Diamond Project, a season filled with brand-new choreography
specially commissioned for NYCB's dancers. I was working on what
would become *Russian Seasons* with a choreographer from Russia
named Alexei Ratmansky, whom no one at City Ballet yet knew much
about. Ratmansky was coming to choreograph for City Ballet after having been the director of the Bolshoi Ballet in Moscow and would soon
be recognized as one of the most talented choreographers to appear on
the dance scene in years.

I've always enjoyed the process of being choreographed on. Being a
part of a new ballet is completely different from learning a ballet that is
already choreographed. When I learn an older ballet, I often have preconceived ideas of how my part should be danced. The ballet might be
one that I've watched for years and seen several other ballerinas dance,
which influences how I'll dance the role. I might like the way one
woman danced it but not another; to my discredit, I might egotistically
think that I have a better way to dance it than anyone who has ever gone
before me (in which I'm invariably proved wrong). But I'm always eager
to learn the steps and see how the choreography fits my body and how it
complements or challenges my way of dancing. It is a chance to explore
how I might bring something of myself to a role already laden with history while still being able to honor the choreography and the dancers
who have gone before me.

There is no history, however, when I'm chosen to dance in a new choreography. I've probably never heard the music and rarely have any idea
of the choreographic concept. I enter the first rehearsal with anticipation
and wariness, not sure what is going to be asked of me but excited about
the challenge and flattered that a choreographer wanted to work with
me. Choreographers usually get to choose whom they will work with,
sometimes with advice from Peter or the other ballet masters.

I've been in good ballets and bad ballets and often cannot tell which category a ballet fits into until after some time has passed. Much of what defines a ballet after it premieres has to do with timing and the reaction of both critics and regular audiences. For me to like a ballet as an audience member, I need to have some kind of emotional response or connection to the work. I want to be surprised by the steps and moved by how the performer makes the choreography into visible music. As a dancer actually involved in a ballet, I've found that some ballets have a certain invigorating feeling about them and the dancers know that the work is going to be good; others feel doomed from the start. I've felt that the choreography was either like my second skin or like an uncomfortable coat that I have to put on, but whether the choreography is comfortable to me seems to have nothing to do with whether the ballet is a success or not. It just means I have to work harder with the uncomfortable ones so that I inhabit them well by the time I have to perform them.

Every choreographer has a different style, and some I enjoy more than others. Some work very quickly, driving the momentum of the rehearsal forward so fast that by the end it is hard for me to remember the steps with which we started. Others move very slowly, painstakingly devising their steps one at a time in the studio while the dancers stand in silence, shifting their weight to stay limber and warm. My least favorite type of choreographer to work with is one who has already choreographed the ballet on himself or on another group of dancers and then arrives at our studios to teach us the steps. Often these choreographers are inflexible with their ideas and see only one way of interpreting their work; there is no sense of collaboration with the dancers. I usually cannot feel comfortable in these ballets because I feel that I'm dancing steps made for someone else's body.

My favorite type of choreographer is one who arrives organized and with a plan but ready to work with the strengths and uniquenesses of the dancers he or she has in the studio. This usually produces a great work environment because the dancers feel affirmed and push themselves to give their all to the choreographer, who in turn feels inspired and energized by their commitment and hard work. These ballets are very satisfying to be a part of; while they are still the choreographer's vision, the dancers feel that they have put a bit of themselves into the ballet as well.

Alexei Ratmansky fits into this last category of choreographers, and being in two of his ballets has been incredibly rewarding for me. The 2006 Diamond Project during which he made *Russian Seasons* was just as crazy as our other Diamond Projects had been—the seven choreographers making new works had to compete for studio space, dancers, and rehearsal time. I'm sure it was probably a frustrating experience for Alexei because he rarely had all of his dancers in the studio at the same time, but the dancers loved every minute of working with him.

That season, I'd been working heavily with two other choreographers, Elliot Feld and Christopher Wheeldon, at the beginning of our rehearsal period. Elliot, a well-established choreographer who had founded his own renowned company, Feld Ballets NY, was staging his 1969 ballet *Intermezzo No. 1* with six of us in addition to the new ballet he was choreographing for the project. The rehearsals were long and intense. For Christopher's ballet *Evenfall*, he had chosen Miranda Weese to be his lead, and I was to be her alternate. She was injured early on, however, and Chris worked with me on one section of the ballet until she was recovered enough to resume rehearsals. So between Elliot and Chris, my days were very full.

Once Miranda was recovered, it was no longer vital that I be at Chris's rehearsals, and I was suddenly called to Alexei's ballet. I didn't know much about him at the time because it was his first ballet for our company. We were all very curious about him, and the word from the dancers already rehearsing in his ballet was that he was great to work with.

My first rehearsal was for a group section that included five women and five men. Alexei came over to me and quietly said hello, put me into my place in line, and then moved away to work with the men. He had already choreographed part of the section, and the other girls tried to quickly catch me up on the steps I'd missed. The music and movements were quick, and I felt like I was dancing as if I'd just been dropped into very cold water: wide-eyed and floundering.

I also felt a little anxious that first day because I wasn't sure if I'd been called on purpose or not. The women's group for that section included one other dancer of principal rank, Sofiane Sylve; one soloist, Abi Stafford; and two corps women, Gina Pazcoguin and Alina Dronova. I ended up toward the back of that group in the formation, which hadn't happened to me since I had become a principal. Usually principal dancers were kept up front and separate from the group. Perhaps Alexei had me confused with another dancer? But I decided to put my ego aside and enjoy the process because the dancing was fun and Alexei's manner was so gentle and earnest. I figured things would work themselves out, and I could enjoy being part of some good dancing in the meantime.

The ballet was eventually called *Russian Seasons*, and it is indeed in many ways an ensemble piece. There are six women and six men in the ballet, and every part is a good part. The music comprises twelve songs by Leonid Desyatnikov, some sung by a soprano in the orchestra pit, that follow the Russian Orthodox liturgical calendar. There is no real corps de ballet but a group of soloists and principals who dance in ever-changing groups and pairs and singles. And though there is no real story, it somehow depicts the journey of life, from youthful beginnings to mysterious endings. Wendy Whelan and Albert Evans were the center of the piece, and Sofiane and I were pulled out of the group for featured dances. In my role as the girl wearing the green dress, three of my dances were ensemble pieces while in four of them I was set apart.

As time went on, I became increasingly grateful to be a part of this ballet. Alexei was wonderful to work with. His demeanor was quiet and reserved, but it was obvious that his passion for choreography ran deep and his brain was always processing and assessing and moving forward. I felt more inspired in his rehearsals than I had in a long time. I had a huge desire to perform above even my own expectations because I wanted to please him and make him proud he had put me into his ballet. His standards were incredibly high; there were plenty of times I thought I'd executed a step perfectly well, only to have him quietly shake his head, say, "No," and give me five corrections to make it better. He could also dance all of his steps better than any of us. With seemingly no preparation, he could suddenly move his body to the extremes of the movement, still maintaining his articulation, and all we could do was watch him and hope we could emulate his style in a satisfactory way.

The role Alexei gave me in *Russian Seasons* was a gift. Not only did I love performing the piece, I also loved the entire rehearsal process because of how it stimulated my imagination and inspired me to grow as a dancer. Alexei constantly pushed us to dance the steps better and to be more musical. He would have us pick up small musical details with just a gesture or a look, adding subtle layers to how both the dancers and the audience experienced the ballet. Even when I started to feel as if I were getting a certain technical or emotional concept, he would challenge me with another area to work on that hadn't even occurred to me. My technique was improving, and the way I looked at ballet in general was being enriched. I often felt as if I would never match up to Alexei's vision, but even when I'd obviously failed to do what he wanted, he just smiled and said, "Keep working on that. Maybe you will get it tomorrow." And I was determined that I would.

The novelties in my life didn't end with new apartments and choreographies. Even as I was being inspired anew by working with Alexei, James and I were talking about what direction to follow as we went forward with our lives. Close to a year after the premiere of *Russian Seasons*, in 2007, I learned I was pregnant. I was stepping into another new role, this time as a mother. With much prayer, James and I had decided to start trying to get pregnant; James felt secure in his job, and I was thirty-four years old and feeling that I didn't want to be too much older when we had our first baby. I knew I would miss opportunities with the company and that returning to the stage after giving birth would be very difficult, but it seemed well worth it to both of us.

A month after we "opened the door," I took a pregnancy test and saw the little window on the wand instantly change into a pink plus sign. I felt a thrill and went in search of James. We were both a little grumpy that morning for various silly reasons, and he had retreated to our bedroom to get ready for work. I walked into the room. He was tying his tie.

"Look," I said, not at my most eloquent. I held up the white plastic wand. He stopped tying his tie and stared at the stick in confusion. I hadn't told him I'd bought the pregnancy tests, and he didn't know what it was that I held in my hand.

I saw realization dawn on his face as his jaw dropped and his face turned first white and then a bright red. He gave a big laugh.

"Wow!" he exclaimed, and then gave me a slow, gentle hug. We stayed that way for a bit, overwhelmed and probably both starting to freak out a bit at the implications of it all. We had figured we would be trying for a while before we got pregnant, but God had other ideas. Here we go, I thought.

How amazing to realize that there was a life growing within me, cells dividing and becoming organs and blood vessels and limbs, all while I walked around carrying on my everyday life. It was a precious secret that James and I treasured together, telling only our families and one or two close friends for the first three months. Almost every night we prayed for our unborn child, and I already felt so protective of the new person inside of me.

Dancing while pregnant was very different for me. Physically, I was extremely tired, which is typical for a woman in her first trimester. Not normally one who can fall asleep anywhere but at home, I found myself collapsing in sleep on my dressing room floor during my breaks and would wake up to a puddle of my drool on the carpet. Up until the moment a rehearsal or performance began, I would think that there was no way I could ever get through it, but once I was standing up and took to the stage, adrenaline would kick in and I'd be fine.

I also had a version of morning sickness that got worse as the day went on. By evening, I would be very nauseated, which wasn't convenient during the performance season. There were many moments when I stood in the wings preparing to go onstage and eyeing the trash cans under the tissue boxes that were attached to the lighting booms. Well, worst-case scenario, I thought, I just run offstage to the nearest trash can. I never had to put my plan into action, but there were a couple of close calls.

Emotionally, I felt a sense of joy in dancing that was different from anything I'd yet experienced. It was amazing to know that I was dancing onstage with another life inside me. I felt a new freedom in my dancing. The sense of freedom possibly came from the fact that the second I found out I was pregnant, I felt my priorities shift into a new focus on my child. There was no role more important than caring for this baby, no step that needed to be executed to an extreme degree if it would endanger the baby. For the next nine months, my body was not my own but rather the vessel that God had chosen for the nurturing of the particular child that James and I had been given. So I would do my utmost to be a healthy and safe vessel for that child. Every day I tested it out: as a principal dancer, I needed to be able to do my job exceptionally well. If I felt I could do an excellent job safely, I danced another day, but I knew that the second I felt the slightest hesitation, I would need to stop.

During the first three months of my pregnancy I also came to terms with my own mortality as a dancer. I wasn't thinking of retiring at the time, since I was thirty-four and I very much wanted to continue performing. However, the median age of retirement for all dancers is twenty-nine, and I knew that once this baby was born, I might be forced to stop dancing. I might not want to leave the baby, or I might not be able to get my body into dancing shape again after giving birth. A few other ballerinas had come back to work after having children, one who had had twins, but I knew that it was very difficult, and I didn't know how I was going to react to it all. It occurred to me that I needed to go through the thought process of preparing for retirement so that if the need did arise, I would be ready. So I danced those performances knowing that they could be my last, and I felt a bittersweet joy in them for that reason.

The company was in Saratoga Springs when I was in my third month of pregnancy. My waist was starting to thicken, making the costumes tight. I knew it was time to tell Peter, because I wanted him to know before the word got out. I was nervous about it—pregnancy is often looked at askance in the dance world—but Peter was extremely supportive and happy for me and told me stories about his own children.

"This is your time," he said. "Take it and enjoy it and come back when you are ready."

I did a couple more performances in Saratoga, changing a step here and there and dancing slightly larger and more out of breath than usual, and then I was done for a while.

I loved being pregnant. I loved feeling the baby kicking inside me. At the five-month mark we found out we were having a girl, and James threw back his head and laughed with happiness. We decided to name her Grace shortly afterward, named for the gift of grace God freely gives us. Her middle name would be Rebecca, after my sister.

The extra time I suddenly had on my hands while pregnant gave me an unexpected opportunity. The Robbins Rights Trust asked me to assist Jean-Pierre Frolich, a ballet master for City Ballet who specialized in the Robbins repertory, with staging *West Side Story Suite* at San Francisco Ballet and the National Ballet of Canada. This meant I would travel to these companies and work with the dancers there, teaching and coaching the ballet. I found that I really enjoyed the work, and loved collaborating with the talented dancers from these other companies.

Pregnancy was also another time of healing for me—a healing I didn't even know I needed. I watched myself gain forty-five or fifty pounds, about the same amount I'd gained during my "dark period," and I was happy about it. My body changed and grew large and ungainly and the farthest

thing from a ballerina I could imagine. Some ballerinas still look like ballerinas when pregnant. I was not one of those women. But I was fine with
it. It was so beautiful to see how God had constructed my body to nurture
the life inside of me.

Grace was born in January 2008. I did the birth naturally because, being a dancer, I wanted to be able to feel what my body was doing and to
experience it all, even the discomfort. Happily I was blessed with a short
labor and a husband who was very involved with helping me through
each contraction and every moment, and Grace was born with no com-
plications.

I remember coming home from the hospital in a car service called
KidCar that was created especially for New Yorkers who have children
and who don't own cars themselves. Grace was in the car seat sleeping,
and the bright winter sun shone Magic Marker bright on pedestrians
going about their normal Manhattan lives. I looked at Grace and
thought, The whole world has changed completely now that she is here.
But nobody out there even realizes the amazing thing that has happened.

I didn't take ballet class for three months after Grace was born. I spent
my days with her, figuring out how to be a mother and worrying over
every gurgle and snort that she made. There was no pressure from City
Ballet, but I'd intended to start class after six weeks, though a physical
therapist had recommended I wait twelve. However, Grace had colic
and didn't sleep well at first, and I was a stressed-out, exhausted, and
overprotective mother. I was afraid to leave her with someone else, even
for an hour. And after spending entire days caring for my precious
daughter, returning to ballet almost felt like a selfish, self-centered thing
to do. At my most emotional moments I considered quitting dance and
just becoming a mother full time.

However, I knew I needed to get back into class because I had committed to the company. I also still needed to work for the paycheck for
now, and I knew that deep down I still loved to dance. So I returned to
Nancy Bielski's ballet class at Steps and began the painful process of

getting back into shape. I was surprised, after the first couple of days, by how good it actually felt to move to music again, and I realized that I wasn't completely done with dancing professionally after all. I busied myself figuring out a way I could balance being a good mother with being a good ballerina.

My first performance back was once again in Saratoga, almost exactly a year after I'd stopped at the three-month mark of my pregnancy. I danced the role of the Coquette in Balanchine's *La Sonnombula* with a young up-and-coming dancer named Robert Fairchild. I didn't know him very well and felt a little insecure in the rehearsals. I had once again been away for a year and was coming back still a little out of shape. I'd chosen the role of Coquette to return with because the costume was a long dress, and the dancing was not too difficult. It seemed like the perfect thing to come back with.

Robbie was extremely sweet, and we had a great time in the rehearsals. The performances went well too, and I was happy that I had made the effort to get back out onstage in Saratoga, even though it was physically a bit of a push. After Saratoga, I had a couple more months before our fall rehearsal period, during which I could fine-tune my strength and weight.

We found a part-time babysitter who would be willing to get her schedule at the last minute, when I got my City Ballet rehearsal schedule. She also had to work only four days a week because James had the weekends off and I always had Mondays off. We worked out a system where I would text the babysitter as soon as I knew my hours, and she would come for just those particular hours. I would run home every chance I got, in between class and rehearsals and before performances, so that I could maximize the time I got to spend with Grace. Since I lived only eight blocks from the theater, I could usually be home fifteen minutes after a rehearsal ended.

It was a lot of running around for me, but I was happy to be doing it. I often still got to spend the majority of my daughter's awake time with her, even while I was dancing and performing, and I didn't feel that either Grace or my work was suffering. I was sometimes run a little ragged, but it was worth it to still be so active in Grace's daily life.

My performance seasons with the company fluctuated. At the age of thirty-five I was now considered one of the company's more senior ballerinas, and I often had very light seasons because I'd matured out of a lot of the roles I'd danced when I was younger. At other times, the performance seasons were ridiculously busy for me because it seemed all of my rep was going, or I was in a new choreography that required long hours of rehearsal. But our family worked out a rhythm to deal with the ebbs and flows of the City Ballet calendar, and it felt like we were doing an okay job of juggling it all. Life was good.

Chapter Nine

~<del></del>~

Sugar Plumgate

In December 2010 I was cast to be the opening-night Sugar Plum Fairy for the company's annual run of *The Nutcracker*. I was very surprised; I'd never in all my years been cast to do the first night, which is traditionally the only night that gets reviewed during our six-week run of the ballet, unless there are new and noteworthy debuts. In the last few years I'd done only three or four performances of *Nutcracker* each season, since so many of us danced the role of the Sugar Plum Fairy. And in general, Peter didn't tend to cast me in the more classical roles requiring tutus anymore; my rep had drifted more heavily into the romantic and dramatic categories, which were my strengths. Perhaps I was the most senior ballerina available that weekend. Or perhaps I had danced so much the season before, a particularly rigorous season for me, that I came to mind when he was casting for opening night. Whatever the reason, I was first cast. And maybe I should have known that God had a reason for letting that happen.

I had mixed feelings going into the performance. I was honored to be chosen for opening night and happy to be dancing with Jared Angle, a principal dancer and one of my favorite partners in the company. And I did love the role of the Sugar Plum Fairy. At the same time, it usually took me one or two performances of the *Nutcracker* to feel totally relaxed within the role, even though I'd done it for so many years. There was something about dancing Sugar Plum, whether because it always came after a period of not performing or because it had been one of my first principal roles, that made me feel nervous for the first few shows.

With the added pressure of opening the season, I was worried that I would be "tight" and not give my best performance.

The performance went very well, despite my apprehension, and Jared and I were both pleased with our dancing. Relieved that the first show was behind me, I set my mind toward the rest of the month, during which I would be guesting with different ballet schools in addition to the other City Ballet *Nutcracker* performances, and starting my Christmas shopping. The only worry that lingered from that first show was the impending reviews. The relatively new dance critic for the *New York Times* was Alastair Macaulay, and his very strong opinions had wounded many dancers whom I admired. There were stories of dancers begging not to be first cast so that he wouldn't review them. I knew the chances were that I would get a bad review, so I prepared myself for the worst.

The morning of November 28, I'd been awakened as usual by the sounds of some wild pretend game that James and Grace were playing involving spaceships and tinfoil gravity boots. I got my coffee from the kitchen and sat down on the sofa, reading the *New York Times* on my cell phone. And there I saw it, on the first page of the Arts section.

My stomach gave a little lurch when I saw that Macaulay had written the review, but I took a deep breath and plunged ahead to read it. I skimmed through until I found my name. My stomach sank even further, and I looked off into the distance for a moment, actually stunned by what he had written: "This didn't feel, however, like an opening night. Jenifer Ringer, as the Sugar Plum Fairy, looked as if she'd eaten one Sugar Plum too many." In all my years of weight problems, not one critic had called me heavy, and now, ten long years after my recovery, this review appears.

James came into the living room, and I said, "Well, it's happened."

He stopped and said, "What?"

"Did you see the review? It's not good." James's face fell with sympathy. "Oh, I'm sorry, honey."

"He said I had 'one sugar plum too many.'"

"*What?!*"

I handed James my phone and he read through the review, uttering some choice words when he was finished. Then Grace called him to continue their game, and he handed me back the phone, saying, "I'm so sorry, Jen. Don't believe him. We will talk about this later when we have a calm moment."

I sat on the couch, trying to process it. The first thought that flashed through my brain was: Am I overweight? All of my insecurities reared up, and I felt ashamed for the first time in a long while. But then I calmed down and thought, No, I'm not overweight. I had worn the same tutu I'd been wearing for a couple of years; it had been made for me, and it fit just the same as it always did. Was I at my thinnest? No: I got to my lowest dancing size only toward the end of a hard perfor-mance season. But I was definitely not heavy and was at a good perfor-mance weight, which Macaulay had seen me at many times before. So obviously this was *his* problem and *his* opinion, not my problem, and certainly not an opinion I had to agree with and take into myself.

So then I thought, Well, IT has happened: what used to be one of my biggest fears. Someone has called me heavy in the most public way possi-ble. But that morning, sitting on my couch, I decided that Macaulay could call me fat if he wanted to—anyone could. And I was fine with it for two reasons: I didn't feel I was heavy, and someone else's opinion of me had no power over me unless I allowed it. My worth came from being a Child of God, a wife, a mother, a daughter, a sister, a friend, and the best ballerina I could possibly be, and that was enough. I didn't need affirmation or ap-proval from anyone except the Lord, and if someone chose to write badly of me, it couldn't affect me, because, really, who cared?

And that moment, for me, was a huge personal triumph. I faced what at one point would have devastated me and driven me into hiding and a pattern of self-destruction. Yet here I was, feeling a surge of strength as I realized once again the depths to which God had healed me. People will remark about that review to this day and talk about it as if it were a horrible thing that happened to me, but I have to tell them that I look at it as one of the high points of my life. It was the day I faced a personal Goliath and knocked him down with a flick of the wrist.

Now, despite the fact that I didn't let the review affect my self-esteem or how I felt the performance had gone, I still felt bad that the review had been written, out there for anyone to see. It was certainly embarrassing. Even though Macaulay's was just one opinion out of the 2,500 who had been in the theater that night, he got to write his opinion in the *New York Times.* All of the other reviews of the performance in other papers were favorable, and of course not one of them mentioned my weight, but I knew that the *Times* would get the most attention. However, I also knew I could get past that; I'd gotten bad reviews before and survived.

Part of being a performer is having to submit yourself to being reviewed by critics. Arts criticism is a very complicated thing and I think it is very hard to be a good and well-respected critic. There are certainly critics out there whose reviews are thoughtful and who don't seem to come to performances with an agenda or preconceived notions of the dancers or choreographers. They don't play favorites or consistently demonize anyone in particular. These critics have given me good reviews and bad reviews, which I respected because I felt that they were coming to each show fresh and ready to comment on exactly what they saw in that particular performance.

The sad thing about most dancers, and perhaps many performers, is that we retain a very good memory of every bad review we have ever read about ourselves, yet the positive comments are quickly forgotten. It probably stems from the fact that our life is spent seeking perfection and correcting infinitesimal errors of line or technique. If something about our dancing is good, we ignore it because it will take care of itself. We fixate on the parts that are wrong. Ask a dancer what her weaknesses are, and she will be able to give you an immediate and very detailed list. Ask a dancer about her strengths, and she has to pause and think about it.

I've gotten more good reviews than bad during my career, at least that I know of, but I could quote the bad reviews to anyone verbatim. I, like many dancers, have actually tried to stop reading reviews about myself; whether they are good or bad, they corrupt how I might feel about a particular performance and may color how I perform the ballet in the future. It is much healthier for me to go onstage, armed with the help of my coaches, and give it my all for the audience that is there that night, and then let that experience become a part of the past that I share with that audience so that I can move forward and dance again the next night, in a new way for a new audience.

When I read particularly nasty reviews of dancers or any other artists, I always feel disheartened; I know how much work and care and thought and effort has gone into any one performance. I've seen how important each performance is to my colleagues, and I know that every time we step onstage, we're hoping that our performance will move the audience and transport them or lift them up in some way. How deflating to put all that physical and emotional effort into something and then see a critic negate all of your work with a clever barb or two! Of course every artist knows that he is putting himself out there to be commented on, whether with approval or disapproval, but surely there is a way to review artists in a constructive and responsible way. Some critics are quite capable of this, but not all of them.

That morning on my couch, as my daughter ran up to me, planted a kiss on my cheek, and demanded breakfast, I thought that in the grand scheme of things, this review was such a little matter. Who really cared? It would have been awesome to get a great review so that my mom could put it in the memory book of clippings she had kept since I was a child, but since I hadn't, I would just try to get over it as I had my other bad reviews: move forward and forget it.

Well, I wasn't able to move forward and forget it for very long. To my surprise, the Internet exploded with outrage. I was shocked, but it did make me feel good to have so many people rushing to my defense. It was almost unbelievable to see the number of bloggers who picked up the story. Even Perez Hilton, the celebrity blogger, wrote about it, saying to Macaulay, "We thought the reviewers were supposed to review the dancing, not someone's stomach. . . . Not cool, man!"

Before I knew it, what I had thought of as my own very private little moment of internal struggle and triumph became a public story about which everyone had an opinion. The review also happened to coincide with the release of the movie *Black Swan*, which I hadn't seen but was basically a psychological thriller set in the ballet world. There was already a lot of attention on the crazy side of ballet, and Macaulay's review was just crazy enough to focus it on me.

Macaulay fanned the flames a bit by writing a second article in response to all of *his* critics on December 3, 2010. He stood firmly by his review. Even though some of the things he said about me in this article were meaner than the first, I just had to laugh at the sheer preposterousness of it all. I actually almost felt sorry for Alastair because so many people were angry with him on my behalf. My family was very upset, of course—my protective father told me he wanted to call down the powers of the U.S. government on Macaulay. He later assured me he was just being facetious. And the dancers of City Ballet told me they thought the review was ridiculous. I've never had so many knights rushing to my rescue, and I felt incredibly supported.

A day or two after the second article was printed, I got a call from Rob Daniels, the head of City Ballet's press department. Apparently, many news programs wanted me to appear on their shows and comment on the review, but he had narrowed it down to the *Today* show. Rob thought it would be best if I went on one show, talked about it once, and put the matter to rest. I agreed, even as I was stunned to realize how much attention this review had garnered.

It came to me that I'd been wrong in thinking, once again, that this issue was just about me. The review had touched a very sensitive spot for many people. It involved weight and body image and the right of society to have power over determining what was acceptable or valuable about an individual woman's appearance, issues that are heightened in the ballet world but are very real in the nondancing world as well. People's reactions to Macaulay's review were so strong that it became clear they were responding to these issues of female beauty and worth not just in the dance world but in the world in general.

About two weeks after the review came out, I woke at the crack of dawn and carefully got ready for my appearance on *Today*. I'd gone shopping to buy a new outfit for the occasion—I wanted to wear clothes that showed my body and made me feel pretty. I'd also bought some new high heels to add a little bit of glamour. I left the house even before my early-bird daughter woke up and went out to the car NBC had sent to pick me up. I felt nervous and odd. James and I prayed before I left, and I knew that I had many friends and family praying for me. I felt that God was going to use this situation to help not just me but other young women who might be struggling with issues like mine. I knew that this would not be happening to me unless He had planned it, so I went along for the ride, determined to do my best.

I arrived at the studios at Rockefeller Center, and Rob met me at the entrance. His face had a "Well, here we go" smile on it as we were led back to the greenroom area by an assistant. I tried not to have a "Gee, golly" smile on my own face as I looked around at everyone bustling about the business of doing a morning news show. As the assistant turned to leave us, I nervously asked if someone would be doing my makeup. I'd only applied light street makeup, and I knew that I would appear very different on television.

"Oh, if you want, someone can touch you up."

"Yes, please!" I exclaimed with relief.

In the makeup room, the familiar face of Suzy Alvarez, who also did makeup and hair for the dancers at the theater sometimes, greeted me. It was great to see someone I knew, and she made sure I was well taken care of. While I sat in the makeup chair, we watched the *Today* show in progress, and I couldn't believe I was about to be one of the guests on the show. What if it went horribly wrong? What if they sat me on a stool and I fell off it on live television? What if they asked me a really hard question and I sounded like an idiot and it got replayed over and over on YouTube? What if I spit when I talked, or drooled? My brain kept inventing ever more fantastic images of the disasters that could possibly happen until I had to force myself to stop thinking about it. And I prayed.

Rob and I had talked about all the possible questions that I might be asked, and I felt pretty prepared for every eventuality. I also knew that I wanted to be positive and not perpetuate the image of the critic-villain that Macaulay had become on the Internet. There was good that could come out of this whole situation, and I intended to help people see it.

Time passed swiftly, and before I knew it I was waiting off set to take my seat onstage during the commercial breaks. It was strange to watch Matt Lauer and Ann Curry as they did their thing for all of America from the tiny television stage. They were both very focused and professional, and though they had done this every day for a long time, they seemed to be on the ball and interested in every subject they discussed. I also loved watching the cameramen and backstage crew as they orchestrated the movement of different guests and different cameras. I'd experienced a lifetime of live performance, but the world of live television was entirely new to me.

It was very quiet on the set, even when the cameras were not on. During a commercial break I was ushered to a chair where I was to sit for a while so they could put me on camera a couple of times for the little "coming up later" moments they do on these shows. While Matt or Ann was telling the viewers my story and that I would be on later in the hour, I was instructed to sit in my chair, which thankfully was not a stool, and smile at the camera.

Now, I found this incredibly awkward and slightly hilarious. The periods of time that I was to stare smilingly at the camera felt endless. I felt my smile changing from normal to strained to embarrassed to pained. Worse, I could see the words of the prompter scrolling up the screen of the camera that I was looking into, and I could hear Matt reading them.

"Ballerina Jenifer Ringer was said to have eaten 'one Sugar Plum too many' by a ballet critic," he intoned, as I gazed lovingly at the camera. A thought flashed through my mind: Maybe I should not be smiling about this? Should I poke out my lower lip and look sad and pathetic? Maybe I should have one of the assistants run and get me a doughnut so that I could hold it up to my mouth, smile, and then shrug? Each time I had to do one of those preview spots, the images of what expressions I could put on my face ran through my head like a comedy reel.

During the breaks, the people out on the sidewalk looking into the show's set were waving wildly at me with excitement. I knew that none of them knew who I was, and had heard that later on in the show Jessica Alba was to make an appearance. Perhaps the onlookers were far enough away that they saw my dark hair and thought I was Jessica? I waved wildly back to them.

Finally, it was the commercial break before my segment. I gathered my scattered thoughts and focused on what I wanted to say. I felt a few butterflies fluttering under a blanket of odd calm. I said a little prayer, asking God to give me the proper words to say to whatever questions I was given.

Ann sat beside me, said hello warmly, and looked over her notes. And then one of the producers counted us down and I saw Ann snap into her on-camera mode, full of energy, similar to how I've seen dancers come alive in the split second between the wings and the stage.

Ann introduced the history of our segment and then turned to me.

"The first moment when you read those words—what was your immediate reaction?" she asked.

"It made me feel bad," I replied. "It is embarrassing to see something bad written about yourself in print. So it did make me feel bad about myself. But I had to tell myself that it was one person's opinion out of the two thousand people who were there that night. So where I am right now in my life, I was able to kind of move past it."

"Do you feel that there is too much pressure on dancers and that they are likely to suffer eating disorders?" Ann asked.

"Well, it is a field where our bodies are important. As dancers, we're taught to be perfect in every way. Technically, and in every way. I think, for me, I was sixteen when I became a professional. I wasn't prepared to cope with being in an adult performing world so my coping mechanisms turned into eating disorders and body image issues. So for me, it was the inability to cope, really."

Ann then asked me if the movie *Black Swan* was representative of the pressures ballet dancers were under.

I told her that I hadn't yet seen the movie. But I added, "It is a physical profession where we're dancing all day long. So when you are dancing all day long—I'm sure Natalie [Portman] lost weight just from dancing eight hours a day—truthfully you can't do the job if you are too thin, and that's where people run into trouble. That was my problem when I went through my eating disorder—with anorexia you are weak and you can't do the job; you can't perform it well."

"So," Ann said, "your reaction to the writer in the *New York Times* who basically said that you should understand that your line and body is something that should be written about—do you think it should be?"

"I think that this is a really complex question," I replied, trying to make every word count. "As a dancer, I do put myself out there to be criticized. A dancer's body is part of my art form. At the same time, I'm not overweight. I guess I do have a more womanly body type than the stereotypical ballerina. That is one of the wonderful things about the New York City Ballet. We have every body type—we have tall, petite, we have athletic, we have womanly, waiflike . . . we really have every body type out there. They can all dance like crazy, they are all gorgeous. And dance should be more of a celebration of that—that we're seeing these beautiful women with these different bodies all dancing to this gorgeous music. And that's what we should be celebrating."

"So do you want an apology?" Ann asked.

I took a breath. "No, it's his opinion and he is a critic and he is paid to put his opinion in the paper. And I know that as a dancer I'm going to get criticized. And again, there were two thousand people out there. He got to put his opinion in the paper, but everybody else may have a different opinion as well."

Ann then wrapped it up with, "And this morning you got to voice yours. Jenifer Ringer, you are really lovely. Thank you for appearing here and helping us start a dialogue."

I felt much more comfortable talking to Ann than I'd expected. Overall, the questions didn't end up feeling that difficult. The only one that took me by surprise was when Ann asked me if I needed an apology. I hadn't thought about it. But it took me only a moment to realize that no apology was needed. It was over and forgiven, and hopefully now we would all move on.

I was ushered off the set quickly when my segment was over, and suddenly I was on my way home. Rob was pleased with the interview, and congratulatory texts poured into my phone from family and friends. I was happy about it, but the whole experience mostly felt surreal.

In the backseat of the car I looked over at Rob and said, "Okay, so do you think it's over now?"

He smiled slightly and said, "No, I don't think it's over. Alastair might feel the need to respond. And I bet there are going to be many others who will want to hear what you have to say on this issue. But I really think this *Today* show interview is enough for now. What you said is perfect, and it was on live TV, so your words cannot be taken out of context and misconstrued. I think you can let it rest for now."

I agreed with Rob's wisdom. It had been important for me to say something, but now I could let my words stand and hopefully let the whole thing go.

After a moment, Rob chuckled and said, "Now, if Oprah calls, we're definitely going to Chicago!"

I laughed too, imagining the unlikely scenario of appearing on *Oprah*. Wouldn't that be something!

As the day went on and I processed the fact that I'd been on a national morning news show talking about weight issues, I began to reflect on the events of my life twelve years before. Those dark weeks when I'd been so convinced that my life was worthless and that I'd failed at everything—what would I have said if someone had told me that I would one day be on television speaking words of strength and affirmation? And how amazing to think that God might be using my experiences to encourage other young women who might be having problems with their own weight and self-image. I could actually use what I went through to help other women on a much bigger scale than just the few dancers with whom I came in contact in New York.

Just how much this issue meant to people began to hit home as the day wore on. E-mails were sent to City Ballet and then forwarded to me, bearing messages of support. Though I was not really active on Facebook, I had an account with just my family members as friends and received hundreds of messages there from strangers speaking of how they were encouraged by my strength. I even heard from some mothers asking for advice for their own daughters. I wasn't able to respond to any of these messages due to the volume, but was so touched by them and wished I could write every one back.

The rest of that morning was fairly normal for me. I picked Grace up from school and focused on being a mom. Later in the day, she and I were playing on the playground across the street from my apartment building when the day took a strange turn. A nice-looking man approached me with an inquisitive expression on his face.

"Are you Jenifer?" he asked.

"Yes," I answered, assuming he was a dad I'd met on the playground at some point and just forgotten.

But then he reached into his coat, pulled out a microphone, and held it up to me. Over his shoulder I noticed a news van on the sidewalk in front of my home.

"I'm with Channel Two News, and I wanted to ask you a few questions."

"Really?" I said, shocked. I couldn't believe that a news van had actually hunted me down. "How did you know where I live?"

"We have services that can find that out for us. Can I interview you?"

I stared at him, speechless. Surely, I wanted to say, there are many more important and newsworthy things for you to be spending your time on tonight!

"I'm with my daughter right now, so I really don't want to talk. I'm sorry."

He was nice but persistent and gave it several tries. I deflected him by suggesting he call City Ballet if he wanted to schedule an interview. With a regretful look, he said, "Well, it is kind of the news cycle *right now*. We would need to talk today, otherwise . . ."

I understood that if I didn't talk to him now, the chance would be forever gone. I assured him that was quite fine with me, and he went back to his van.

The most disconcerting thing was that the van stayed where it was for another half hour. As I played with Grace on the playground, I felt uncomfortable and worried about going back home. Would there be more of them waiting for me there? This must be a small taste of what famous people feel like, I thought. And it was not pleasant.

The next day I was a tabloid headline. After dropping Grace off at her preschool, I walked to my local Trader Joe's to buy groceries and saw a picture of myself on the front page of *AM New York*. "Fat Ballerina Says 'I'm Not Fat!,'" the caption read. I guffawed out loud on the sidewalk. What was happening? It was too strange for me to grasp, and I just went about my normal life, hoping it would all blow over.

Rob and I agreed to turn down other offers for television appearances, and eventually things seemed to die down. But a month later, in early January, I saw Rob in a hallway of the theater.

"You won't believe this, Jenny, but Oprah called," he said.

Well, it was not Oprah herself, but a producer who was interested in the story and wanted to do a phone interview with me. I was certainly game to do it. Oprah had such a huge audience—I started to wonder what God was doing here. Perhaps He had cast me for opening-night *Nutcracker* just so that this whole Sugar Plumgate, as we had come to call it, would happen. Perhaps God wanted there to be a discussion in the dance world about weight and body issues and eating disorders, and the review from Alastair Macaulay was the perfect catalyst. Whatever the reasons, I was in it for Him.

I did the interview with the producer from *Oprah* by phone. From the start I resolved to just be myself and be honest about my past. I figured that if this was something God wanted to happen, then it would happen and be used for a good purpose. Sure, I wanted to meet Oprah—how cool would that be? But it was not a desperate need, and I could live with or without it.

A few days after my phone interview, I was asked to appear on the show. But first, a producer would come to New York for a couple of days with a camera crew to spend a day following me around and interviewing me. They would get unprecedented access to the backstage area of our theater during classes and performances. The company understood that this was a wonderful opportunity for City Ballet to reach a bigger American audience than they'd ever had.

My parents were visiting at the time, and we had our little apartment set up for guests. When we learned that the camera crew would be spending time with us at home, my poor parents ended up in a hotel so that I could make my apartment look decent.

The producer was a very nice young man named Jason who also happened to have a young daughter at home named Grace. He and the camera crew were very easygoing and patient. They were also troopers—just as they arrived, a snowstorm hit, and none of them had any decent snow gear. Jason spent the whole time in New York tramping around the slushy sidewalks in sneakers that were constantly soaked through.

The team arrived at my house early in the morning to film my family's wake-up routine. James and I tried to be as normal as possible with a camera crew squeezed into our small apartment, and Grace was oblivious to everything but the delightfully fuzzy microphone. Then they followed me to work. I had to do silly things like leave my apartment twice so that they could get the view of my leaving from both inside the apartment and outside in the hallway. They watched company class and a stage rehearsal of *I'm Old Fashioned* by Jerome Robbins, which I would be performing that night. Then they filmed me leaving the theater and returning home to take over the care of Grace from our wonderful babysitter, Michelle Hoag.

The crew filmed me returning to the theater, in the snow, and then filmed all of my preparations for the performance. Then they shot the ballet from backstage. It was a strange experience for me and everyone in the theater to have the camera crew around. The crew was very respectful of the dancers, and the dancers were accommodating about the unusual event, even as some of them took the opportunity to good-naturedly tease me when the cameras weren't looking. I also had to remind myself, right before going onstage, that my focus needed to be on the performance and the two thousand people in the audience that night, not on the cameras backstage.

The next morning the crew came back to do our interview. My family and I prayed beforehand that I would be given the right words to say when it came to the difficult questions. I really wanted my situation to be used to help women who might be feeling shame or self-hatred because of their weight or food issues, and I didn't want to waste this opportunity to be honest about myself if it would in turn help start the healing process in others. I felt very calm during the interview and had no difficulties with the questions. It felt a little strange to be exposing such personal details of my struggles, but it also felt right. Afterward, I felt a sense of peace and knew that God was working.

I was scheduled to fly to Chicago about a week later for the taping of

Oprah. My transportation was arranged, and I was released from re-hearsals with the company. Rob would be accompanying me, for which I was grateful.

A few days before I was scheduled to go, a big blizzard was predicted for the Chicago area. We got a call from Jason that they wanted us to come out a day early to beat the storm. James and I scrambled to prepare for my absence from home. Grace had just turned three and was still in the high-energy stage of toddlerhood. My mom would extend her visit to help James take care of Grace, which was a huge relief. I packed a bag with clothes for the show as well as workout clothes and dance clothes, since City Ballet was in the middle of its winter season. I couldn't just take days off in the middle of the week without rehearsing, if only on my own. When I returned to New York, I was scheduled to dance the role of Spring in Jerome Robbins's *Four Seasons*, which was a very de-manding part. I needed to stay in shape.

The night Rob and I got to Chicago, the blizzard hit, and it was a doozy. My hotel room was on a high floor and I could feel the building swaying in the wind. I woke up the next morning to a white world bro-ken up by sideways snow. Oprah was forced to cancel her day's tapings because of the storm, and everything had to be pushed back. Jason called and said that it was a scheduling nightmare and they had to rear-range everything. Could I stay two more days?

Of course I said yes. And so I spent four days in Chicago with nothing to do. It was a strange little mini-vacation for me. In New York, I'd been spending my days running around between Grace's school, ballet classes, *Nutcracker* gigs, rehearsals, and City Ballet performances. I rarely sat down to rest. Now suddenly, I was in a nice hotel room with no family dinners to make, no toddler snacks to pack, no rehearsals to run to, no three-year-old to bathe and put to sleep. I didn't know what to do with myself.

I tried to sleep late the first morning but made it only to about eight fifteen. I woke up and had coffee and read the paper, a novelty in itself. I watched the progress of the blizzard, both outside my window and on the local news. I went to the hotel gym to ride the bike and walk on the treadmill. I watched *Oprah*. I even did a ballet barre in the hotel room, thinking people would certainly think I was crazy if they could see.

It occurred to me that the Joffrey Ballet was located in Chicago, and that if anybody would continue business as usual in a blizzard, a ballet company certainly would. I got in touch with them and received permission to take company class with them while I was in town. I tramped ten blocks through the snow my second and third days in Chicago and really enjoyed taking class with the company. The Joffrey dancers were beautiful, and the teachers taught their classes in a more classical style than City Ballet, with longer and more complicated combinations. On the way back to the hotel, I shopped the Magnificent Mile for some earrings to wear for *Oprah*.

I also watched *Black Swan*, which Jason strongly urged me to do. He said that Oprah was bound to ask me about it, and he had been a little frustrated that I hadn't seen it yet. I've always been that way: reluctant to spend my time watching or reading about ballet when so much of my day is already focused in that direction. But here in Chicago, I really had nothing else to do, so I ordered in room service and rented the movie on my hotel television. So many people had told me that the movie was scary that I decided to rent it in the afternoon, since scary movies tend to give me bad dreams. I didn't want to have to try to sleep after the film, in case it was too disturbing.

The movie had the opposite effect on me, however. I admit that I found it pretty humorous at times, but that isn't a reflection on the movie itself, which I thought was very well done. Indeed, I thought the first half of the film was a pretty accurate depiction of how the ballet world can be, and I admired Natalie Portman's portrayal of the ballerina. She actually learned how to carry her upper body like a ballet dancer, something that takes a great deal of training. But when the movie turned into a thriller, I couldn't help but get the giggles. Probably anyone seeing their workplace dramatized in such a way would have a similar reaction. Seeing what I do every day for a living turned into a scary movie with evil, tutu-wearing murderesses was just too much.

Finally the day of the taping arrived. The producers had added an extra taping that day to make up for the missed ones, so this would be Oprah's third show of the day. Rob and I would do the show and then head immediately to the airport for our ride home. We met early before the car arrived to take us to Oprah's studios, and Rob ran me through scenarios for the show so that I would feel prepared. Jason also promised to give me an idea of the line of questioning Oprah might take.

When we got to the studios, we were greeted by the very friendly staff and shown to a little waiting room of our own. Someone came to do my hair and makeup. I'd been asked to bring a pair of pointe shoes so that I could put them on if Oprah wanted me to. I'd also brought a pair of pointe shoes for Oprah in her size so that she could put them on if she wanted. Someone came to lead me to the stage so that I could try out my pointe shoes on the surface there to make sure it wasn't too slippery.

I walked through the backstage area in my socks, since the other shoes I had with me were either snow boots or high heels. The audience and stage area was actually much smaller than I'd expected, and the whole set had a rather intimate feeling. I tried the shoes on and did a little dance. The surface would be no problem. I suddenly started to have visions of myself dancing around and then tripping and falling on Oprah.

I turned to Jason. "Do I have to walk out onto the set in front of the cameras?"

"No, you'll already be sitting after the commercial break," he replied. "Why?"

"I was afraid that as I walked out I'd slip and have a really awkward moment."

Jason thought it was funny that a ballerina, of all people, would be afraid of tripping as she walked. But what he didn't realize was that we ballerinas can be very clumsy "on land" when trying to do such simple things as walking—especially this ballerina.

We went back to our waiting room, and Jason came in to go over the questions with us.

"Now, these are what we think Oprah will ask, but we can't guarantee it. Sometimes her brain will go in a different direction or something in particular will capture her interest and she will follow it. But this is my best idea of how it is going to go."

None of the questions were very surprising, which was a relief. Suddenly music sounded from the television monitor in the room, and we saw that this taping had started. Oprah came onto the set to talk to the audience, and a few moments later the cameras were rolling.

Watching the first segments of the show, I couldn't quite believe where I was and what I was about to do. I didn't have a chance to meet the other guests on the show that day; they must have all been in their own waiting rooms. I felt a little nervous and strange, especially after having been isolated in a hotel for almost four days. But mainly I felt excited about the experience. I was going to meet Oprah and be on her show! I was determined to just relish the adventure and be myself. I had no need to put on any persona but my own and no need to feel nervous. I prayed that God would use me to His purposes and hoped that good would come out of all this. I also planned to have fun while it was happening and didn't want to waste my time being nervous.

When it was time, Rob left me to go and get a seat in the audience. I was led to wait off set and stood joking with Jason and some of the other producers while we waited. Before I went on, an initial video segment of my life in New York was shown, and I chided Jason for including the shot of my not-so-picturesque ballerina feet. But I was impressed with what a great job they did with the backstage filming and told him so.

Very soon I was told to go up to the stage. Oprah was sitting in her chair, and I was led to sit beside her. She shook my hand and was very welcoming and nice, seeming genuinely happy to see me. She thanked me for staying longer because of the storm. Then it was time to start the interview.

The conversation felt very natural; Oprah was very focused and pleasant, even though it was her third show of the day and she must have been tired. If it hadn't been for the people in the audience, I would have thought I was sitting in her living room having a nice talk. We spoke about *Black Swan*, body image, and age, and I put on my pointe shoes and danced around a bit. I'm not sure I was very dignified once my pointe shoes were on, but it felt weird to be in my street clothes and pointe shoes dancing around a television set. I gave Oprah her shoes, and she had me sign them. I enjoyed every minute of it.

After the show she stood up to say good-bye to the audience and I stood beside her, surprised by how tall she was. She took a few steps off-stage, and I thought I should let her go alone so that she could make a grand exit; I figured I would slink off to the side afterward. But she grabbed my hand and said, "You're coming with me."

So we walked off together, hand in hand. She looked majestic and in control as she greeted some audience members. I did a weird, shuffling duck-walk in my pointe shoes with an "Aw, golly" smile plastered across my face. We descended the stairs from the set, and with a wave, Oprah was whisked away to her car, her assistant assuring her that traffic looked good.

And that was the end of that. I was given a gift bag with an Oprah sweatshirt and water bottle, and Rob and I were packed up and sent off to the airport. Rob was thrilled, and I was happy. I'd had a good time and now was excited to see the show. I felt like I was already forgetting some of the details because I'd been so swept up in each moment. I returned to New York and resumed life as usual, getting back in time to put my daughter to bed and perform *The Four Seasons* the next night.

After the show aired, I received many more messages on Facebook from people who had been inspired by the story or wanted help with their situations. And every now and then when the show repeats or is shown in a foreign country, I'll get a new batch. I continue to be amazed by what God has set in motion with the whole Sugar Plumgate situation, and I don't even know the half of how He might have worked through the events that began in December 2010 with that *Nutcracker* review. But what a faith builder, to know that God could use one of the darkest periods of my life to bring joy and healing not only to me twelve years later but also to an unknown number of strangers across the world. And I know that my problems, in the grand scheme of things, are very slight and insignificant when compared with things that others have gone through, but eating disorders and depression are very real and debilitating problems that can ruin people's lives and leave them caught under a dark net of shame and isolation. It is gratifying for me to think that through my experiences and with God's help I can possibly help others who may suffer with issues similar to mine.

Chapter Ten

⚛♥

Dancing *Dances at a Gathering*

⚛I'm often asked about my favorite roles and ballets. Dancing the principal roles in Balanchine's *Serenade* as well as the experiences I had originating roles in Alexei Ratmansky's *Russian Seasons* and *Namouna: A Grand Divertissement* will always be highlights of my career. But another ballet has been a part of my ballet life almost from the beginning of my time in the company, and as I've grown and matured as both a dancer and a person, I've moved through the different women's roles in it. Indeed, this is one of those ballets that can take a lifetime to fully appreciate, from the stage or the audience. As I near the end of my career as a dancer, my experiences with this ballet take on a new richness and meaning, because I find that the ballet can be a metaphor not only for real life but also for the life of a professional dancer.

Jerome Robbins's *Dances at a Gathering* is a masterpiece that requires many viewings to begin to grasp its depth and complexity. Though it has no story or plot, it is about living and interacting and experiencing human relationships in all of their forms. And because this work of art is a ballet, its mysteries and nuances are fluid; each live performance is different. Every time a new or different dancer is introduced into the cast, the dynamics of the piece change. Every time a new pianist comes onstage to play the series of Chopin waltzes, mazurkas, and études, his or her tempos and phrasing directly influence how each dance is performed. *Dances* is a ballet I've never tired of watching or dancing.

To audiences used to twenty-minute pieces, *Dances* may seem long. It is a solid hour of dancing. But each of its individual parts, choreographed for different groupings of the ten dancers who make up the cast, is different in tone and texture. You can watch relationships being developed and then revisited throughout the piece. I find it mesmerizing, and I've been told that when Robbins began choreographing *Dances*, which premiered in 1969, he showed some of the parts to George Balanchine, who said, "This is like popcorn. I want more!"

My own relationship with *Dances* started early in my career, after I'd been in the company for only a couple of years and before my struggles began. *Dances* is typically danced by principals and soloists, and I was a very new corps member. But Jerry Robbins, who was still alive then and overseeing rehearsals, was known for picking dancers without regard to rank, so it was really not that unusual that I was called to understudy the ballet.

Each dancer in this ballet, each "character," has a different personality and manner of dancing, and I've been blessed to have an experience with each of the five female roles. The women are distinguished by the color of their flowing chiffon costumes: blue, pink, apricot (also called yellow), mauve (or purple), and green. The five men are dressed in different-colored tights and blouses with matching ballet boots. My first assignment was to learn the Blue Girl. The Blue Girl is in many ways the juvenile of the group and does not have as much stage time as some of the other dancers. Her relationship to the others in the ballet is similar to that of a younger sister. This was as true for me as a dancer as it was for the role when I was called to the rehearsals. The other dancers were experienced in their roles and already knew their steps, so I just stood in the back and watched, trying to pick up what I could.

It was intimidating to be in those rehearsals at first. The studio was filled with principal dancers in their prime: Kyra Nichols, Jock Soto, Damien Woetzel, Peter Boal, Maria Calegari, Lourdes Lopez, Helene Alexopoulos, and Wendy Whelan. None of them had ever even acknowledged my existence, and I kept myself in the farthest corner of the room, out of everyone's way. I really didn't want to be noticed at this point; Jerry was at the front of the room rehearsing, and though he was generally in a good mood for these rehearsals, I'd heard stories and I was pretty scared of him. I don't remember much from those first re-hearsals because I think I was so overwhelmed to be watching these great dancers rehearse with this great choreographer.

After a couple of weeks, there was a *Dances* rehearsal on the compa-ny's daily rehearsal schedule that called only two names, and mine was one of them. Victor Castelli, the ballet master for *Dances*, would be with us. I assumed that I was now actually going to be learning the steps for the Blue Girl, not just watching others dance them, so that I would know them if I was ever needed to fill in.

However, when we arrived for the rehearsal, Victor informed us that we were to be learning the Green Girl. Now, the Green Girl is an oddity in the ballet. She does not arrive until halfway through the ballet, and when she does appear, it is only to dance a witty, stylized solo. My friend Pascale Van Kipnis, the other dancer at the rehearsal, and I were both young corps dancers and were a little wide-eyed to be learning this part. But Victor jumped right in and started telling us about the Green Girl's character. Her solo was almost like a monologue. She was supposed to be an older ballerina telling stories about her greatness.

Using her body, Victor told us, she would "say" things like "Here, I would take a great leap, flying through the air, and when I landed the audience would go crazy! I would bow and then do a beautiful port de bras that would leave them weeping . . ."

The solo was very subtle, with nothing overtly difficult. The chal-lenge lay in controlling the movements with the correct nuances and instilling the right feeling and meaning into the steps. There were deli-cate timings and musical phrasings with combinations of steps that turned on a dime and moved instantly from quick to slow, matching the staggered rhythms of the music. It was really fun to dance, and Pascale and I were red-faced and breathless by the end of the rehearsal, proba-bly because we both held our breath throughout much of it.

We rehearsed it all the way through one more time and then were told that Jerry would be coming to see us the next day.

I was full of adrenaline for the rehearsal. I couldn't believe that I was going to be showing something to Jerome Robbins. Pascale and I were both in the studio early so that we would be fully warmed up and prepared. Jerry and Victor came in, Victor smiling and Jerry looking at Pascale and me warily. He obviously wasn't going to give his approval easily.

The studio felt silent and empty with only the four of us, plus the pianist, in there. Jerry had us begin dancing the solo together, each of us taking one side of the room. The first thing the Green Girl does is to walk slowly in a half circle, opening her arms up to the audience. Jerry stopped us immediately.

"It's more like this," he said, demonstrating how he wanted the walks done. The way he walked had gravity and texture, and the expression on his face conveyed the character's sense of self-importance and grandeur. Pascale and I had to try several times before he allowed us to move on to the next step, which simply involved shifting our weight from one foot to another.

We confidently executed this move, probably not putting much thought into it, and Jerry clapped his hands to stop the pianist again.

"No," he said, "you are showing off your costume."

Jerry again demonstrated for us, becoming the character. As he danced the steps, he looked up at the "audience" in the mirror and said, as if he were the Green Girl, "See this? When I danced before the Queen I wore this beautiful gown. Everyone gasped!"

I started to realize that the solo was not about the seemingly easy steps at all; it was all about the richness of the character Jerry had created. The dancer performing the Green Girl needed to understand *who* it was that Jerry was attempting to reveal to the audience. This was my first inkling that with Jerry, it was rarely about the steps themselves.

In the thirty-minute rehearsal, we didn't even make it once through the entire solo, which is in reality probably only one or two minutes long. Jerry wanted to stop and talk about every step. When our time was up, he looked at Pascale and me and said, pointing his finger at us, "Keep working on it, keep working on it." Pascale and I looked at each other, both amazed at the fact that we had just had a private coaching session with Jerome Robbins. It was extraordinary, but it was also obvious that we still had a lot of work to do.

Shortly after that rehearsal, I was told that Jerry had decided to switch me to Apricot, also known as the Yellow Girl. I think I was just too young to grasp the nuances of the Green Girl's persona. This was not something to be worried about; he often switched dancers from part to part until he felt that he had found the right fit between a dancer's personality and the character of a certain role. He also tended to use his favorites in everything. I never did perform the Blue or the Green Girl onstage, but I'll never forget that initial rehearsal with Jerry. His way of working appealed to my way of dancing; I wanted ballet to be about more than just the perfect execution of technical steps. I wanted there to be an inner dialogue going on inside the performers' heads, even if there was no real story line to be followed. I wanted there to be a reason why I was doing certain steps, and Jerry's choreography gave me that reason.

It was in the role of the Yellow Girl that I first performed *Dances at a Gathering*. The Yellow Girl is a complete change of pace from the Blue and Green Girls. Her personality is bubbly and free, vivacious and playful, with hints of a darker drama at times. For a season or two I just understudied, watching Lauren Hauser and Wendy Whelan be coached to perform the role. Jerry loved both of these dancers and rarely had much to say to them, especially because they had both performed the part before. And seeing that they each had different takes on the role of the Yellow Girl, I came to understand that another thing Jerry valued was a *genuine* quality in his dancers. He wanted dancers to be true to themselves, as they inhabited his choreography; any hint of pretense, tension, or acting would drive him crazy. He wanted to see thoughts and emotions come to the surface in an organic way that was evident through the layers of his choreography and the dancer's own personality.

The Yellow Girl has a piece called the Wind Waltz, a pas de deux at the beginning of the ballet in which she dances with the Green Boy. We were supposed to dance as if the wind were pushing and pulling us along, and our steps often echoed and overlapped as we moved in staggered repetition of each other. Mastering the Wind Waltz essentially taught me how to be a "Jerry Dancer." It was while I was learning it that it was drummed into me that eye contact with my partner was more important than almost anything.

Jerry's pas de deux are rarely about a bravura presentation to the audience. They are about some relationship or dialogue or experience shared between the two people onstage; the audience is allowed to watch this relationship and find satisfaction in the very human emotions the dancers are feeling. For that reason, Jerry wanted partners to focus on each other, without sidelong glances toward the audience for approval.

During my first rehearsals for the Wind Waltz, I rarely got very far into the choreography without being stopped. We would dance about eight counts of music and then hear Jerry's hands clapping in a signal for the pianist to stop.

"You need to look at each other *all* the time," he would say.

We would start over. *Clap clap.*

"You took your eyes off of him. Never take your eyes off of him."

We would begin again. *Clap.*

"No. You must look at her no matter what."

Soon, my partner and I were twisting our necks at impossible angles in order to maintain eye contact no matter what direction our bodies were facing. We were dancing the steps horribly, but we were concentrating so hard on looking at each other that we were disregarding our ballet technique.

Jerry didn't care. "Okay, you are starting to get it," he finally said.

It dawned on me that this was a lesson. Jerry didn't expect us to actually dance the pas de deux this way. We were dramatically distorting the choreography in order to look into each other's eyes. But he wanted the *feeling* that we would never take our eyes off of each other. He wanted us to be constantly aware of each other and never to lose sight that we were dancing together, for each other, and not for the audience. And if there was even the possibility within the choreography that we could make eye contact, then we should be compelled instinctively to look at each other. Technical execution of the steps took second place to the emotional connection between the dancers.

My experience learning the Yellow Girl's mazurka was completely different. This was a solo, so I had no partner to look at. But I soon discovered that my partner was in fact Chopin's music. The solo was very brief, but somehow Jerry had stuffed complicated rhythms and changes of tone into a very short musical moment. It was important to be right on the music so that his choreography would be very clear.

During one section, all the Yellow Girl did was some stylized walking right on the beat of the music. She was to step on the first, third, and fifth counts of the very fast six-beats-per-measure music and there was a slight emphasis on the fifth beat. I can still hear Victor's voice counting in my head, "ONE two THREE four *FIVE* six ONE two THREE four *FIVE* six!"

If I blurred my feet at all or got late on the music, I was sent back to the beginning to try again.

I loved the challenge of trying to force my body into the parameters of the musicality and initially had to put a great deal of concentration into getting the choreography exactly right. Soon, however, it became second nature and I couldn't imagine doing it any other way. And there was nothing like the feeling that I was dancing right on top of the music, visually exposing the rhythms for the audience so that they could appreciate the music on a whole different level. I often danced that solo with the feeling of some force propelling me from behind, pushing me forward so that the music never got away from me. It was exhilarating.

During one stage rehearsal for *Dances*, after I'd been performing the Yellow Girl for a while, I came out of the wings to take my opening pose for the mazurka solo. I looked at the pianist across the stage, and we started simultaneously. After I'd danced only the first rapid six counts, Jerry, standing at the front of the stage, shouted out, "HEY!"

I stopped in my tracks, standing flat-footed while the pianist stuttered to a stop. I looked at Jerry anxiously. He had never lost his temper with me, though I'd certainly seen him lose it with others. This is it, I thought. I'm finally going to be yelled at by Jerome Robbins. I girded my loins and told myself not to cry.

Then Jerry laughed and shrugged, looked around, and said, "It's fun!"

I kept looking at him a moment while the other ballet masters on-stage laughed, a little nervously. Then, smiling weakly, I walked back to my starting position on watery knees, gave the pianist a look, and we started the solo from the beginning.

Now, when I dreamed of becoming a ballerina, I never thought I would be thrown into the air by one man to do a double spin before landing upside down in another man's arms, but that is exactly what the Yellow Girl does halfway through *Dances*. She participates in the Grand Waltz, one of the bigger group dances in the ballet, with six of the ten dancers onstage at one time. At the end of the dance is a series of throws where the boys toss the girls through the air to each other. The three girls have successively more exciting jumps, with the Yellow Girl being the last girl. I was pretty daunted by the prospect of these throws when I first learned about them.

My "thrower" was to be Jock Soto, the strongest man in the company, and my "catcher" was to be Kipling Houston, a seasoned soloist very comfortable in the Robbins rep. Both had done the part many times with many different girls, so they approached my first rehearsals very casually. I tried to appear nonchalant as well, even though I was terrified inside.

Jock gave me some simple instructions. "Take off in this position and then don't do anything. Let me do everything," he said.

"And then pray that I'll remember to catch you," Kip added with a smirk.

I was supposed to keep my arms up and my legs together like a pencil while I was hurtling through the air, but I think the first time Jock let go of me, I screamed and immediately spread-eagled, making it very difficult for Kip. So much for trying to appear calm.

Jock and Kip were very patient with me, and after a couple of tries I was able to get a decent version down. Soon enough, after some rehearsals and performances under my belt, I got very comfortable with the throw and knew I could trust my partners completely. It would only make me a *little* nervous when Jock would look at me very seriously and say darkly, "I'm going to throw you *so high* . . . ," and then Kip would walk by rubbing his elbow and loudly complain, "My arm is really hurting tonight. I'm not sure I'll be able to catch Jenny in those throws . . ."

I danced my most memorable Grand Waltz while on tour with the company in Palermo, Italy, in 1994. It was summertime, and we were performing in an outdoor theater. The stage, like many in Europe, was severely raked, or slanted, with the part closest to the audience being lower than the back. This meant that during the throws, Jock as the thrower was at the top of the "hill," and the catcher, who in this performance was James, was at the bottom of the hill.

As I approached Jock in preparation for my throw, having seen him toss the Blue Girl away toward James, I saw a look in his eye that said he was going to really *launch* me this time. I wasn't worried, because James was strong and reliable and I knew that I was in good hands. But as I left Jock's hands and completed my first revolution in the air, my mind took a snapshot of James in the split second before I went around for my second spin.

This is what I saw: Pascale, as the Blue Girl, was not in her normal finishing position but was instead on her hands and knees on the stage, trying to get up. James had his hands on her waist and seemed to be trying to disentangle himself from her costume as he glanced at me over his shoulder with a look of horror in his eyes. With that picture in my mind, I went around for my second spin, tipping upside down and really hoping that James would in fact be there to catch me.

He was, though I really have no idea how, and we were all certainly more cautious the next performance in Palermo when the throws came around.

After performing the Yellow Girl for several years, I began to get the sense that it was time for me to move on. I didn't want to be out of

Dances completely because I loved the ballet. But the Yellow Girl's role involved a great deal of youthful running about, and I started to feel too mature for the part. Though I was a principal by this time, I was still uncomfortable requesting roles, something I've hardly ever done. Jerry had passed away a few years earlier, but luckily the ballet masters had the same feeling that I did. I was called to learn the Mauve—or Purple—Girl.

I'd seen the taller, more statuesque dancers of the company dancing this role. Lourdes Lopez, Maria Calegari, and Helene Alexopoulos were all long-legged beauties who brought glamour and mystery to the part. I was shorter than these other dancers, and more long-waisted than long-legged. The Purple Girl's signature sections were adagio pas de deux that required a sense of gravity and lyricism. I knew that I would need to change my approach to *Dances* to do justice to the part of the Purple Girl, and concentrated on adding a sense of weight to my steps, as if I were moving through very thick air.

In addition to her other dances, the Purple Girl opens the Scherzo section with an untamed solo. The Scherzo is the last real dancing in the ballet, because the actual finale of the piece is filled mostly with contemplative walking. I knew this music well long before I danced to it because it was one of the piano pieces my sister had played; I used to lie under the piano while Becky practiced it, loving the feeling of being surrounded by such wild and tempestuous music.

Before her solo, the Purple Girl waits for the stage lights to change, and in silence she runs out to center stage. The pianist watches from the onstage apron and strikes a dramatic chord right when the Purple Girl hits an elongated lunge, her arm pointing diagonally out toward the audience. After that, it is as if the Purple Girl is losing her mind, alternating between wild dancing and controlled moments of stillness. I had to struggle to control myself when dancing to this music because of the wild choreography and passionate notes flying from the piano. There were plenty of rehearsals where I actually did lose my balance completely, and several performances where I thought I might end up rolling around the stage but managed to keep it together. It was a thrill to dance.

After dancing the Purple Girl for a while, I was asked to take on the only role I hadn't yet learned: the Pink Girl. I've always loved watching what Jerry made for the Pink Girl. She has wonderful choreography that allows her to be playful, sweet, and tenderly loving. Her pas de deux with the Purple Boy in the middle of the Scherzo is, I believe, one of the most beautiful combinations of music, choreography, and placement in a ballet that exists. For years I'd watched Kyra Nichols and my friend Yvonne Borree dance this part, and I felt terribly honored to be given the chance to dance it myself.

The Pink Girl has three pas de deux in addition to her group dances. One of these is the Études Pas de Deux, a dance with the Brown Boy. This pas de deux is very satisfying to dance because it has some flashier dancing at the beginning and end of the piece, with big jumps and a lot of traveling around the stage. I always felt a sense of freedom when I could come out onstage and dance the first diagonal that traveled from one corner to the next with a flying *tombé coupé grand jeté*. The two dancers challenge each other and seem to relish their energy and strength. The boy puts his hand out, palm down. The girl puts her hand higher. Then the boy puts his other hand higher, which forces the girl to put hers even higher. They then take their hands away and make a gesture as if to say, *No one won that one, so let's do something else.* But in the center of the pas de deux, the music turns quiet and the Pink Girl and Brown Boy have the opportunity to dance together in a gentle, loving way. It is as if they set aside their joking relationship to finally reveal their true feelings to each other. But soon enough, they return to safe ground, playing with each other until the music once again winds down.

Then they come to a resolution. The Brown Boy once again puts his hand out and the Pink Girl adds hers, but this time they link arms so that they are connected. The boy then swirls the girl up onto his shoulder so that she looks like a bird in flight, and he takes her off the stage.

The Pink Girl's last dance, like the Purple Girl's, is the Scherzo, which takes place right before the finale. She is caught up with everyone else in the storm of wildness, but then she is able to make a connection with the Purple Boy during the eye of the storm. The Purple Boy is bent over, not looking at her, and she runs to him and gently taps him on the arm. But after the tap, she begins to fall, as if that tap were her last bit of energy. The Purple Boy turns to catch her, lifts her high into the air, her body reaching for the sky, then places her down to kneel with him on the floor.

Then, after all of the tempestuous movement that preceded it, there are six slow counts of stillness. The Pink Girl sits back on her heels, looking into the distance. The Purple Boy kneels beside her, looking into her eyes. Then he slowly offers her his hand. She sees it, places her hand in his, and together they rise to walk slowly in a half circle, arms stretched out as if to trace a beautiful sunset. What follows is an incredibly tender pas de deux, with the two dancers exchanging expressions of fragile devotion and seeming to cling to the hope of an everlasting love. The Pink Girl is constantly trusting the Purple Boy's strength and steadfastness as she falls back blindly into his arms. They do a slow, extended bird lift, where he presses her all the way above his head, and she floats over him like an angel.

Dancing this pas de deux will be an everlasting joy to me. I was privileged to dance it with Jared Angle, my friend and one of the best partners in the company, and I was able to truly trust him and relax into the peacefulness of the pas de deux without worrying that anything would go wrong. During the times we danced that pas, it felt as if we were alone in another world, and it really didn't matter if there was an audience there or not.

But something happens at the end of the pas de deux that seems to signal a breach of trust. A discordant chord sounds from the piano, and the relationship is broken. The Purple Boy reaches for the Pink Girl's hand, but she takes it from his grasp and runs away. The other dancers return to the stage and the couple rejoins the group, their future left up in the air.

I think one of my reasons for loving *Dances at a Gathering* so much is the feeling of dancing with friends. The ballet is all about relationships, and it's just so meaningful for me to interact and respond to another dancer, without words, whom I've either known for many years or am just then, in the rehearsals and performances, getting to know. What I'll take away from this ballet career, when it is finished, is the friendships I've enjoyed with these other extraordinary artists, both onstage and off, as we all walk the path of being a dancer together, dancing through our own individual struggles and triumphs, side by side.

I've always found *Dances* to be such a satisfying experience, no matter which part in it I dance. During the hour of the ballet, so many different feelings are exposed by the happenings onstage, and many of them cannot be clearly expressed. There is no story to the ballet, yet many stories unfold as the dancers interrelate with one another. Some casts gel completely, and it almost feels as if a family or a group of very close and old friends have met to dance together for a day; the audience is forgotten, and we all dance for one another, completely in the moment. As I come out of the wings to walk my pattern at the beginning of the finale, I always feel a sense of completion and gratefulness, both for the dancing I've just been allowed to do and for the other dancers with whom I've shared the stage. A performance of *Dances* is like a journey that we've all been on together, and once it's over, I've found that the cast often lingers offstage to talk about particular moments, whether they were good or bad. It's as if we're trying to hold on to a feeling that was already lost and gone the moment the curtain lowered and the music ended. No matter how hard we might try to re-create it, that performance, that experience, is over, and it becomes just another echoing memory, adding layers to the history of that stage.

Chapter Eleven

❧

Facing Away

❧Often, before we get to the stage rehearsal of a particular ballet, the dancers will decide that it is time to "face away," which means we'll dance not toward the mirror but rather toward the back wall of the studio, which becomes our "audience." Thus we relinquish our dependence on the mirror and the habit we all have of checking to make sure things are looking as perfect as possible; instead we focus on one another, and start really dancing together.

For me, the ultimate experience of "facing away" is being a mother, and it's what I've loved most in my life so far. I feel so blessed every day I've been allowed to be a mother, and I'll never regret the hard work that goes into it because, oh, what joy it brings. And not because it is any easier than my "day job." Being a ballerina, with all of its difficulties and anxieties, in no way prepared me for some of the rigors of motherhood; I'd never cared for something so utterly and completely until I had a child. The one thing my dance experience has taught me, however, is that there is no way I can ever be a perfect mother, so every day is just an exercise in doing my best with the situations presented to me.

When my daughter, Grace, was around three years old, James and I began talking about trying to get pregnant again. Grace had brought us more gladness than we could have ever imagined, and we wanted to expand our family. Grace began her second year of preschool the same fall as Sugar Plumgate, and after all of the hubbub settled, we made a plan to "open the doors" again in the spring and see what God might have in store for us. We knew that we wanted one more child, and since I was turning thirty-eight in the spring of 2011, time seemed to be running out. Becoming pregnant again would mean missing another nine months of dancing, but since I was rarely injured, I hadn't missed any performances in years. The time seemed right for us to try for another child.

In late August we were thrilled to learn I was pregnant again. I danced the fall season with City Ballet, feeling the same symptoms of tiredness and nausea I'd felt with Grace. I showed a baby bump a little earlier with this second baby, so costumes got tighter a little quicker. I also felt more tired; with a three-year-old at home wanting constant attention, I didn't have the luxury of all the naps I'd taken when I was pregnant with Grace. There were a couple of bath times with Grace when I felt myself nodding off and would snap awake when my head hit the side of the tub. I also tended to fall asleep while putting Grace to bed. Grace, who was a precocious reader, now read her night-night books to me, and I was often awakened by her tapping my head at the end of the book and saying, "Did you miss the story, Mommy? Should I read it from the beginning?" I assured her that I'd heard her reading it in my dreams.

I stopped dancing after the fall season of 2011 but kept busy teaching at the School of American Ballet, filling in as a teacher for company class and helping to teach a new cast my role in Alexei Ratmansky's *Russian Seasons*. I enjoyed the teaching opportunities because I found I always learned a lot myself whenever I taught, no matter what the level of the dancers. I also loved sharing *Russian Seasons* with the dancers new to the ballet because it was such a special ballet to me. I'd felt so inspired by Alexei, while still feeling like I was investing my own personality into the part, and I was eager to pass my love for the ballet on to other dancers. Though I was sad not to be dancing it, I got a lot of satisfaction out of examining it in a different way and explaining it to the new cast.

I also spent time writing this book and would find quiet places to sit and write for a couple of hours while our babysitter, Michelle, was taking care of Grace. All in all, I kept pretty busy, and my due date approached unexpectedly rapidly. We found out we would be having a boy and decided to call him Luke Douglas, the Douglas after my father. James and I decided to make our foyer into Luke's bedroom, which meant a whole new round of renovations. Oh, the machinations we New Yorkers have to go through to fit children into our small spaces. Luke's "room" would only fit a crib and a chair, but at least he would have his own space.

With Luke's pregnancy, I had a few false alarms when I thought I might be going into labor, and I'd gone to the hospital unnecessarily twice. Another such false alarm happened ten days before my due date, and I was once again sent home. Throughout that day, I was having contractions, but I felt like the Woman Who Cried Baby and wanted to be sure that I was actually going to be delivering a baby before I went back to the hospital again. I lingered at home, reluctant to admit that I was really in labor, until the contractions became so regular and uncomfortable that it was obvious that it was time to go and give birth for real.

It was a good thing I decided to go when I did, because we barely made it to the hospital in time. Fortunately, my mother had come to town to watch Grace and help us adjust to life with a new baby, so James and I went to the hospital right after Grace went to bed. We walked through the hospital doors at 8:00 p.m., and Luke was lying on my chest, screaming, by 9:30. He was bluish and swollen but healthy and so very precious. It all happened so fast that after he was born, the nurse blinked at me and said, "I need to check you in. What is your name?"

Getting back into shape after both babies was ridiculously hard, but I'd done it once before, and so had a lot of dancers. I gained about fifty pounds with each pregnancy, even though doctors recommend gaining only about twenty-five to thirty-five pounds. The first time around, I just enjoyed myself and didn't think about the weight gain at all. With the second pregnancy, I was determined not to gain as much weight and to stay in better condition so that I wouldn't have such a hard time getting back into shape. Despite my efforts, my weight gain was the same, so perhaps that's just what my body does when it is pregnant.

After Grace, I joined a gym and would spend two hours a day there after my ballet class, taking cycling classes and doing weight training. In addition, I would push Grace in the stroller for hour-long walks along the Hudson River. By the time Luke came, James and I were trying to save money, and I didn't want to spend our resources on a gym. I jogged and speed-walked in the park and went up and down the seven flights of stairs in my apartment building.

I also took ballet class, of course—so many little muscles we use in ballet are not used in everyday life, and I had to rediscover and strengthen all of them. Some days I thought I'd never dance again, and I certainly felt like giving up often, but I kept going, telling myself to do what I needed to do each day and that eventually my efforts would bear fruit.

The determination to regain my dancing form, of course, brought back to life some of my old feelings about my own image, and my body. I still, and probably always will, struggle with perfectionism. It may be part of what makes me a good performer, but it is also the part of me that I'm always trying to temper, the voice that I'm trying to override with other, God-centered priorities. I often feel that I'm trying to do too many things in a day, that none of them are things I'm doing well enough, and that everything ends up being accomplished in a subpar fashion. When those thoughts creep in, I have to remind myself that I need to depend on God for my strength and resources and that His grace is the only way I can make it through the day. My strivings, without God, amount to nothing.

In terms of dancing and weight, I know that there is a standard image that's still upheld in the ballet world, and I know that I'm one of those dancers, miraculously, who breaks that standard, which isn't an easy or comfortable place to be in much of the time. While I dance at a good, lean weight now, I still don't have the too-skinny look that is the norm for ballerinas. If I were more focused on ballet and more willing to make certain sacrifices of time and will, would I be a better dancer or have had a better career? Probably. If I were bonier, would I have gotten more critical praise or been cast in better, more serious roles? I really don't know about that. But I do know for certain that I would be insane. I believe our souls are wired to seek something to worship, and for me, ultimate focus on ballet would have eventually made ballet my god again. It would have, I believe, destroyed me. And to me, it isn't worth the cost.

I have hopes that the ballet world will change and become more welcoming to all body types; it is so amazing to see dancers of every shape using their bodies to move to music in such extreme and beautiful ways. Things are changing, even in the lean ranks of New York City Ballet. Every body type is represented among the elite ballet dancers of this generation, but those who don't fit the mold often feel dissatisfied with their appearance. I've talked with many young dancers who struggle with the fact that their bodies don't meet the ballet standard. And I know that change doesn't happen in a hurry, especially in a profession so wrapped up in a particular look or shape or image. But I do hope that the dancers themselves can become healthier and not give ballet aesthetics power over their own self-esteem.

In the fall of 2010, the magazine *Dance Spirit* asked me to write a letter to my teenage self. It distills what I wish I had known when I entered the ballet world at the age of sixteen, but it also contains lessons I remind myself of on a daily basis even now.

Dear Jenifer,

When you choose dancers whom you want to emulate, either as artists or as people, don't feel like you have to be exactly like them. You are unique and have gifts that were given to you alone. Explore those gifts and relish them, even as you appreciate the gifts that you see in others.

You will be taught to seek perfection, and while it's all right to strive for brilliance, no one will ever be perfect. If you feel that perfection is the only way to succeed, you will only ever feel like a failure. Focus instead on artistic interpretation, musicality and understanding technique, and remember that if you keep joy in your dancing, others will feel joy when they watch you.

Much of your time will be spent in dance studios lined with mirrors. Sometimes it will feel like all you see are the things about your appearance that you find ugly. Try not to focus on the parts of you that you hate—accept those parts and discover what about yourself you find attractive. Remember that God gave you this body as your instrument, and to Him, it is beautiful.

Finally, while a great deal of your life will revolve around dance, it does not define you and is not the source of your self-esteem. There is a large and rich world out there, and you are a multifaceted individual who can get involved in many different pursuits. Continue learning about everything you can, and if you're feeling down, help somebody else. It will make you feel better. [As seen in *Dance Spirit*.]

After Luke was born in April, and ever so slowly, my weight did come off, and I started to feel like a dancer again. My goal was to make it back to the stage for City Ballet's fall season, but there were no ballets going in that season's repertory that I danced. I would have to wait for *Nutcracker*.

I did make it back for two performances of the Sugar Plum Fairy the last week of December 2012. It seemed like it took a lot more work on my part to make it back from the second baby, and there was an added pressure because I was returning to a role that was not only technically demanding but also required that I appear in a tutu—no long skirts to hide under. And there was, of course, the added ghost of Sugar Plum-gate hanging over my memories of *Nutcracker*.

But I had a wonderful time. It was great to be back onstage, and I was once again dancing with Jared, whom I trusted to see me through flawlessly. I had very high expectations for myself: I wanted to look and dance as if I'd never left, and prove that I could get back in shape once again. Perhaps I was being a little too prideful; my first performance back after Luke had a significant bump, literally.

The very first thing the Sugar Plum Fairy dances in Balanchine's *Nutcracker* is her solo. She arrives onstage in the beginning of act 2 with the children playing Angels, leads them in a long, gliding circle, and then dances to the famous music played over and over in every store during Christmastime. Before my entrance, I was feeling more nerves than usual, but once I got onstage, I looked at the little Angels' faces and felt myself relax. I pictured them actually being giant real angels and imagined that the theater was God's throne room—I would dance for Him. As the solo went along, I felt comfortable and strong and started thinking, This is fun! I feel great!

Then, just before a moment when the music stops and then changes to a faster rhythm, there is a simple jump, a *pas de chat*, that takes the Sugar Plum to center stage front. I thought, I'm going to jump *really* high!

I didn't. Something happened on the takeoff, and I landed on my bottom, with a thud and a bounce, front and center.

It was shocking. And embarrassing. And, well, funny. I stood up to resume dancing and got applause for my recovery. I finished out the solo with no further mishaps. When I got offstage someone joked to me, "Well, after that, you can do no wrong! The audience is going to love you no matter what!"

And I think maybe God was helping me to remember that I don't need to be perfect. I don't need to prove anything to anyone. I can just dance—yes, I have to, and want to, put the work into it and do my best, but at the end of the day, once I'm onstage, the performance is about just dancing.

As I turn forty, I've returned to a place in my dancing where I'm simply appreciating the experiences I've had both onstage and off, and my thoughts turn again to *Dances at a Gathering*. Jerry gave his dancers a wonderful gift with the last movement of his ballet. *Dances* does not end with a robustly uplifting finale in the traditional sense. The music is soft and contemplative, and all the dancers from the ballet, together onstage for the only time, wander in from the wings slowly, walking and pausing as if to look at and remember the space that they are inhabiting. At one point, the Brown Boy crouches down and softly presses the floor with his hand as if he is touching something extremely precious; all the dancers stop to watch him and consider what he has done.

Then there is a moment in the music when it seems that something momentous has suddenly taken place offstage. All the dancers stop where they are and look to the front left corner of the stage. They then stand still and follow an unseen *something* with their eyes and faces as it travels up the left side, across the top of the theater, and then down the right side of the stage. Next, something else, also invisible, high in the center of the space in front of them captures their attention. They all gaze at it, and some take a few steps forward to get closer to whatever it is. Then the dancers slowly let their gaze drop down until their chins have lowered toward their chests.

The music then resolves itself into a melody that sounds like dawn and hard-won knowledge and growth after a loss. The dancers all do a very simple port de bras together, lifting their arm across their bodies in an arc and gently opening their palms to the sky to catch something hopeful in their hands. They move to the back of the stage and separate into two groups, one of men and one of women. The groups gaze at each other across the stage, then exchange bows of greeting. They reach to their partners, in some cases dancers with whom they have not yet danced in the ballet, and then form a circle to bow to each other again. Finally, arm in arm, the couples begin walking, off to another experience, as the curtain lowers.

Everybody seems to have their own explanation for what exactly it is that we're supposed to be seeing when we all stop and turn to gaze upward in the finale. Even Jerry himself changed his description from time to time. I was told we were following a flock of birds as they winged across the sky at twilight. Another time we were told we saw a zeppelin in the distance. The explanation for the finale that resonates most with me is that this is the last time we will be in this particular space, and we're remembering the experiences we had there. After being a part of *Dances* for so many years, I treasure each performance and am often moved to tears during the finale because I never know when it could be the last time I perform it. Injuries could happen, or it could go out of the repertory for a few years and not return before I've retired.

I've used the finale of *Dances* to say good-bye to certain theaters on tour, knowing that I probably will not be coming back to them again, and to individual dancers with whom I might not perform again. And every performance of *Dances* is in fact a last of sorts, because each combination of cast, pianist, and audience is unique and can never be repeated. For an hour, we live a small life together, and when it is over, we all move on to experience other things. It is bittersweet because we have shared such a rich time together, yet we know that it will never happen in exactly that way again. *Dances at a Gathering* is a complete journey, but one whose ending is actually the beginning of another path. It lifts up both the dancer and the viewer, urging them to relish life with all of its passions, losses, and light and then to have the courage to face a future filled with even more of the same, yet different, experiences.

I feel the same way about my dance career as I begin contemplating the end of it. In the Bible, it says that David danced before the Lord with all his might (2 Samuel 6:14). It does not say that he danced before the Lord with perfect execution; it just says that he danced with all his might. And I've been given the gift and the chance to do the same. I feel so grateful that I've been allowed to dance for a living, and grateful for the lessons I've learned and am still learning as I travel through this ballet world. I would change nothing that I went through, because it has made me who I am. I would not have the blessings I have now without the trials I experienced before. I'm grateful that I get to share this gift with the people around me, and that I get to reflect the gift back to God. When I look in the mirror now, I see God's grace and mercy accepting and eradicating my failures and imperfections. For it is my Savior, inside me, who is beautiful, and what I see shining back at me from the mirror now, covering all of my brokenness, is Him.

And how I want to burst when my five-year-old daughter hears some favorite piece of music in our apartment and rushes toward me in her Supergirl costume, hair and bare feet flying, arms outstretched and crying, "Dance with me, Mommy!" I pick her up and twirl her around, the two of us doing some inspired mother-daughter moves, and then we turn to include my one-year-old son, who shrieks and chortles as he watches us and does the "toddler bounce" on his short, chubby legs.

What a gift.

Chapter Twelve

‿✑‿

The Mirror

⬭Dancers are surrounded by mirrors. They fill our dressing rooms and line entire walls of our studios. We're constantly checking ourselves: What looks right? But much more often, what looks wrong? What needs to be fixed or changed or hidden or eradicated? Even if we're alone in a studio, working on something just for ourselves, we cannot get away from the mirror. It is there, projecting a truth that can be easily distorted by the dancer's mind's eye.

Somewhere along the line, I gave the mirror way too much power. It became a malevolent presence in my life, always lurking around corners to suddenly appear on a wall or a door and taunt me with evil images of myself. There was a certain seduction it wove over me that drew my eyes ever toward it, even while the rest of me was constantly trying to run away. I hated the mirror, but I was still ever trying to please it, hoping that one day it would gaze back at me with approval.

When I was a child, the mirror was my friendly companion as I discovered myself and became aware of my appearance. The mirror brought me nothing but entertainment as I watched how my limbs moved or saw how my body bent when I was sitting down. It helped me experiment with my facial expressions as I sat in front of it and tried to act out the exotic feelings I would read about in my beloved books: dismay, shock, horror, euphoria.

In my pretend stories, I was always a princess of some sort who had to escape from being captured by some villain. Princesses were always beautiful and perfectly behaved. I clearly remember being devastated one day when I looked in the mirror after dressing up in my red velvet princess dress and tiara. I had the chicken pox, and my face was covered in spots. Princesses were not supposed to have spots.

When I started to take ballet, the mirror became my compass. Was I going in the right direction with my positions? Did I need to make adjustments to where I put my arms or how I held my shoulders? Were my legs going as high as I wanted them to? In the mirror I saw my actual self overlaid by my vision of myself as a perfect ballerina, and I constantly strove to reconcile my reality with my ideal. The mirror was a source of hope and a promise of what I felt I could achieve.

Slowly, subtly, without my noticing, a darkness crept over the mirror like an oily film. As my body began to change into its womanly form, the mirror showed me shapes I didn't recognize or want. I was not matching up to the ideal I'd always assumed I would eventually reach. I still felt the same—why was the mirror showing me something different? The mirror became something for me to distrust; it was no longer showing me a princess or a perfect ballerina, and no matter what I did, all I could see staring back at me was an ugly stranger.

The mirror had betrayed me. It was now something hateful to be denied and avoided, but I still had to use it and was confronted by the necessity of it every day. Gazing into any mirror was a torture, but I could never tear my gaze away. I would stare at myself, lingering on the distasteful parts of my body that the hateful device would flaunt defiantly, displaying my failure with awful clarity.

Finally there was a break. I stopped dancing. I stopped looking at anything but my face in the mirror. I struggled for a new identity, a new worth divorced from my appearance. I withdrew inside myself and there found God, in whose image I am made. It is the reflection of His glory that brings me joy, and it is the striving for His image that brings me identity and humility.

As I mended, I warily struck up a new relationship with the mirror. It was one of fragile acceptance and even, finally, approval for just the normal, imperfect person that I was. I was not a princess, and I had good, beautiful parts along with weird, ugly parts, all making up a whole being who was just fine. I'd taken away the mirror's power.

And now I can use the mirror as the tool it is meant to be. I often forget to look into a mirror all day long and then catch my reflection and find my hair sticking out in a funny direction or baby food stains on my shirt. After a wild morning with a grumpy toddler and too much to do, I force myself to use the mirror to make sure I don't leave the apartment in a state that would embarrass my family. Grace is starting school, and I want her to be proud of her mother.

I also now have the precious privilege of teaching my daughter how to use the mirror, and I hope to infuse her with physical self-confidence as well as the knowledge that her appearance does not define her worth or her identity. Grace already has a tender, kind heart and a generous spirit, and I hope to teach her to always look to the heart of a person when she is making decisions about the people she meets.

Often as she is getting dressed, she will pause and stare at herself naked in the mirror, her face a neutral expression of curious interest.

"Oh, Grace," I'll say. "Look at the beautiful body you have. It is so strong and healthy and can do so many interesting things. God gave you exactly the right body for *you* because He knew what you needed. And inside that body is your beautiful, precious soul."

And I'll see her expression change to one of pride and pleasure as she gazes at herself and wriggles around, shaking her arms and legs and twisting to see her tummy and back.

"Yes," she will say with the confidence of a child. "God gave me a beautiful body. Watch me, Mommy!" And she will dance before the mirror, beaming with joy, her beautiful spirit shining out through her eyes.

ACKNOWLEDGMENTS

I never expected to write a book about myself, and I must thank Todd Gold and my agent, Dan Strone, for having the idea and getting it all started. Also I want to thank my friend Robert Lipp, who is responsible for creating the Dance On scholarship for City Ballet dancers, through which I was able to get the college education that gave me the confidence to write this book myself. In fact, Bob is the one who introduced Todd and me in the first place.

I want to thank my amazing editor, Wendy Wolf, as well as Margaret Riggs. Wendy gave me the freedom to "just write," and then somehow she and Maggie made sense of the large quantity of pages I gave them, blessedly cutting much out. Thanks also to Brianna Harden, who crafted such a beautiful jacket cover. I am very grateful to Elisa Rivlin, Carolyn Coleburn, Kate Griggs, Carla Bolte, and everyone else at Viking. I also so appreciate the efforts made on my behalf by Dan's assistant, Kseniya Zaslavskaya, and all those at Trident Media Group. To Steven Caras, Paul Kolnik, Rosalie O'Connor, and Joe McNally I give my gratitude and admiration for their ability to capture dance in a way that makes still images seem to move. Thank you to Rob Daniels, director of communications at City Ballet, for his guidance and wisdom, and to my friends from the ballet world who have been so supportive.

I extend so much love and appreciation to my Monday Mom's Group from Redeemer Presbyterian Church for their prayers and support, and for the examples they all are to me of Godly women, wives, and mothers. Their vulnerability, senses of humor, and insight have helped me through so many days. Particularly I want to thank Katharine

Cluverius for reading this book and helping me to better approach writing about my faith.

Last, and most important, I need to thank my family. My sister, Becky, is ever my ally and advocate, empowering me to be courageous and be myself. My parents are always my supporters and read several versions of this book, offering suggestions and encouragement with love and sensitivity. They have continuously prayed for me about every part of my life. I hope I can be just like my mom and dad as I parent my own precious children on their own life journeys. And my husband, James, continues to be my hero in ways big and small. Without his thoughtfulness and selflessness and wisdom and patience, this book would never have been finished.

There is nothing like writing a book about yourself to make you realize how far you still have to go and how many people have helped you get to your current spot. I have accomplished nothing on my own; it is only with God's help and the amazing people in my life that I have done anything, and to them I am humbly grateful.

BALLET GLOSSARY

Adagio—movement that has a slow, fluid quality

Apprentice—the lowest rank of dancer at New York City Ballet; performs only a few ballets in a given season. Although most dance companies follow similar rank structures as City Ballet, some have no apprentices; others have first and second soloists; some have Etoiles, which are above principals; some have no ranks at all.

Arabesque—ballet position in which one leg is extended directly behind the body and one arm is often stretched out to the front

Balanchine style/technique—the stylistic way of dancing created by the choreographer George Balanchine that features a unique precision, quickness, and efficiency and incorporates elements of neoclassicism

Ballet master/mistress—the instructor in a professional company in charge of a particular ballet or rehearsal

Ballonné—a step that slices the working leg first away from and then into the standing leg, done either as a jump or in pointe work without a jump

Barre—the horizontal bar often made of wood that is fastened to the walls of a ballet studio for the dancers to hold on to during the initial exercises of a ballet class

Bourrée—a step where the dancer glides in any direction using many tiny steps *en pointe*

B-plus—a standing pose where one leg is bent and crossed behind the other with its toe placed on the floor

Center/Center work—exercises done in a ballet class in the center of the room, away from the support of the barre

Classical—the traditional style of ballet established in the nineteenth century

Corps de ballet—the first official rank achieved by most full-standing company members; the largest group of dancers in a ballet company that primarily does the ensemble dancing

Demi-soloist—a role in a ballet that is more prominently featured than the role of the corps de ballet

Divertissement—a short dance or interlude in a ballet

En dedans—a pirouette revolving inward, toward the supporting leg

En dehors—a pirouette revolving outward, away from the supporting leg

En pointe—to dance in pointe shoes; the act of rising up onto the toe box, or front section, of a pointe shoe

Grand battement—a high, controlled kick

Grand jeté—a *jeté* in which the dancers make a split with their legs in the air

Jeté—a jump from one foot to the other

Jeté battu—a *jeté* in which the legs cross over each other once and then switch places before landing

Mazurka—a Polish folk dance in ¾ time

Movement—a section of music within the whole composition or a part of a ballet within the whole piece

Neoclassical—a style of ballet that is less formal and rigid than classical ballet and usually has no narrative

Partnering—when a man supports and assists a ballerina as she dances

Pas de deux; de trois; de quatre; etc.—a dance for two, three, four, etc.

Pirouette—a turn on one leg

Plié—to bend the standing leg or legs

Port de bras—how the arms are held and carried; the positioning of the shoulder, elbow, wrist, and fingers as they move through the air

Principal—the highest rank attained by a ballet dancer at New York City Ballet; dances the most important roles

"Puff"; "puffed"—a part that is very hard and causes the dancer to become out of breath; to be out of breath

Repertory—the list of ballets shown during a performance season

Saut de basque—a traveling jump in which the dancer jumps from one foot to the other while revolving in the air

Scherzo—a sprightly musical composition usually in quick triple time

Soloist—the middle rank, between the corps de ballet and the principal at New York City Ballet; usually dances featured parts

Soutenu—a smooth turning step where both feet are on the floor

The tape—the voice machine that dancers at New York City Ballet used to call for their daily schedule

Tombe coupé jeté—a traveling step that involves first a turning step on the floor and then moves into a large jump from one foot to the other

Turns—a series of steps in which the dancer spins or revolves

Understudy—one who is covering a role but would perform it only if the primary dancer scheduled to do the part is unable

INDEX

❧

PHOTOGRAPH CREDITS